INSUBSTANTIAL PAGEANT

JEFFREY L. LANT

Insubstantial Pageant

CEREMONY AND CONFUSION AT QUEEN VICTORIA'S COURT

HAMISH HAMILTON
LONDON

To my parents

First published in Great Britain 1979
by Hamish Hamilton Ltd
Garden House 57–59 Long Acre London WC2E 9JZ

Copyright © 1979 by Jeffrey L. Lant

British Library Cataloguing in Publication Data
Lant, Jeffrey L
  Insubstantial pageant.
    1. Pageants – Great Britain – History –
  20th century
    2. Great Britain – Kings and rulers
  I. Title
  394'.4'0941   GT4043
  ISBN 0-241-10317-7

Printed in Great Britain by
Western Printing Services Ltd, Bristol

CONTENTS

	Acknowledgements	vii
	Foreword	ix
	Introduction: Golden Jubilee Day, June 21, 1887	1
1	Uncertain Ceremonial	17
2	A 'Disgraceful Debate'	34
3	Confusion in the Abbey	58
4	Housing the 'Royal Mob'	88
5	Paved with Good Intentions	117
6	State or Semi-State?	150
7	In Quest of Honours	177
8	The Armed Forces' Salute	201
9	Sixty Years a Queen	215
	Epilogue	247
	Notes and Select Bibliography	257
	Index	261

ILLUSTRATIONS

Between pages 54 and 55

The Golden Jubilee, June 21, 1887
1 Queen Victoria in the dress she wore at the ceremony *Windsor*
2 The Thanksgiving Service, Westminster Abbey, seen from the organ loft *Illustrated London News*
3 Two drawings by Spy:

(a) William Henry Smith, M.P.
(b) The Hon. Spencer Ponsonby-Fane
4 (a) The Earl of Abergavenny. From the drawing by Ape
(b) Sir John Richard Somers Vine. From the drawing by Spy
5 (a) The Queen's Jubilee Drawing Room *Mary Evans*
(b) Queen Victoria unveils a statue of herself at Windsor, June 22, 1887 *Windsor*
6 (a) The Royal procession in Westminster Abbey *Mansell*
(b) A Mug from the Queen for Good Conduct *Mary Evans*
7 Jubilee Festivities:
(a) Garden party at Buckingham Palace, 1887 *Mansell*
(b) Pageantry at Wakefield, Yorkshire *Mansell*
8 Queen Kapiolani of Hawaii (seated) with her sister-in-law, Princess Liliuokalani. The Queen is wearing her famous dress of peacock-feathers *Hawaii State Archives*

Between pages 182 *and* 183

9 (a) Lord Skelmersdale, 1877
(b) Colonel Henry Ponsonby, 1861
10 (a) Arthur, Duke of Connaught, 1887
(b) Lord Esher, 1907

The Diamond Jubilee, June 22, 1897

11 (a) The Queen's procession enters Pall Mall from St. James's Street *Mansell*
(b) Arrival at St. Paul's *Mary Evans*
12 (a) The Queen drives out during the celebrations *Mansell*
(b) Illumination of the Fleet, Spithead *Mary Evans*

Death of the Queen, January 22, 1901

13 (a) Embarkation at Cowes *Mary Evans*
(b) The cortège at Windsor *Mary Evans*
14–15 (above) The procession leaves Buckingham Palace *Mansell*
(below) Royal mourners at Paddington Station *Mansell*
16 The funeral service in St. George's Chapel, Windsor *Mansell*

ACKNOWLEDGEMENTS

I am grateful to Her Majesty the Queen for graciously allowing me access to the Royal Archives at Windsor Castle and for permission to reproduce certain photographs from the Royal collection. Miss Jane Langton, Registrar of the Royal Archives, has been most helpful in my work as has been Miss Frances Dimond, Assistant Registrar.

I am indebted to the following for allowing me to use manuscript material in their possession or to which they hold the copyright: the Duke of Norfolk, the Marquess of Salisbury, Sir William Gladstone, Bart., and the Trustees of the British Museum.

During the course of my research many individuals have been most kind to me. I am glad to be able publicly to mention the following from among them: Mr. E. G. W. Bill, Librarian, Lambeth Palace Library; Miss Agnes E. Conrad, State Archivist, Hawaiian State Archives; Dr. J. F. A. Mason, Librarian, Christ Church Library, Oxford; Mr. Robert Montgomery Scott, formerly of the United States Embassy in London; Mr. E. K. Timings, formerly Assistant Keeper, Public Record Office; Sir Anthony Wagner, Clarenceaux King of Arms; and Miss Vera Watson.

I should also like to point out the assistance I have been given by the staffs of the following: Bodleian Library, Oxford; the British Library (especially at the newspaper collection at Colindale), Home Office Library, Royal Mint and Trinity College Library, Cambridge.

Finally, I should especially like to thank three individuals who have been most important to the publication of this book. James A. Woods, S.J. allowed me the time to finish this project when I was an administrator at Boston College. Mr. Roger Machell, my editor, has been unfailingly kind and thoughtful. Finally, Mr.

George Dangerfield, ever my mentor and dear friend, has over the course of many years and particularly during the writing of this book given me the benefit of his erudition and enlightened good sense. I am grateful to them all, as I am grateful to all those who helped me whether mentioned here or not.

FOREWORD

The great pageants of English history punctuate a good many volumes both weighty and frivolous. So often cited as occasions of brilliance and display, they have nonetheless been very little studied. In part this neglect has come about, I suspect, because of their very prominence. So obvious, they have not seemed sufficiently recondite to suit the taste of many historians. Moreover, because documents relating to them are unusually fragmentary and dispersed, ceremonies are not easy events to research. No less lethargic than others, historians have simply avoided the necessary work involved in recreating them. Finally and perhaps most importantly, modern pageants are designed to have a popular dimension. Historians who wish to be thought serious have therefore avoided them, fearing that their own grave purposes might be questioned by handling such common subjects. Thus events in which multitudes participated have been largely disregarded.

This book is designed to set matters right.

It began as a doctoral dissertation at Harvard University, but most of the work in assembling it has been done in Great Britain. There, upon examining documents, the most important of which are held by the Public Record Office and never before systematically studied, it became clear that Queen Victoria's Golden Jubilee of 1887 is a far more interesting and significant event than is generally thought. It was then that the broad outlines of royal ceremonial organization were laid down after decades of persistent bungling and confusion by the court. To be sure, the Golden Jubilee was often hilariously mismanaged, but it at least pointed the way towards an unwonted efficiency and unprecedented sureness of touch in these matters.

Despite many mistakes, it seemed clear on the occasion of the Diamond Jubilee ten years later that royal officials at last knew what they were doing. If this event was relatively well ordered, however, it was otherwise with the Queen's funeral in 1901. The seasoned officials who had previously been employed and who were responsible for the impression of expertness were displaced by order of the new king, Edward VII. He gave direction of the programme to the woefully ill-prepared members of the College of Arms, who had had no part in the previous learning process. The result was most unfortunate, the muddle and disarray traditionally associated with royal occasions being carried with a flourish into the twentieth century, unexpectedly remaining to challenge the ingenuity of the new reign.

This book, drawn from a wide range of source materials, most new, some hitherto insufficiently examined, gives, I hope, a new perspective on the amateurish Victorian court and the difficult sovereign at its centre. In a subsequent volume, I hope to do the same for the monarch, so very different, who followed.

Cambridge, Massachusetts   J.L.L.
April 4, 1979

INTRODUCTION

GOLDEN JUBILEE DAY, JUNE 21, 1887

BY THE time Queen Victoria boarded the royal train at Balmoral on June 17, 1887, beginning a trip to London which would end in the celebration of her golden jubilee on the throne, she felt decidedly put upon. There were, after all, a number of last minute details still demanding attention, and she was ridden with anxiety about the forthcoming festivities which were so excitedly anticipated in the metropolis. A shy woman for all that her reserve was well alloyed with the traditional Hanoverian exuberance and high animal spirits, the Queen on this occasion had been 'trembling' for months at the prospect which awaited her arrival.

Never a woman to suffer in silence, the Queen vented these feelings in a letter to 'dearest Bertie,' her son Albert Edward, Prince of Wales, only a few days before she left Scotland. 'I am so overburdened with work that I have hardly any time for anything & am thoroughly knocked up already. . . . I really think we will be *ill* if it goes on!'[1]

Members of her staff, well aware of how the Queen felt about the jubilee, must have heaved a collective sigh of relief as she started her journey to the south, the quicker to have done with it all.

Even as she travelled, however, there were continuing signs of the enthusiasm felt by the country towards the event, which had not touched the Queen. Perhaps most poignantly, the Countess of Jersey, member of a family long connected with the Court, noted in her diary groups of peasants standing mute in the early hours of the dawn on June 18, waiting to catch the merest glimpse of the royal train as it sped by on its way to Windsor, where the Queen was to rest and deal with final arrangements until ready to proceed to her capital. Having done so, on June 20, the eve of the jubilee, she moved on to London.

Immediately upon her arrival, Queen Victoria was given a good idea of what was in store for her on jubilee day itself, for the city was bright with unwonted colour and decorations and dense with roving throngs of inhabitants and visitors newly arrived for the occasion. Once they caught sight of their sovereign at Paddington station, these 'enormous crowds' gave way to the 'immense enthusiasm' that was to characterize the London pageant. Even the Queen, while still not able to shake off her anxieties about the morrow, was gratified by the reception.

More indication of what she might expect when she drove to Westminster Abbey on the morning of June 21 was given during a breakfast party at Buckingham Palace which preceded her departure. There the Queen was joined in the Chinese room by her third son, Arthur, Duke of Connaught, and her daughters Helena, Princess Christian, and Beatrice, Princess Henry of Battenberg, who was also allowed to bring her husband.

Throughout this nervous meal telegrams of congratulation arrived, and as troops passed in front of the palace, the royalties heard the 'constant cheering' of a crowd which had been forming outside since hours before the metropolitan police and the 8,000 military guards took up their positions at 7 a.m.

To be sure, these interrupting cheers were not yet for the Queen herself but rather for those guests who had been put up elsewhere and were now entering the courtyard of Buckingham Palace to take their places in the procession.

How these august personages should be greeted upon their arrival at the palace had been one of the hundreds of details which proved so vexatious to the responsible officials. When Lieutenant Colonel Hatton of the Grenadier Guards asked Sir Spencer Ponsonby Fane, Comptroller of the Lord Chamberlain's Department, how the guards band should salute the royalties, whether the King of Saxony ought to be greeted by his own national anthem or by some bars (but how many?) of that of the German Empire of which his state was a part, Ponsonby Fane was stumped.

In the event, that seemingly infallible authority on the minutiae of pageantry, the Prince of Wales, sensibly decided that snippets of the British national anthem would do for all.

Otherwise the complications would have been considerable, not least because the bandsmen would have no means of properly (and quickly) identifying who was driving by. 'For he might have been a Roosian, a French, or Turk, or Proosian, or perhaps Itali-an!'

By mid-morning the processions which had been so taxing for Colonel George A. Maude, Crown Equerry, to arrange were being marshalled. The first to be put in suitable order was named after Princess Mary of Cambridge, Duchess of Teck, the Queen's cousin and contained a heterogeneous collection of minor royalties not important enough to be given places in either the Kings' Procession which left Buckingham Palace at 10.30 or in the Queen's which followed, somewhat delayed, at 11.30.

Shunning her robes of state and the full accoutrements of monarchy, Queen Victoria was driven in an open landau drawn by six of the famous cream stallions. She wore mourning relieved only by a lavender bonnet in the shape of a crown trimmed with white *point d'Alençon* lace and diamond ornaments.

As the diarist William Allingham noted, the overall effect of these processions was wonderful, the liveries and trappings being likened to a 'glittering river.' 'It was a really magnificent sight,' Queen Victoria thought. But it was the 'continuous hurrahs' greeting her progress which so thrilled the Queen and at last assured her that her many anxieties had been needless.

Not that there were no contretemps even in such a moment of triumph. The Marquess of Lorne, the Queen's son-in-law by virtue of his marriage to her daughter Princess Louise, was thrown from his horse in the courtyard of Buckingham Palace and so could not ride with his princely relations along the route. It was rumoured at the time, though, that rank-conscious European princes thought it fitting that Lorne had been thus removed, for he was after all merely a commoner, though heir to the proud Scottish dukedom of Argyll.

It also seemed a pity that many of the notables had been shut up in closed carriages which made it difficult for the crowd to see them. Such arrangements were especially unfortunate in the case of the splendidly overdressed Indian princes, the effect of whose extravagant costumes and masses of jewels being lost inside their cramped conveyances.

While the Queen's procession moved along the route to Westminster Abbey, those favoured with places inside waited. They had been instructed to arrive well in advance of the service, but the press of traffic had been such that the doors had to be kept open long after officials had hoped to have everyone locked up inside.

Mr. Gladstone, like the Queen, had been met with something very like a demonstration on his way. As that most ungladstonian newspaper *The Times* noted with satisfaction, however, 'An occasional chorus of loud groans showed that there are some things which an English crowd cannot forgive even when excited by an almost feverish spirit of exultation.' It meant, of course, Gladstone's attempt to secure Home Rule for Ireland, a policy about which the Unionist *Times* could never be condemnatory enough. As for Victoria herself, she later commented that while she knew her great *bête noire* had been somewhere in the Abbey, she had thankfully missed seeing him.

Edward W. Benson, Archbishop of Canterbury, had also had difficulty in getting to the Abbey, though his was more prosaically exasperating. When his coachman was stopped by a policeman while attempting to pass along the processional route, the Archbishop found he had forgotten the necessary permit enabling him to continue. When the officer showed every sign of refusing to allow Benson to drive on, his grace leaned out of the window, and, perhaps with a note of asperity in his voice, bluntly informed him, 'They can't begin till I get there.' Only then was he allowed to pass.

Guests arriving at the Abbey had plenty of time to review the decorations. There had been some suspicion about the work being done by Messrs. Banting and Son for the Office of Works, not least because Bantings' principal line of endeavour was undertaking. Allowed to scrutinize their preparations the day before the ceremony, *The Times* found that 'The imposing effect of the edifice has been impaired, but happily it has not quite been destroyed.'

On jubilee day itself such grumpy opinions were less common, if only because the massed uniforms and official costumes of the gentlemen along with the colourful toilettes of the ladies disguised the effect of the lurid Bath red which constituted the main decorative colour. Archbishop Benson, who had been appalled by the changes he had witnessed during a previous inspection trip, was considerably relieved. 'The Abbey was not spoiled or rendered unecclesiastical, as it seemed likely to be, by the arrangements.'

Early in position for the service, the guests had to while away the morning as best they could. Many brought picnic lunches and the morning papers; most simply sat uncomfortably on their hard wooden seats.

Lady Monkswell, wife of the second baron, found that the Office of Works had squeezed so many seats into the Abbey that she and her husband had difficulty in making their way past other guests. They finally managed to climb to their places, where they found each was allotted 19 inches of board, without a back rest. Put in the section reserved for peers, she found herself behind Baroness Burdett-Coutts, the banking heiress, who kindly advised Lady Monkswell to hold onto her shoulders whenever she felt like standing up to see what was happening, 'as we did on the slightest provocation, we got so bored with waiting. . . .'

To pass the time, some people took to changing places. Lady Monkswell noted the 'very old and funny' Baron Crewe (then aged 75) clambering along the benches looking for a better seat, while Lady Burdett-Coutts held his stick and Lady Monkswell attended to his cocked hat.

Even the most important fared little better. Lord Cranbrook, Lord President of the Council, and Lord Halsbury, Lord Chancellor, seated near to the Queen's position, could scarcely see because of a high enclosure around the dais. Seated close to the Lord President was the Marchioness of Salisbury, wife of the Prime Minister, who was particularly put out about the enclosure. Lord Cranbrook recorded that 'Lady Salisbury said she should like to hang the man who put it up—probably the Dean. . . .' With all the difficulties it is no surprise that the *Daily News* in its account of the day noted that 'a general air of lassitude and ennui began to replace the look of eager expectation and vivacity.'

At last, however, long after the minor royalties and the Queen's guests had been seen to, the crowd inside the Abbey became aware of rising waves of noise outside. It was, of course, Queen Victoria approaching the great west door. As the *Daily Telegraph* reported, 'The processional pageant may have been striking elsewhere but its magnificence was surely never seen to such advantage as when massed and intensified at the Abbey front.'

There was in fact a burst of church bells, spontaneous and even thunderous applause, the rising notes of the national anthem played at its full length over and over again. Finally the Queen succeeded in making her way through this pandemonium, entering the Abbey by means of a long dark tunnel designed to take her beneath the newly constructed rows of temporary seating.

Considering that there had been no rehearsal of the processional arrangements, all had gone very well indeed.

The Queen's procession to the altar was led by the minor canons and canons of Westminster resplendent in copes, the wearing of which had alarmed High Churchmen throughout the land. The Queen herself was preceded by the chief officers of her household, the Lord Steward and the Lord Chamberlain, who walked, as they must in the presence of the sovereign, backwards. It was thought that the Earl of Lathom, Lord Chamberlain, 'accomplished his difficult feat of pedestrianism very deftly and gracefully.'

From a strategic vantage point, Sir Spencer Ponsonby Fane, Comptroller of the Lord Chamberlain's Department, directed the musical proceedings with blue and red flags. First he waved a signal to the State Trumpeters, who responded with a flourish on their instruments. Then with a red flag he alerted Dr. Bridge, the Abbey organist, that it was time for the national anthem. With that the procession to the altar commenced, the Queen nodding from side to side acknowledging the obeisance of her assembled subjects, most of whom would only be able to see her as she moved to and from her place for the service, the Coronation Chair of Edward III, specially refurbished for the occasion.

Once there, while the sounds of a Handel overture crashed around her, Victoria gave way to a characteristically nostalgic reflection. 'I sat *alone* (oh! without my beloved husband, for whom this would have been such a proud day!). . . .'

The service itself lasted about forty minutes, but for most of those present the procession to the coronation chair had been its most interesting feature, not least because it was difficult to follow what came after. Not only did the enclosure around the Queen's dais impair sight of Victoria, but despite a massed choir and the full use of the Abbey's organ by Dr. Bridge, there were considerable difficulties in hearing what was going on.

From an artistic point of view the guests may not have been missing much, as *The Musical World* evidently thought so little of the way the music was handled that it skipped the subject entirely in its review of the occasion, apparently deciding on discretion rather than critical candour. Nonetheless the poor quality of the sound was most provoking.

Even so Archbishop Benson, who had been involved in the arrangement of the service and was of course a leading participant, was pleased at its conclusion, though he, too, neglected to mention the music. 'The ecclesiastical part of this noble celebration seems to be regarded, thank God, by all, as deeply devout & church like. The manner of the Queen was most reverent.'

More often remarked than Victoria's reverence, however, was the touching way she accepted the homage rendered by her own family, particularly those marked by tragedy as her son-in-law, Prince Frederick William, Crown Prince of Germany, already a voiceless, dying man though dazzling in his white army uniform with its silver breast-plate and eagle crested helmet, and the Duchess of Albany, young widow of the Queen's youngest son, Prince Leopold. To Victorians, endlessly interested in death and the paraphernalia of mourning, the salutation of a cancer-stricken prince and the kiss of two widows, one of them still in the most sombre weeds, were notable events. And that Princess Beatrice and the Grand Duchess Serge of Russia, one of the Queen's grandchildren, sobbed through the Prince Consort's 'Te Deum' was only fitting.

Once this bitter-sweetness was over, the procession reformed and, to the sound of Mendelssohn's 'Athalie', recessed through the Abbey's nave. The Queen then returned to Buckingham Palace cheered along her way by crowds reported as being larger and more enthusiastic than before.

Luncheon, understandably served later than usual that day at the palace, was designated a family affair so that the black Queen of Hawaii and other visiting non-European royalties might be excluded, so jealous were western princes of the precedence accorded the orientals. At its conclusion, the Queen went on to the balcony of the Blue Room and watched a march past by naval bluejackets, a characteristic inspiration of Lord Charles Beresford, one of the Lords Commissioners of the Admiralty, a man who missed no opportunity to promote his service. Victoria then went indoors to accept presents from her household, guests and family.

Later in the year a selection of them, catalogued by the Lord Chamberlain's Department, was presented to the public in the red and gilt state rooms of St. James's Palace. The Queen insisted that there should be no charge, so that her subjects might freely see the offerings of the great and the humble.

The Emperor of China sent two boxes of tea. The Thakore of Morvi presented a charger and a set of valuable trappings. A certain Miss Sedley gave a blue velvet pincushion she had fashioned herself, while the Oratory in South Kensington sent the complete works of Cardinal Newman in 35 volumes, a gift which Queen Victoria, a plainspoken Broad churchwoman, may not have fully appreciated. These and other gifts of widely varying sorts drew some 432,000 people to the exhibition at St. James's Palace and at the Bethnal Green Museum in London's East End where it was also mounted.

By the end of the jubilee afternoon the Queen was much fatigued, but still managed to appear at a state dinner that evening in a dress with a woven pattern of rose, thistle and shamrocks, symbols of her three kingdoms, and her large diamonds. After this affair, which was attended by all the chief jubilee guests, she made the *cercle* of the Ballroom receiving Indian princes, members of the Corps Diplomatique, special envoys and suites attendant on the various princes. 'I was half dead with fatigue . . . but felt truly grateful that all had passed off so admirably, and this never-to-be-forgotten day will always leave the most gratifying and heart-stirring memories behind.' Before retiring the Queen went to the window of her chamber for a glimpse of the general illumination of her capital, the world's greatest city, *en fête* for her and her reign of fifty years.

For jubilee night vehicular traffic had been prohibited in the West End, and a vast concourse of people roamed the streets. It was the first time that electric illuminating devices were widely used, and there were blazing electric lamps and patterns featuring loyal mottoes and symbols everywhere.

Public houses remained open until 2 a.m. despite the misgivings of temperance advocate Sir Wilfrid Lawson, M.P. Lawson, was a long-time member of the House of Commons, who, devoted to radical crotchets and slogans, had attempted to filibuster the Commons into the small hours of jubilee day. Arguing that Sir Charles Warren, Chief Commissioner of Metropolitan Police, had exceeded his powers in granting an extension of hours he rose to warn, '15,000 people would be employed in making the people drunk tomorrow night.'

In fact, no such general stupor occurred, the Home Secretary, Henry Matthews, assuring members afterwards that there had been a 'very remarkable absence' of riot and disorder. Later still the Chancellor of the Exchequer, G. J. Goschen, attributed to the jubilee such an immense jump in the beer revenues that he found no need to ask for supplemental estimates for the army for 1887–1888.

Thus jubilee day passed off successfully in London and indeed around the world wherever loyal Englishmen were to be found. Consulates were illuminated, though the Foreign Office banned any lavish expenditure. Ambassadors, however, were allowed a freer hand and gave grand dinner parties in full fig.

There had been much worry, of course, about what the Irish would do both at home and abroad, especially after Nationalist members of Parliament under the leadership of Charles Stewart Parnell attacked the jubilee estimates. The British consul general in New York reported that loyal British residents of that city had been forced by local hostile Nationalist opinion to give up a proposal to raise a permanent memorial to the Queen's jubilee in rivalry to the French donated Statue of Liberty which had been presented in October, 1886.

Moreover, on jubilee day these same Nationalists met in public meeting and denounced the Union with England, Mr. Arthur Balfour, the Chief Secretary, and the Dublin Castle regime. To conclude the anti-jubilee activities in New York there was a mass 'for the repose of the souls of the 1,500,000 persons who have perished from hunger and eviction during the fifty years of England's misrule in Ireland.'

As is still so often the case, Nationalists in the United States were much more outspoken in their anti-British sentiments than their colleagues in Ireland. While Irish Americans were organizing their demonstrations in New York, Parnellites M.P.s were doing no more than boycotting the thanksgiving service in Westminster Abbey. Their followers at home in turn stayed away from the limited celebrations scheduled for Dublin, attending neither the parade of troops in Phoenix Park nor the special church services. The result was a day not unlike most others, for as the *Daily News* reported, 'Of popular manifestations of loyalty there were none, neither was there any demonstration of disloyalty.'

On the day after the jubilee, the Queen's strenuous round of activities did not abate. In the morning she called on 'Poor Old Aunt' Cambridge in her apartments in St. James's Palace. Princess Augusta, Dowager Duchess of Cambridge, was then 89 and infirm, so the Queen came to her. While there she accepted a gift from her other Cambridge relations led by Prince George, second Duke of Cambridge and including his sister Princess Mary, Duchess of Teck.

In the afternoon she received a deputation of ladies at Buckingham Palace who presented a congratulatory address along with 35 boxes containing nearly three million signatures of those who had contributed to the Women's Jubilee Offering. Lady Londonderry, wife of the Lord Lieutenant of Ireland, presented an additional coffer containing the names of nearly 150,000 women and girls of Ireland.

Having accepted these, the Queen then gathered up the Prince and Princess of Wales, the Crown Princess of Germany, her second son Prince Alfred, Duke of Edinburgh, and Princess Christian, and drove to Hyde Park for a Children's Jubilee Fete. This was a late addition to the jubilee activities. Edward Lawson, proprietor of the *Daily Telegraph*, had announced the scheme only on May 19, scarcely a month before it was to take place. Nonetheless it prospered because he had gathered together a distinguished committee headed by the Prince of Wales and including the Dukes of Cambridge, Bedford, Portland, and Westminster, the Prime Minister and Lords Hartington and Rosebery, and because it was also announced that the Queen would attend.

The fund for which Lawson solicited contributions, principally through his newspaper, was designed to provide a treat in Hyde Park for about 30,000 children aged from 10 to 14, selected from the London board and voluntary schools. Unlike most other collection schemes associated with the jubilee, it was greeted with immediate enthusiasm; even the gadfly radical journalist and M.P. Henry Labouchere gave it his blessing in his irreverent periodical *Truth*.

Some of this widespread support may conceivably have resulted from a misconception that the treat was for the indigent. Even Queen Victoria, having attended, thought she had seen '30,000 poor children.' Some people had misgivings about the intentions of its chief organizer, Edward Lawson. Editor and principal proprietor of the *Daily Telegraph*, Lawson was a man anxious to get on in the world; to do so, he had made a determined alliance with the leading powers in the land, becoming in the process an advocate of every cause reckoned loyal, patriotic and generally stand-pat.

While such a stance brought him a golden harvest of good opinions from those whose interests lay in maintaining the status quo, it earned Lawson the suspicion of the radicals, to whom Lawson's motives seemed clear: the *Pall Mall Gazette* promptly dubbed the affair his 'Jubilee Baronetcy Fete.'

Although Lawson undoubtedly had an eye cocked in the direction of No. 10 Downing Street, being anxious to secure some kind of official recognition, he was frustrated. While the Prime Minister had determined to make a press award in his jubilee honours, he and his advisor in these matters, the first Marquess of Abergavenny, had already decided to give this first Fleet-street award to Sir Algernon Borthwick. Borthwick was not only proprietor of the influential *Morning Post* but was already grumbling about an unnatural lack of consideration for his support of the Unionist cause. Lawson had to wait until 1892 before he got the baronetcy he so evidently desired in 1887.

Other apprehensions about the fete included whether the services of hundreds of teachers should be volunteered without bothering to ask them; there were also questions about what dire consequences might be attendant upon mixing these large numbers of boys and girls together, and the difficulties of providing adequate—and decent—sanitation facilities.

A certain Mr. Runciman wrote to the *Standard*, 'To me, when I think of that mixed horde this question is portentous ... Either you must disfigure the Park, or London must submit to seeing a scandal.' Agreeing with the likes of Runciman that a disaster was looming, the *Church Times* joined the *Pall Mall Gazette* in an unlikely alliance, urging the cancellation of the scheme. But their opposition did not signify as £7,300 was collected, more than enough to cover the cost of the party, on which some £6,500 was spent.

The Duke of Wellington had once said it would tax the resources of a great commander to move 30,000 men into Hyde Park in an orderly manner and bring them out again. For the fete, the task of leading the 'mixed horde' into the Park fell to Colonel Howard Vincent, M.P. of the Queen's Westminster Volunteers, a zealous advocate of amateur soldiery. Undeterred by Wellington's opinion, Howard divided the children into two small armies and marched them to their destination under military command. One division gathered in St. James's Park and the other in Regent's Park. On arrival in Hyde Park the children found a series of tents had been set up, staffed by such fashionable ladies as Lady Randolph Churchill and the Duchesses of Abercorn and Westminster. Even the redoubtable Louisa, Duchess of Manchester, had been prevailed upon to attend and hand out bags of food to the children, not a task ordinarily associated with this notoriously haughty grande dame.

Once the contents of the 30,000 paper bags had been devoured, most of them were released to the winds. Loyal to its proprietor, the *Daily Telegraph* found even these clouds of windswept litter beautiful. 'By and by,' the paper wrote, 'the surface of the Park was whitened with driving clouds, thick as leaves in Vallombrosa. . . .' Diverting games had been provided for the children, such as 25 punch and judy shows with live toby dogs and 86 peep-shows with themes both uplifting and amusing. 'Oh dear, oh dear, I wish it would never be night,' exclaimed one small thing in a white mob cap. 'I shan't be able to play at half the things here.'

In mid-afternoon, aeronauts added another distraction by going aloft in a great coloured balloon suitably named the 'Victoria.' As it rose over the curious, craning faces below, one little girl was heard to remark, 'Look! There's Queen Victoria going to Heaven!' The comment was premature; a few moments later, the Queen arrived in Hyde Park to the enthusiastic cheers of the milling children.

The only one Victoria actually spoke to was Miss Florence Dunn, selected for presentation because she had a perfect school attendance record. Miss Dunn was given a special jubilee cup. This was an idea of the Prince of Wales, who had brought it back from the marriage of the Tsarevitch. 'Can any child, after that memorial mug, invite her to join in a game of hop scotch or skipping rope?' the *Daily News* wondered. The Queen did not mention Miss Dunn in her journal, noting merely that the massed children sang 'God Save The Queen' 'somewhat out of tune.'

Once the singing was concluded, the Queen drove back to Buckingham Palace, leaving the drafted teachers to pry their charges away from the amusements and get them safely home. As Victoria left the area a man standing at the barriers was heard by that voluble diarist Augustus Hare to remark, sorrowfully, 'I have made Socialist speeches for years . . . and the last two days have shown me how useless they have been, and always must be, in this country.'

Later that afternoon, the Queen left London, having remained at Buckingham Palace not a moment longer than she had to, and began a triumphant progress to Windsor. At Slough, where she changed from train to carriage, she was met by the third Duke of Buckingham and Chandos, Lord Lieutenant of Buckinghamshire, and a deputation from the county, who presented her with a congratulatory address.

On her way to the Castle, Victoria made a brief stop at Eton College, where loyal addresses were presented as well as the aged Mr. Wilder, the Vice-Provost, who had been one of the boys sent from the college to congratulate King George III on his golden jubilee in 1809.

Outside Windsor Castle, the Queen unveiled a jubilee statue of herself fashioned by Boehm and given by the citizens of the town. *The Times* was enthusiastic about this work by one of the Queen's favourite artists praising its 'imposing appearance,' but others, closer to the truth, dismissed it as being heavy and lifeless, a bronzed dumpling of a thing. The Queen's opinion of it is unknown, but if she had a favourite jubilee statue of herself it was probably the one placed next to that of the Prince Consort in the grounds of Balmoral.

In the evening of June 22 a torchlight procession of Eton boys marched to the Quadrangle of the Castle carrying flambeaux and Japanese lanterns. With these accompanied by the school bands, they performed flaming figures both 'weird and novel,' according to an account in *The Times*.

One of the songs the boys sang before the Queen was composed especially for the occasion by A. C. Ainger. Eric Parker, an old Etonian who marched that day, later recalled that the previous afternoon neither words nor music had yet been written. But by 8.30 on the day of the march, after a night of febrile inspiration, both were ready to be rehearsed. In these circumstances, it is scarcely to be wondered at that the result was less than memorable: 'Sing together, one and all/Shout together great and small/Victoria! Victoria! Victoria! Our Queen!' The Queen's comments, however, were charitable: 'They did it so well and it had a most charming effect.' Having thanked the boys personally, she sent them home cheering.

On June 25, the Queen addressed a letter to her people; it was published in a special edition of the *London Gazette*. 'I am anxious to express to my people, my warmest thanks for the kind, and more than kind, reception I met with in going to, and returning from Westminster Abbey . . . the enthusiastic reception I met with then, as well as on all these eventful days in London, as well as in Windsor . . . has touched me most deeply.'

The Queen's letter showed she was genuinely pleased by what had been done for her—as well she might be. After all her nervousness before the event, the enthusiasm of the demonstrations which attended her every movement had taken her completely by surprise. Her letter of thanks was much more than a formal expression of gratitude. It was a most personal missive of great sincerity and warmth so 'admirably composed' that the Duke of Cambridge wanted it posted throughout the land. 'This feeling,' she continued, 'and the sense of duty towards my dear country and subjects, who are so inseparably bound up with my life, will encourage me in my task, often a very difficult and arduous one, during the remainder of my life.' Queen Victoria profoundly meant these words as well as the benediction which concluded her letter: 'That God may protect and abundantly bless my country is my fervent prayer.'

After the jubilee and until the end of her reign, there was never again any serious doubt that her countrymen responded to their sovereign's sentiments in loving kind. Yet in the early months of 1887 such happiness ever after had been by no means predictable, not least because the public wish for a brilliant national pageant was being thwarted, largely at Victoria's own wish. What of course provoked people was the apparent meagreness of the programme rather than the hints of its disorganization and confused arrangements which kept reaching them through the press. This was simply because muddle was reckoned to be so usual a part of the business of royal pageantry as to cause no surprise.

CHAPTER ONE

UNCERTAIN CEREMONIAL

AT QUEEN VICTORIA'S CORONATION in 1838, to start at the beginning of the reign, mistakes were very much in evidence, many but by no means all the result of ecclesiastical ineptitude.

The Bishop of Durham, Dr. Maltby, in charge of the orb, symbol of temporal sovereignty, proved, in the Queen's words, 'remarkably maladroit and never could tell me what was to take place,' while Benjamin Disraeli, a spectator in Westminster Abbey, faulted both the bishop's spiritual and lay colleagues who 'were always in doubt as to what came next.'

Unprepared through lack of rehearsal, when the Bishop of Bath and Wells turned over two pages at the end of the order of service, he did not realise he had done so and informed the Queen she might retire, the proceedings being finished. After having trooped off in all her monarchic regalia to the Confessor's Chapel, however, the Queen found the Sub-Dean of the Abbey, in charge because of the Dean's infirmity, insisting that she return and properly finish the ritual. Characteristically, Lord Melbourne, the Prime Minister, preferred to leave matters as they stood—'What does it signify?' he asked the Sub-Dean—but Lord John Thynne was adamant, and so the Queen trooped out again from the debris of the chapel where bottles of wine and sandwiches cluttered the altar.

With such contretemps regularly punctuating the lengthy coronation service, it is little wonder that the girlish and entirely inexperienced Queen Victoria should have beseeched Archbishop Howley of Canterbury for help. 'Pray tell me what I am to do, for they don't know.'

Matters had not improved by the time the Queen married Prince Albert of Saxe-Coburg and Gotha on February 10, 1840.

Albert's movements during the ceremony had not been plotted, and so from one moment to the next he had no idea what was expected of him: should he sit or stand for his bride? Bow to the archbishop or ignore him? Follow the stage whispered advice of the dowager Queen Adelaide or pretend he knew better?

The want of preparation was seen again when the bride arrived in the Chapel Royal at Buckingham Palace; her twelve attendants were so tall they had to take tiny, mincing steps to avoid tripping over each other as they carried a train that was far too short for such a group.

Once the marriage was over, there was further avoidable embarrassment when the twelfth Duke of Norfolk, Earl Marshal, who was himself partly responsible for the poorly arranged ceremonial, insisted upon signing the register first, holding up everyone else while he fumbled to find his spectacles.

The advent of Prince Albert with his efficient habits and head for management led by 1845 to a considerable reform of the way household officials functioned. Insisting that the responsibilities of the Lord Steward and Lord Chamberlain be rationalized, Albert improved the quality of life in the royal residences and also economized. His reforms mainly concerned these officials' domestic duties. The way they handled royal ceremonial was largely, and in the case of the Earl of Marshal, who as an hereditary officer of state felt free to ignore the prince's rationalizing tendencies, entirely untouched, leaving them at liberty to carry on in the careless, casual fashion which had embarrassed the prince at his own wedding and threatened to turn so many other stately events into farces.

At the opening of the Great Exhibition in 1851—this time the responsibility of the Lord Chamberlain, the second Marquess of Breadalbane—such methods led to an astonishing error.

As Handel's 'Hallelujah Chorus' was being performed, a Chinese stepped forward and made a low bow to the Queen. As the *Examiner* recorded, 'this live importation from the Celestial Empire managed to render himself extremely conspicuous, and one could not help admiring his perfect composure and nonchalance of manner.' Seeming to expect a cordial and respectful reception, he was naturally accorded one by officials confident he had been sent at the last moment by the Emperor of China who was otherwise without a representative. He was thus conspicuously placed in the stately procession of ambassadors, though no one knew who he was.

Uncertain Ceremonial

Afterwards this imposing figure in a blue satin robe proved to be something other than he seemed. His name was Hee Sing and, sputtered Henry Cole, one of the Exhibition's chief organizers, merely 'a sea captain who brought his junk into the Thames for exhibition, and got a good deal of money.' Remembering the embarrassing scene made by the Prussian Minister concerning his precedence in the procession, Cole and his colleagues fumed about how the malevolent Court of Berlin would get back its own by magnifying the story of Hee Sing's prominence. As for Prince Albert, he noted the by now unexceptional 'terrible trouble over the arrangements.'

The next year there was more of it, and worse.

On September 14, 1852, after feeling unwell during a drive to Dover, the famous Duke of Wellington commanded his man to 'send for the apothecary.' Expiring shortly thereafter he plunged the inhabitants of Walmer, where he was in residence as Lord Warden of the Cinque Ports, and Deal into a 'perfect stupor' in the words of *The Times*, and obituary writers into a frenzy as they attempted to crown his hallowed memory with ever more laudatory epithets. Since there was never a question that this 'very type and model of an Englishman' deserved a public funeral, his death also plunged royal officials into uncertainty because they had no idea what to do, although the duke's death at the age of 83 might have been anticipated.

At first the lack of any plans for the funeral seemed fitting rather than lax, especially as the duke's heir, Lord Douro, was out of the country at the time of his father's death. After a week, however, *The Times*, feeling the proprieties had been fully observed, began to wonder what was causing the delay, listing a number of topics causing dissension in the nation: disagreement as to where the body should be buried, a fear there would be an unsufficient number of troops to line the way, and—a notion *The Times* summarily rejected—that somehow gorgeous pageantry reeked of the benighted past and was therefore unsuited to the present advanced age. *The Times* soothingly concluded that within five or six weeks these questions would have been resolved yielding the impressive and solemn obsequies everyone desired.

Following the established pattern in these matters, behind the scenes there was uncertainty and even chaos about what should be done, even though officials had providentially been given extra time to work things out.

Because Queen Victoria had not wanted to give the impression that the funeral was the result of royal favour alone but rather sprang from the respect of the nation, she wanted Parliament to give its approval to the proceedings. Parliament, however, would not be in session until November 11 and could not easily be recalled beforehand, not least because ministers of Lord Derby's 'Who? Who?' government were uncertain of their majority and had no wish to hurry back.

The delay, however, was not enough to rescue either the beleaguered Earl Marshal or harassed Lord Chamberlain, the second Marquess of Exeter, who were responsible for different aspects of the arrangements. Working without an effective precedent (for Nelson's funeral in January, 1806 did not provide much guidance beyond where the body might ultimately be interred), preparations lurched forward with the utmost uncertainty, while the press and public rained suggestions about what should be done. Towards the end of September, the *Illustrated London News* caught the prevailing mood: 'Throughout the realm of Britain, all questions and topics of conversation have temporarily merged into one—when, where, and with what state and ceremonial the great Duke of Wellington shall be buried?'

Towards the middle of October *The Times* growled, 'Nobody can say that anything has been done.'

Most of the trouble stemmed from the fact that there was no one person in charge to harness the different, competing authorities more often concerned with maintaining departmental independence than with finding out the most effective means of raising a successful pageant. *The Times's* words in a strong editorial on November 2 might have been applied to any of the great royal occasions. 'It must be borne in mind that hardly anything is yet positively and absolutely fixed, though the preparations are pushed forward as much as possible, and that what is announced one day as agreed upon may be altered the next. . . . From the number of persons having independent authority in carrying out the arrangements of the ceremonial, much confusion and delay are caused even at present, and more will in all probability arise hereafter. The Lord Chamberlain, the Earl Marshal, the Board of Works, the General Commanding-in-Chief, the Commissioners of Police at Scotland Yard and in the City, the Lord Mayor, and the Dean of St. Paul's, all claim jurisdiction in a matter which essentially demands for its proper execution the control of a single guiding authority. The consequence is that nobody entrusted with the actual execution of details seems to know exactly where he is, what he is about, or how far he may go.'

As a result, occasions such as the Duke's Lying-in-State at Chelsea Hospital, undertaken by the Lord Chamberlain, were lamentably arranged, not only because the trappings were, in the words of that busy diarist Charles Greville, 'gaudy and theatrical', but because the rooms were too small and badly arranged for the large numbers of the public who wanted admittance. As a result, in the crush to gain entry at least three persons were pressed to death.

On November 18, the day of the funeral, things were no better, and organizational confusion marred the proceedings throughout.

The Lord Chamberlain's Department had, for example, issued far too many cards for St. Paul's Cathedral where the funeral service was to take place and did not bother with a seating plan so that invited notables found they had to arrive early, scramble for places, and remain long in the draughty cathedral, many of them standing for lack of seats.

Indeed their wait was further prolonged because the massive bronze funeral car, twenty-seven feet of assorted allegory, shaking violently as it was drawn along the route, kept getting stuck in the rich metropolitan mud. Designed after a sketch by Gottfried Semper and only cast at the last minute when the initial plans by Banting the undertaker proved impossible to carry out, the car caused a succession of difficulties on the day of the funeral, the last a delay of over an hour before the Cathedral when the coffin was transferred to the bier on which the duke's remains were borne inside. Not anticipating such a problem, the military bands stationed under the Cathedral's portico had been issued with only one item of music, so that at intervals the chorale 'To Thee O Lord' from Mendelssohn's *St Paul* was played over and over again.

Inside the Cathedral, with the congregation shot through

with the cold of November, the ceremony, the last in which heraldry was prominently featured, took place with only one further mistake. When Garter King of Arms, Sir Albert Woods, recited the Duke's staggering array of honours, he gave Wellington one he did not in fact possess: Duke of Brunoy in France. Louis XVIII had offered such a title it is true, but Wellington had diplomatically turned it down.

Why didn't Prince Albert, so thorough and methodical, angered by inefficiency and muddle, and so concerned about the image of the monarchy do something to change matters? He tried to.

As long before as 1838 Albert, with his Germanic sense of how monarchy should be seen, introduced a number of changes into the Court balls, including a throne from which the Queen could receive her guests, so that these functions were no longer as badly arranged and undignified as Greville had first found them. By the time his favourite child, Victoria, Princess Royal, married Prince Frederick William of Prussia in 1858, Prince Albert had for several years been recognized as the effective agent of the crown and so experienced no difficulty in overseeing Vicky's wedding arrangements himself. Ticklish problems of precedence Albert handled himself, also settling the vexing question of how large a suite each royal guest might bring. As a member of the royal caste himself he could do so more easily and with less likelihood of angry opposition than any official could.

Sadly, however, Albert had too many calls upon his time to follow up this success with a thorough-going reform of the disordered way royal pageants were arranged, even though he was beside himself whenever the final result was less than flawless. He knew the Duke of Wellington's funeral, for instance, was a fiasco, and privately complained to Baron Stockmar, his confidential advisor, that he had been 'torn to pieces' at Vicky's wedding by the 'many little details that had gone wrong.' By the time the Prince of Wales's wedding took place in 1863, fifteen months after Prince Albert died, matters had reverted to their traditional confusion.

With the Queen sunk in deep mourning and used to relying on her dead husband in all things, there was no one to take command of the arrangements for this great state ceremonial.

Police arrangements were deplorable on the day the Prince of Wales fetched his future wife, Alexandra of Denmark, from Gravesend and brought her to a tumultuous reception in the capital. At one point officers beat back the crowd with their truncheons, causing a number of bloody injuries; at another, the Life Guards charged into the panicking crowd with sabres drawn.

At Windsor, where the marriage was celebrated in March, 1863, the precedence of the guests bedevilled royal officials who knew that any unsuitable arrangement of the Prussian and Danish princes present might exacerbate tensions already high because of the Schleswig-Holstein affair which divided the two countries. Throwing up their hands, they left the difficulties to be sorted out by the Count of Flanders, brother of the heir to the Belgian throne, who was prevailed upon to marshal the procession entering St. George's Chapel. He gave pride of place to the Maharajah Duleep Singh, former ruler of the Punjab, a stroke of genius on the Count's part which gave the Europeans a collective feeling of injustice and focused their irritation on the exotic maharajah rather than on each other.

Once inside, the service went smoothly enough (one could scarcely blame officials for the fact that five year old Prince William of Prussia kept biting his uncles' legs), though as the Archbishop of Canterbury concluded the Exhortation the reverent atmosphere was shattered by the musicians, including the organist, tuning their instruments for the recessional. The congregation had to hush them into silence before the archbishop gave the benediction, after which the procession rushed out in rather poorer order than it had come in.

Once the royal guests had departed, the lack of proper planning became very evident as great ladies in tiaras and feathers and gentlemen in ribands and stars looked for a way out of Windsor. At the railway station pandemonium had already broken out, assisted by a sudden rainstorm and hail which delayed the guests from getting there. Crowding on to the platform, they found that too few carriages had been ordered for the special train which had already left without taking on board most of the distinguished travellers for whom it had been intended.

When at last an ordinary train pulled in there was a rush to find a seat, which resulted in such pushing and shoving that the Archbishop of Canterbury was lucky to find a place in third class. There he came across a relieved Lady Cranworth who cried out upon seeing the sorely tried archbishop, who had been much buffeted, 'Oh, I am so glad to see you, my lord. I felt so ashamed of my place. Now I am satisfied.'

Others did not feel so complacent, however: the Austrian Ambassador, angry that he and the other ambassadors had not been invited to the wedding breakfast, found his wife literally pulled off his arm and swept away. Ultimately Countess Apponyi was rescued by Benjamin Disraeli and thrust into a carriage with his wife, on whose lap the former Chancellor of the Exchequer was forced to perch all the way back to Paddington.

With the passing of time, the purpose for which ceremonial events were mounted underwent a subtle though crucial change. Traditionally these functions had been arranged as courtly pageants, in which the bulk of the nation neither expected nor wanted to participate. At best, people were meant to be passive spectators content with the merest glimpse of gorgeous trappings. In such circumstances mistakes were relatively unimportant, however annoying, since few people would know about them and even fewer care. But with the development of a widely read and influential national press, a sense of actual presence and participation could be imparted to everyone no matter how far removed from the scene.

Moreover, with the introduction and development of Prince Albert's concept of a sovereign above party and of the crown as the representative not of a faction but of the entire nation, mystically embodying the national will, pageantry as the symbolic image of monarchy took on an enhanced significance.

Mistakes, confusion and sloppiness were therefore much less tolerable than before because they now besmirched the nation as a whole.

When the Prince Consort died prematurely, worn out by his unflagging and ultimately destructive overwork, the Queen was both unwilling and very likely unable to carry his work to its logical end. Instead, ironically, she thought she was honouring his memory by retreating behind the walls of Windsor, littering the countryside with statues of the prince, and, on account of her prolonged mourning, severely cutting back on the pageantry which was the most vivid and appealing aspect of monarchy. Prince Albert would have been appalled by this course and recognized its danger to the system he had fashioned. Without the prince to bring the Queen to her senses, she adopted a course highly detrimental to the future of the throne. Moreover, with the Prince of Wales, debarred from any useful activity by his mother, sunk in a life of pleasurable dissipations and self indulgence, the unfortunate effect was compounded. The Prime Minister, William Gladstone, an ardent monarchist, rightly fretted about the continued well-being of the crown as he looked at its grave circumstances. In December, 1870 he wrote to Lord Granville, his Foreign Secretary, 'To speak in rude and general terms, the Queen is invisible, and the Prince of Wales is not respected.'

Matters continued to worsen in the wake of the notorious Mordaunt divorce case in which the Prince of Wales was subpoenaed and forced to testify in open court that he had not been involved in any way with Sir Charles Mordaunt's wife. In this instance, since Lady Mordaunt was probably insane, the Prince was justifiably cleared. Even so the whole incident fed the burgeoning republican movement which was led by the very able and ambitious Sir Charles Dilke, M.P., a young man of talent Gladstone could simply not dismiss out of hand.

Under circumstances which the Queen showed no signs of understanding as she vetoed schemes for the Prince of Wales's useful employment in a viceregal capacity in Ireland and refused to lighten her own mourning, it was a godsend that the heir to the throne fell seriously ill just as Dilke was in the midst of a major speaking tour arguing the establishment of an English republic.

Diagnosed, after a visit to Lord and Lady Londesborough's place at Scarborough, as typhoid, the prince's illness (which was first reported in the press on November 22, 1871) took a dramatic course which was made even more compelling when the seventh Earl of Chesterfield, who had been at Scarborough, died, followed by a groom who had also been there.

After a visit from the Queen and her retinue to Sandringham House, the prince's fever waned, and with it public interest. But on December 8, without warning, his condition seriously worsened, and three days later he was on the verge of death. The Queen rushed back to Sandringham with other members of the Royal Family to wait by the prince's bedside for four days and nights while he fought for life, every phase of his illness being reported by the press to a public now anxiously aroused.

Despite Bertie's strong constitution, he gradually weakened; at one point the Queen and Princess Alice, her daughter, were lugubriously assuring each other that there was no hope. Yet on December 14, as the bleak anniversary of Prince Albert's death came round, the fever finally broke and it became obvious the prince would survive after all.

No monarchist needed to be told to what use the Prince of Wales's illness could be put. Even the Duke of Cambridge, perhaps the least imaginative of men, wrote to his mother, 'The Republicans say their chances are up—Thank God for this! Heaven has sent this dispensation to save us.' And *The Times* made use of the occasion to urge the prince to lead a more serious and useful life as behoved a man snatched from the grave. 'We can well believe that it [his recovery] will be followed by a resolution that the years of his maturer manhood shall be given to the service of the people who have shown themselves so anxious for his welfare.'

The first requisite was a suitably splendid ceremony of thanksgiving designed to express the gratitude of the sovereign and her heir to the Almighty, and, not so incidentally, to provide a show for the people who had wanted their prince to live and who had sadly missed the public functions of monarchy since the demise of the Prince Consort.

The idea for the thanksgiving service may have come from the Prince of Wales himself; it was enthusiastically received within the Royal Family. Gladstone and his government were delighted that such an event should take place; predictably, however, Queen Victoria, who had herself only just overcome a feverish rheumatic infection, was with difficulty persuaded to comply.

Once the Queen had consented, however, Gladstone and most of the members of his Cabinet were eager that the event, which was a neat way of reinforcing the throne and dishing Dilke, should be a truly regal occasion and make use of the full panoply of monarchic pomp. At the beginning there was by no means total agreement on who should be made to bear the expense; Robert Lowe, the often irascible if brilliant Chancellor of the Exchequer, flirted with the idea the Queen should pay for it herself from her Privy Purse, a scheme which would confound the radicals, who wondered along with an anonymous contemporary pamphleteer, 'What Does She Do With It?' Since he had a suspicion this idea would not prove popular at the palace, he indicated he would be willing to go to Parliament for the money if pressed.

When the third Viscount Sydney, the Lord Chamberlain, learned that the Queen might be asked to pay for the ceremony herself, he immediately went to Gladstone assuring him in the strongest terms that if Victoria were so solicited, the entire plan was likely to be vetoed, since the Queen was searching for any excuse to squash the proceedings. Though there was no stauncher advocate of cheese-paring than the Grand Old Man, he instantly told the Lord Chamberlain that his government would ask Parliament for the cash.

Working out the details for the ensuing ceremony fell entirely to the Lord Chamberlain's Department, for the Queen made her approval contingent upon the thanksgiving being a ceremony in semi rather than full state, enabling her to dispense with the full impedimenta of monarchy and proceed in relatively informal style.

Semi-state had never been used for such an important ceremony; nor had it ever been used when Parliament had been asked for a grant to cover expenses. Such events, to be sure, were part of the royal calendar, but the open carriage and morning clothes which distinguished them were understood to be correct only for comparatively minor occasions, such as dedicating a building or opening a bridge. The Queen's decision thus flew in the face of precedent and had the not unimportant result of cutting the Earl Marshal, who could only be employed on state occasions, out of the business of pageantry for the time being.

Precisely how novel the Queen's decision was, Garter King of Arms, the Earl Marshal's chief deputy, himself was able to verify when asked to search through his records for a recent precedent of the sovereign entering the City of London (where St. Paul's is located) to render thanks to God. Only one of those which Sir Albert Woods discovered was sufficiently documented to be of use, and it did not support Victoria's position. In July, 1814 the Prince Regent (later King George IV) had entered the City to give thanks for the successful termination of the war between England and France. Garter's records showed it as a splendid ceremony in full state in which the members of the House of Lords, the Great Officers of State, the Archbishops of Canterbury and York, the members of the College of Arms and the Princes of the Blood Royal had all taken part.

In the circumstances Victoria's determination to dispense with the rich regalia of the English crown seemed almost insulting and was certainly unwise.

Dedicated as he was to reinforcing the throne and stemming the criticism against the Queen, Gladstone found himself in a difficult position because of Victoria's obstinacy, moreover his Cabinet, as Sydney informed Ponsonby Fane, was 'very much disturbed' by what was happening.

Gladstone, of course, was most sympathetic to such opinion. He was also well aware of sentiments like those of Sir Thomas Biddulph, the Keeper of the Queen's Privy Purse, who candidly informed Ponsonby Fane, 'I am afraid the Queen is getting alarmed about there being an idea that she is going in *State* to St. Paul's, so please make it understood that it is only half state. The difference to her, whether she went in one or the other is nil, but she has peculiar fancies.'

Most accustomed to these 'fancies', the Prime Minister knew that too strong a representation to Victoria on the matter might result in the cancellation of the thanksgiving with serious adverse results and would certainly undermine his still good working relationship. That the Queen wanted to end it all or at least stay out herself was clear after she had asked him on January 13 for an escape clause to be included in the announcement to Parliament in case she decided not to participate. And throughout their subsequent correspondence in January and February she let it be known with what alacrity she would withdraw.

Because the Queen was adamant and Gladstone did not want to jeopardize the thanksgiving, he allowed Lord Sydney to make the kind of arrangements Victoria wanted. Disappointed, facing an irritated Cabinet and the first hints of criticism from the press, Gladstone reluctantly told Sydney that semi-state might do well enough if it did not rain and if the horses moved at a slower trot than usual so that the people could see.

At the same time, the Queen was making it abundantly clear precisely what kind of ceremony she wanted. On January 22, 1872 she informed the Prime Minister that she would have a small and simple affair of short duration. 'Ostentatious pomp,' she assured Gladstone, was 'utterly incompatible' and 'unsuitable to the present day,' an argument which was nothing more than rationalization on the Queen's part, pure and simple.

Sydney therefore arranged that the procession to St. Paul's would be handled in the same fashion as that organized when Blackfriars Bridge was opened in 1869, and the Queen kept a close surveillance to make sure nothing more elaborate was done. A few carriages, none of them state equipages, were all that was allowed, and a short processional route was authorized. Between 7,000 and 8,000 people were to be invited to the cathedral.

Sydney had good reason for suspecting that these arrangements would not satisfy the public. It was against his better judgment, therefore, that Ponsonby Fane was permitted to announce how many persons were to be accommodated in St. Paul's. When the almost paltry figures became known, there was an immediate outcry. If this was the total of those being invited, how elaborate could the other plans possibly be? At once there were demands for a release of the full prospectus.

The announcement of the number of guests to be invited to St. Paul's resulted in a torrent of criticism being directed against the impending thanksgiving service, now set for February 27. There were those (including *The Times*) who believed that up to 18,000 had been present in the same edifice on the occasion of the Duke of Wellington's funeral. This probably large overestimate was not easy to refute, no precise count of tickets ever having been made. Those better informed, such as F.C. Penrose, Architect to St. Paul's, estimated the figure at between 12,000 and 13,000.

Even so *The Times* and the London Court of Common Council thought the figures for this occasion far too low, and when the Prince of Wales actively intervened, the Lord Chamberlain was forced to make the first of what soon became a whole train of significant modifications: he raised his estimate to 13,000 places and instructed the contractors in the first week of February to alter their plans accordingly. Gladstone told the House of Commons that he was delighted by the development.

The processional route, already announced in the *London Gazette*, was the next item to be challenged. *The Times* led the attack against what was generally deplored, citing the inappropriateness of the Embankment, the level surface of which would allow only one row of spectators to be accommodated and these at great risk because pickpockets roamed the area at will. Oxford Street was preferable. While *The Times* supported its position by printing a spate of letters to this effect, behind the scenes discussions were taking place involving the Prince of Wales and finally even the Cabinet, which resulted in Oxford Street being added and the Embankment dropped.

The immediate result of the change of route was a threat of resignation from Lord Sydney, who by now had had quite enough. He had been embarrassed by the changes in the number of guests to be invited and by the alteration of the processional route, both of which suggested his superintendence was at fault. In fact, of course, Sydney was not personally responsible for the contretemps. He was unhappily caught between the wishes of his sovereign and those of the government and public. As Ponsonby, the Queen's Private Secretary, wrote to assuage his hurt pride, 'The real truth is that the thing has grown. She has consented to do much more now than originally could have been proposed.' Having been assured of the Queen's continuing regard, Sydney decided to stay on.

In the meantime, however, newspaper opinion was letting it be known that still more changes were needed. Beginning on February 8, *The Times* began its campaign for the organization of a brilliant pageant 'with all that constitutes a show in the eyes of the people.' Again and again it made its position clear, in one editorial writing, 'We cannot let a day pass without again urging that the Royal procession be made more worthy of the occasion than is at present intended.'

On February 19, *The Times* spelled out in detail what it thought fitting for the occasion: The Lord Chancellor and the Speaker of the House of Commons as well as deputations from both Houses of Parliament, ministers, judges and other eminent persons should be asked to join. 'The Royal Family,' it stated unequivocally, 'should be followed or preceded by something more than their attendants and a squadron of Life Guards, and those who have the ordering of this matter should use all forethought and spare no pains to render the procession as imposing and interesting as possible.'

Gladstone, wanting something grander than the Queen contemplated, entirely agreed with these opinions and because of them was at last able to say so. Five days before the event, he informed Victoria, 'The truth is that there is a great & signal outburst of loyal feeling & affection, which however does not readily brook disappointment & Mr G cannot doubt that any addition to the forepart of the procession . . . wd be very acceptable to Parlt as well as the public.' The Prime Minister was, as always, most courteous, but the Queen could not have missed the point that whoever pays the piper feels justified in calling the tune. With the utmost reluctance, Victoria agreed to the participation of the Lord Chancellor and the Speaker of the House.

Having done so, however, she refused to sanction the use by the Speaker of his splendid state coach suggesting that its ostentatious bulk would slow down the procession which she wanted to end as quickly as possible. The Queen may well also have feared that the Speaker's state, compared to her own, would occasion adverse comment. Again there was opposition, Gladstone, a rigorous House of Commons man, informing her that members would not permit their official representative to appear in a mere town carriage. Again the Queen was forced to give way.

Though suggestions for alterations went on being made, few more were adopted. The second Duke of Wellington, Lord Lieutenant of Middlesex, was not to be included in the procession, although Victoria's cousin the Duke of Cambridge, Field Marshal Commanding in Chief, was invited on one condition. As Ponsonby telegraphed to Lord Sydney, 'This is to be considered final arrangement.' At the same time Victoria wrote to Gladstone, 'The Queen is looking with much alarm to the ceremony of the 27th—the fatigue & excitement of wh she fears will be vy great & she has been grtly annoyed at the constant new suggestions wh are being made.'

To one suggestion that was made to her, the Queen remained adamantly opposed: the Prince and Princess of Wales should not, she insisted, ride in a carriage by themselves but would drive with Victoria herself. As Ponsonby shrewdly guessed in a letter to Gladstone, he suspected the Queen felt Alix and Bertie would be more enthusiastically received than she would be. In this instance Gladstone wisely acquiesced.

In fact one more change was made before the day of thanksgiving, but it did nothing to relieve continuing criticism of the arrangements. On February 23, the departure time was moved up by a quarter of an hour, evoking strenuous protests from the police at the disruption of the published plans. As *The Times* wrote on February 26, having surveyed them, 'The show itself will be a trifle—infinitesimal. . . .'

Nonetheless on February 27 most people made the best of the situation, despite such unsatisfactory aspects as a dearth of soldiers, the absence of bands, the fact that most of the royal carriages were closed because of a chill rain, and the use of streets like the Old Bailey—surely, wrote *The Times* reporter, 'the most gloomy and dilapidated of thoroughfares.'

Then, too, the service at St. Paul's was not felt to be above reproach. 'Why,' asked *The Times* in evaluating the 'Te Deum' and Anthem of Mr. Goss, 'should we be condemned on a State occasion of unprecedented solemnity to the official compositions of the St. Paul's organist?'

Still, the Queen, who never minded gusts of cold air, allowed her own carriage to be open, which pleased the crowds along the way even if it exposed the haggard condition of the still convalescing Prince of Wales.

Despite the many justifiable criticisms, most opinion was inclined to praise the national thanksgiving—once it was over. Victoria, for instance, who herself had made so many difficulties, wrote, 'I have no time to describe at length the long progress, the millions out, the beautiful decorations, the wonderful enthusiasm and astounding affectionate loyalty shown.' Even *The Times*, which had been most outspoken about how poorly things were being arranged, changed its tune after everything had taken place. 'The Thanksgiving Day has come and gone, and universal opinion proclaims that it has exhibited one of the grandest and most impressive ceremonies ever witnessed in this country.'

Loyal though such sentiments were, they were not in the long run very helpful, for they could only confirm in the Queen's mind the notion that she had been quite right to stand against the tide desiring the grandest pageantry possible. Now she could argue, if the matter arose again, that semi-state, though simple, was sufficient, entirely forgetting how insistent most people had been that it was inadequate, even insulting for any occasion of significance.

'Those who say the British people do not love shows mistake them sadly, and no less mistaken are they who would abolish them as at issue with civilization.' Thus had *The Times* concisely stated the case on thanksgiving day itself.

When the matter arose again, however, as was inevitable, the Queen was found to be as unheedful as before, which was, of course, one reason why her golden jubilee proved so difficult to arrange. Why did her government not intervene to right matters?

CHAPTER TWO

A 'DISGRACEFUL DEBATE'

BY JANUARY, 1887 the second ministry of the third Marquess of Salisbury had been in office only a few months, yet the Queen was firmly attached to it. In large part her fondness was the direct result of the prospective alternative, an administration headed by her now notorious bogeyman, Mr. Gladstone. Gladstone's relations with the Queen, as all the world knows, had been severely troubled for years, but his advocacy of the Irish Home Rule cause made them poisonous. 'For long I stood up for his motives,' Victoria wrote disingenuously in the summer of 1886, 'but now they are activated by vanity, ambition & malice & shew signs of madness.'

Gladstone's adoption of Home Rule not only assured him the undying enmity of his sovereign, but brought down his third ministry, split his party and ushered in a fascinating period of political turbulence and uncertainty. As the dust began to settle, two hostile coalitions faced each other in the land: the dominant 'Unionist' party made up chiefly of orthodox Conservatives headed by Lord Salisbury and joined by such former Liberal stalwarts as the Whig leader Lord Hartington and the pride of the Radicals, Joseph Chamberlain. Facing them were the shattered Gladstonians now firmly allied with the forces of Irish Nationalism headed by that cool enigma, Charles Stewart Parnell.

Resounding party names notwithstanding, these coalitions were nothing more than loose, shifting groups of men, whose precarious balance might easily be upset as the politics of instability unfolded. As was to be expected, developments from Ireland provided the first test of their ability to endure.

By the summer of 1886, the agrarian situation in Ireland had reached a parlous state with livestock and agrarian prices greatly depressed and the means of credit to tide people over too limited for those in need. The dark undercurrent of rural violence, never far from the surface of Irish life, emerged with vengeful forcefulness against the landlords, whose most glaringly apparent member was that rent-racking eccentric, the second Marquess of Clanricarde, enjoying in London the staggering profits from wide estates in County Galway.

As this situation took form, both Lord Salisbury and Parnell adopted characteristic postures: the Prime Minister, pledged to a strong law and order policy, quickly dispatched General Sir Redvers Buller to the southwest of Ireland to squash outrage, making the slightest bow in the direction of reform by appointing a study commission to review the land situation. In his turn, Parnell offered an amendment to the address at the opening of Parliament in August drawing attention to the pitiable conditions of Irish tenants and the exactions of Lord Clanricarde. Shortly afterwards, he produced a Tenants Relief Bill designed to give the land court power to suspend the eviction of persons of proved insolvency.

Both Salisbury's position and Parnell's response raised doubts among their allies, who were accustomed to supporting other policies, but in the end the need to preserve the still very fragile coalitions proved persuasive. A hesitant Gladstone led his party in voting for tenants' relief, while the Liberal Unionists, no doubt hoping that the study commission would advocate a more tender policy, supported the government's position, thus assuring it a majority of 95. Just as Parnell had predicted, this result produced further chaos in Ireland, where the Plan of Campaign followed as a matter of course.

Inspired by an article in *United Ireland* by Timothy Healy, M.P., towards the end of October, the Plan of Campaign was a scheme designed to support tenants facing eviction. Its leading idea was to withhold rents deemed excessive and to use them to help individuals facing ejection. In the difficult times of the autumn of 1886, it proved an instant success, quickly engulfing most of the 116 estates which it ultimately affected.

As the Plan of Campaign moved from success to success in Ireland, the parliamentary coalitions in England were again challenged by these unsettling developments. This time, however, it was Parnell who gave way to Gladstone, moving against the agitators of the land war so as to preserve the

Nationalist alliance with the Liberals. At the same time, the Liberal Unionists adopted the policy of the government by refusing to allow any extension of the principle of revision of rent by direct intervention of the state.

The resolution of these two potentially threatening situations might have led dimmer observers to suppose that the political situation was returning to the equilibrium which had characterized it in mid-Victorian times, and that the government which Lord Randolph Churchill had likened to 'a rickety infant, requiring the most careful handling' was growing up into a secure maturity. As the more acute were aware, however, it was Lord Randolph himself who stood in the way of this development.

Having blazed into prominence during Gladstone's second ministry as the master of a suave and cutting irreverence, and leader of the so-called 'Fourth Party', made up of gilded young men in a hurry, Lord Randolph had after the Home Rule elections gained such a heady position that Lord Salisbury felt he had no choice but to make him Leader of the House of Commons and Chancellor of the Exchequer, a stunning achievement for a man of only 37 whom the Prime Minister profoundly suspected.

Lord Salisbury's doubts were redoubled, once the unpredictable Churchill was in the Cabinet, where he proved to be a stinging nettle to his rather hidebound colleagues. He inclined to Russophilia; the Cabinet was strongly Rossophobic. He wanted to impose parliamentary closure by majority vote; other ministers found it a dangerous, threatening innovation. Quickly becoming a staunch Treasury man, he zealously emulated Gladstone's cheese-paring ways; the rest of the government thought his frugalities extreme and short sighted. In the end, such disagreements, disheartening to both the Prime Minister and Lord Randolph, could not last, but when Lord Randolph decided to provoke a crisis, he so foolishly chose his ground as to make Lord Salisbury's victory an easy one.

Churchill made the precipitate decision to resign his positions due to some trifling differences over expenditures between himself and the heads of the services, W. H. Smith at the War Office and Lord George Hamilton, First Lord of the Admiralty. Insisting that he was 'pledged to the eyes' for retrenchment,

Churchill told Salisbury he must go unless reductions were ordered. Salisbury, stunned by his supreme good fortune in having Lord Randolph choose to make a stand upon such a narrow and unstirring subject, instead quickly called his bluff. In a whisk the resignation was accepted, and the Prime Minister's Christmas at Hatfield House was turned into an event of high hilarity and great good spirits, for it was nearly certain that Churchill had himself destroyed a spectacular, bothersome career.

The immediate result of Churchill's resignation was the need for Lord Salisbury to reorder his administration, a prospect so alarming to Joseph Chamberlain, who feared the end product would be unbearably reactionary without Churchill, that this 'man who killed Home Rule' immediately made a gesture of conciliation to Mr. Gladstone, thus launching a round of earnest talks between Gladstone and Liberal Unionists to see if a satisfactory rapprochement might be fashioned.

These talks added yet another unsettling factor to an already confused situation, but Lord Salisbury had even more pressing problems in the new year than whether Chamberlain would return to the Liberals. Could he fill the Treasury post? The Leadership of the House of Commons? And by doing so somehow strengthen a vulnerable government with uncertain prospects? Lord Randolph had, of course, gambled that Salisbury could not, and that having confounded the political world by his resignation, he would amaze it by his swift return to office, his indispensability sweetly confirmed by the Prime Minister and the 'Old Gang' Conservatives. Having 'got rid of a boil on the back of his neck,' however, Salisbury was resolved to do whatever was necessary to insure against its return. Relying on the help of the Queen, who was much put out by Churchill's 'extraordinary conduct', the Prime Minister finally managed to draw in G. J. Goschen, a former Liberal First Lord of the Admiralty, the man about whom Lord Randolph had forgotten. He took the Exchequer.

For Churchill's leadership of the Commons, Salisbury picked W. H. Smith, a worthy, unimaginative figure, now known mainly for his railway bookstalls and the fact that he is thought to have been the inspiration for the Right Honourable Sir Joseph Porter, K.C.B., First Lord of the Admiralty in *H.M.S.*

Pinafore. Historically, he wasn't, though the caricature is apposite enough, since Smith had been Disraeli's First Lord and had as little naval knowledge as Porter. If as *The Times* wrote, 'Mr. Goschen will take Lord Randolph Churchill's place in more senses than one', Mr. Smith just took his place.

At the same time, Salisbury took advantage of Churchill's resignation to remove the plodding first Earl of Iddesleigh from the Cabinet as Foreign Secretary, taking on the office himself. As in domestic affairs, the foreign situation was a most troubled one at the time. Yet, he reasoned, when England was faced with some prospect of war, who could deal with the situation so well or more prudently? He may also have felt some obligation for alleviating difficulties for which he himself was not without responsibility.

Uncharacteristically audacious, Lord Salisbury, then, too, Foreign Secretary, had during his 1885 'Caretaker' government managed to contrive the creation of a new Bulgarian principality under the leadership of Prince Alexander of Battenberg. It was a neat move simultaneously erecting another barrier against Russian expansion in the Balkans and designed to shore up the Ottoman Sultan's control over the remainder of his European empire, but it led to a squall with Russia, whose Tsar was convinced that England had become his principal antagonist. He therefore worked assiduously to destroy the Bulgarian creation, finally ordering the kidnapping of the prince himself when all else failed. So long as Lord Randolph, with his known leaning to St. Petersburg, his unalterable opposition to European involvement and his determination that large cuts had to be made in military spending, remained in the Cabinet, Salisbury was handicapped in what he might do about such 'simply piratical' actions. As soon as Churchill was gone, however, the Russians feared he might consider war.

The truth is, however, that Salisbury wanted peace and quiet both at home and abroad, and as soon as he took the Foreign Office he set out to contain the tensions. He did so by helping to fashion the Mediterranean agreements, an understanding between Britain, Italy and Austria (with some German backing) for the defence of the status quo in the area. These treaties neutralized any threat from either Russia or France, nations which could only be truly menacing when supported by a member of the Triple Alliance, all the members of which Salisbury had now squared. As soon as they were signed, therefore, later in 1887 a countermovement towards a general normalization of relations set in.

Busy as both Prime Minister and Foreign Secretary, Salisbury had to cope not only with the shifting alignments of parliamentary politics but also with the intricate manoeuvres on the international scene. He had also to deal with continuing agrarian difficulties in Ireland as well as unparalleled obstruction by Nationalist members in the House of Commons, who objected to the measures the government was adopting to deal with the situation. Then, too, he had to worry about whether Joseph Chamberlain would withdraw, and whether his alliance with the Liberal Unionists could be made to run smoothly. And then there was always the uncertain menace of Lord Randolph Churchill to consider. Given all these considerations, Lord Salisbury may perhaps be excused for letting the Queen's impending golden jubilee slip his mind from time to time. Victoria, of course, was not pleased when it did, irritably remarking throughout the spring on her Prime Minister's general ignorance about the arrangements. After he had paid her a visit to Windsor in late March, 1887, for instance, she wrote in her journal that they 'talked of the Jubilee arrangements some of which he did not seem to understand till I explained them to him. . . .'

Even had he had time to concern himself with this matter, Lord Salisbury was not sufficiently interested to do so, for all that others considered how fortunate it was that such an event, which could be used to boost the cause of Unionism, had fallen to his time in office.

Bearer of an historic name, master of wide acres, accustomed to the substance of power, Robert Arthur Talbot Gascoyne-Cecil, Marquess and Earl of Salisbury, Viscount Cranborne, Baron Cecil, had no more than a polite interest in stately pomp and circumstance, ribands and stars, the pageants and *on dits* of the Court. He accepted the Garter in 1878 only because Disraeli had made it a condition of his own acceptance that Salisbury should have it, too, and consistently declined a dukedom from Queen Victoria, who periodically pressed him to change his mind.

Very likely he preferred his chemical experiments and the tricycle on which he made excursions through the vastness of Hatfield House. Baubles and gewgaws from the fountain of honour were of slight consequence to him, and he seems never to have understood why other men would persistently scheme to get them. Of course, given the wealth of such trifles which he himself accumulated over a lifetime it is hard not to smile at Lord Salisbury's professed indifference to the insignia of rank.

When it came time for the jubilee his lack of interest in matters of ceremonial was so rooted that he could not even simulate curiosity about what was to take place. Nonetheless, Salisbury had to give it some attention. When he reluctantly turned from his other more pressing work to do so, one thing was uppermost in his mind: the jubilee should be handled in such a way that both he and the House of Commons should be bothered by it as little as possible.

To realize this ambition, in December, 1886, Salisbury asked William Henry, fourth Earl of Mount Edgcumbe, to head a special jubilee committee to superintend the occasion. Long associated with the Court, beginning with his appointment as Lord of the Bedchamber to the Prince of Wales in 1862, Mount Edgcumbe had previously been both Lord Chamberlain and Lord Steward before the Prime Minister again named him for the second time to the latter, premier post in the Household in August, 1886.

It was evidently Salisbury's intention that Mount Edgcumbe should assume direction of all jubilee activities, coordinate the various government departments involved and establish some sort of central bureau which would keep the Prime Minister abreast of all developments with a minimal effort on his part. It was a sensible, overdue idea, but presented its own problems, not the least of which in Mount Edgcumbe's opinion was that if he, having long served the Prince of Wales, were to head the committee, it might prove difficult to resist the 'somewhat extravagant' notions the Prince was expected to propose. Since in any case the Lord Steward did not expect members of the Cabinet to follow the orders of a mere member of the household without demur, he therefore earnestly hoped Salisbury would appoint a minister chairman, allowing Mount

Edgcumbe to serve as a simple member instead. If, however, Salisbury decided to persist in his original scheme, Mount Edgcumbe urged him at the very least to name the members of the committee himself. Otherwise it would not have enough authority to act.

Nothing seems to have been done by the Prime Minister before the first meeting of the jubilee committee was convened at the Board of Green Cloth towards the middle of January, 1887. Salisbury's failure to respond to Mount Edgcumbe's letter threw a pall of uncertainty over this first gathering at which Mount Edgcumbe was joined by Lord Lathom, Lord Chamberlain; Earl Sydney, who had been Lord Chamberlain at the time of the national thanksgiving in 1872, and, in an advisory capacity, Sir Spencer Ponsonby-Fane and Edward Hamilton of the Treasury.

Once gathered together, they were uncertain about what they could do and spent their first meeting drawing up questions designed to elicit from the Prime Minister a summary of their powers and responsibilities. These were submitted in a memorandum drawn up by Mount Edgcumbe on January 14.

Were members of the committee appointed 'personally, departmentally or as representing the Government?' they wanted to know. 'What evidence of delegated authority of any kind can be given to insure our recognition by the various Departments & officials with whom we may have to communicate?' 'Is it contemplated that we should take the initiative in any such communications, or . . . has [it] been arranged that the Heads of the various Departments will communicate with us in the first instance when they want us to do anything?'

These were matters of such concern to the committee that 'Both Lord Lathom & Lord Sydney feel as strongly as I do that we can take no action whatever—even in seeking information—until our authority for doing so is fully defined & recognized....'

Salisbury's response was not what they had hoped for: he did no more than get the Cabinet to appoint them as an official committee of the government, a response which left its members as uncertain as ever about what to do.

Mount Edgcumbe summed up the committee's disappointment in a sorrowful letter to Henry John Manners,' the Prime Minister's secretary, on January 2, 1887. 'I am bound to say that at present the Committee hardly see how they can be of much use—as everything will be undertaken by the particular Depart^t under which it comes.' In short, without explicit sanction from the Prime Minister, there was no way for Mount Edgcumbe to exercise the coordinating function Salisbury originally intended.

Salisbury evidently accepted these arguments, at least in part, for he later allowed Cabinet members to serve on the jubilee committee. By then, however, it was already too late, for once preparations were begun each department was reluctant to place itself under the jurisdiction of the overseeing committee. As Mount Edgcumbe informed Salisbury in April, even Lord Lathom, directing preparations for the service in Westminster Abbey, would not cooperate, though he was inferior to the Lord Steward in rank. As the jubilee broke down into the traditional muddle of conflicting authorities, Mount Edgcumbe could only wail, 'There does not seem to be much for the C^tee to do. . . .' In fact, as matters advanced, there was more need than ever for such a superintending body, but without the explicit authority which Lord Salisbury seemed unable to give, Mount Edgcumbe hung back, allowing things to take their uncertain course. Understandably, he felt rather guilty about his failure to take action. On June 3 he wrote rather defensively to Lord Salisbury, 'I hope you don't think that I have been remiss in not keeping the Jubilee Committee at work. I think that if it had continued to meet it might have been useful for the discussion of some doubtful questions & for registering what was settled from time to time. But as Lathom regarded everything connected with the arrangements for the Thanksgiving day as strictly belonging to his Department, & preferred consulting the Queen & the Government independently . . . and as nothing else in the way of Jubilee celebration could be entertained for want of money, there was nothing for the Committee to do.'

Mount Edgcumbe need not have been so apologetic, as Salisbury's failure to pay proper attention to the committee was as much responsible for the result as his own exceeding caution about what he should do. In consequence, of course, the jubilee lurched forward in the confused fashion typical of English royal events. This disorganization was generally provoking but not of enough interest to Lord Salisbury, who let matters regarding the committee take a drifting course.

Perhaps the only thing to make him abandon his indifference to the committee might have been some indication that it could assist his government in satisfactorily arranging jubilee matters in the House of Commons. But in the absence of any such indication, Salisbury allowed what might have proved an important innovation to founder, while he himself was forced to consider how legislation needed for the jubilee could quickly and easily be brought through one of the most turbulent and obstructed Houses of Commons ever assembled. An editorial in *The Times*, admittedly a rabidly Unionist organ, on March 4, 1887, gives some indication of what was happening.

'A robust and unwavering faith in the vitality of Parliamentary institutions is indispensable to the peace of mind of any public-spirited Englishman who watches what is happening from day to day in the House of Commons. It is not only that obstruction, once the patented invention and private property of a few irreconcilables, is now widely spread and unblushingly avowed among politicians closely associated with distinguished party leaders. It is not only that new methods of delaying public business are continually introduced and adopted with zeal or regarded with chastened resignation by responsible statesmen. The mischief goes far deeper and is much more dangerous. Obstruction, even in its most insidious forms, may be encountered by changes in the rules of the House, but it is difficult to see how any such changes can prevent the subversion of order, authority, and law which is wrought by the ruinous influence of faction.'

What had caused this situation?

Early in the session the government had introduced the Criminal Law Amendment Bill, a tough coercive measure designed to provide for the prosecution of boycotting, intimidation, criminal conspiracies against rent, unlawful assembly, resistance to eviction, or the incitement of others to commit such crimes, all to be dealt with in courts of summary jurisdiction. It also allowed for the transfer of cases involving trial by jury so that local feelings of leniency might be countered, and it gave the Lord Lieutenant the power to declare by proclamation that the act was in force in listed parts of the country or that specified associations were 'dangerous' and their members therefore liable to be prosecuted. More ominously from the Irish standpoint, the act, unlike those which had gone before, did not have to be submitted periodically to parliament for renewal. It was designed to be a permanent menace.

With the introduction of such a measure, the stage was set for one of the most disruptive parliamentary sessions in history, as the Irish Nationalists and some Radical Liberal allies tried every obstructionist technique to stall this legislation, including filibustering against every measure which preceded it on the calendar. Eager to minimize all such opportunities for delay and to force the House of Commons to deal with this issue, it was the Salisbury government's policy to present as few other matters for debate as possible. This prohibition applied, too, to the jubilee where it was the ministry's plan to ask for House of Commons action only on the matter of supplies for the occasion.

Ironically, however, it was that staunchest of Unionists, the Queen, who foiled this sensible plan, forcing the government to bring in another, unexpected piece of legislation especially for the sovereign.

Often reminding people that she was the daughter of an army man (her father the Duke of Kent had been Colonel of the first Royal Scots), Queen Victoria had always taken an interest in her military forces and had often regretted her inability to serve. It was a disability she intended to make up for in the life of her son Prince Arthur, who from the time he was named after his godfather the Duke of Wellington was destined for an army career. Like any proud mama, of course, Victoria wanted to ensure that it was a successful one, and therefore was never shy about pressing for the Duke of Connaught's steady promotion to positions of real power.

In 1885 such a position opened up, Commander-in-Chief of the forces of the Indian presidency of Bombay. At once, the queen laid siege to Lord Salisbury's 'Caretaker' Administration, making the utmost effort to persuade the Prime Minister to authorize this appointment before the Liberals returned to office and (she was sure) gave it to someone else.

Lord Salisbury was under no illusions about the Duke's credentials. He was at best only a conscientious, unimaginative man, and the Cabinet therefore considered the post too important for him and moreover knew that ordering him to it would provoke outraged accusations from the Opposition about unwarranted patronage and truckling to the Queen. Its members therefore unanimously voted not to accede to Victoria's request.

Inevitably, of course, the Queen protested against this decision, and had her cousin, the Duke of Cambridge, Field Marshal Commanding-in-Chief, write to the War Secretary to do so, too. In time a succession of such moves brought about what the Queen wanted, although none of Lord Salisbury's misgivings had been allayed. Even so, the Queen was ecstatic: 'It is a splendid command,' she noted in her journal, pointing out that the prince would have 36,000 men under him and would be able 'to do whatever he likes, as to promotions, &c, not having to refer to anyone.' Such a post was well worth the struggle she had had to make. Imagine the Queen's surprise, then, when she was told that if her 'favourite son' came home for her jubilee, he would automatically lose it.

Due to a statute passed during the reign of William IV, the departure of certain high ranking officers from India, including the commander-in-chief of Bombay, brought about their immediate resignation. The Queen's response to this situation was automatic: it was a foolish, archaic law and ought to be changed. Surprise turned to outrage, however, when Victoria was told that Lord Salisbury considered the parliamentary situation so difficult he could not recommend amending the law in order to permit the Duke to return home. At once, Victoria's back stiffened as she ordered her private secretary to inform the Prime Minister on March 1, 'As it [the bill] need not consist of more than one clause repealing a former clause, there will be very little room for obstruction and if a limited number of members use offensive language she cannot help that.'

The Queen's position on what she was soon to describe as this 'most amazing difficulty' put the government into a difficult situation not only because the course she recommended would necessitate a postponement of the Crimes bill, the most important measure of the session, but also because adopting her view would force the ministry to defend an appointment it had only reluctantly agreed to make in the first place. After consulting with W. H. Smith and other Unionist leaders, therefore, Salisbury told Ponsonby on March 2 that such a bill in this session was an 'absolute impossibility.'

Refusing to accept the Prime Minister's advice, Queen Victoria ordered Ponsonby back to the attack pounding home one constant theme: 'H.R.H. *must* come home.' As a postscript to one of the many letters thus directed to Salisbury, Ponsonby, a man of humour and common sense, wrote, 'H.M. observed in the warmth of debate that if her favourite son could not come home she would give up the Jubilee . . . I am afraid I did not weep.'

Faced with a storm threatening to overflow its teacup, Salisbury recommended that the Duke resign and be reappointed after the jubilee. Knowing full well he was unlikely to return to Poona if she adopted such a course, the Queen reacted with vehemence to the suggestion. 'She became very indignant,' Ponsonby wrote Salisbury, '& said she would not speak to any one about it as she would lose her temper. . . .'

Unhappily, faced with the Queen's obstinacy and growing anger, the Cabinet capitulated, Lord Salisbury informing Victoria he intended to bring in the bill she desired. A month later, on April 8, W. H. Smith introduced 'The Duke of Connaught Leave Bill,' and the Unionists in the House of Commons prepared for the attacks of Irish Nationalists and Radical Liberals who were certain to make the most of the fact that the Duke's return from India on three months' leave indicated precisely how little he was needed there. It was an argument the Liberal *Daily News* was pleased to highlight; in an editorial on April 21, it wrote, 'If it be shown that the forces in the Presidency of Bombay can get on very well for three months without the presence of a Royal Prince as Commander-in-Chief, the question may arise whether it would not be better that promotion by merit and long service should invariably take its course, undisturbed by the personal claims of Royalty.'

The irony, of course, was that the leading members of the government all agreed with these Liberal arguments but were now forced because of the Queen's intransigence to contravene them as best they could.

A 'Disgraceful Debate'

Sir John Gorst, Under Secretary of State for India, opened the debate for the government on the second reading of the bill on May 12. Turning his Nelson eye to Lord Salisbury's earlier suggestion, Gorst said that the ministry ought to be commended for taking the path of strict correctness in this case. After all, the Prime Minister might have suggested the Duke resign and be reappointed later, a course which some people might have thought an improper evasion of the statute. Because the government had a fastidious regard not only for the letter but also for the spirit of the law this course had not been adopted.

Gorst continued by announcing that while Prince Arthur would get his leave if this bill passed he would get neither pay nor other emoluments while he was away from his post. Also, if the Viceroy should think it necessary for reasons of defence to keep him in India, the prince would not return home. Finally, to counter any hint of favouritism, Gorst announced to the House of Commons that while this measure was undoubtedly privileged, the government now pledged itself to bring in as soon as possible a general bill extending the same prerogatives to the other enumerated officers. Under the circumstances, Gorst had done a creditable job defending a position no one in the government agreed with.

Originally on a bill of this kind the ministry in power could have expected the full cooperation of the opposition. It was, after all, not a particularly important piece of legislation. A hint of what would have happened in former days was given when Hugh Childers, a former Chancellor of the Exchequer, arose from the Liberal benches and, having been assured again that a general measure was forthcoming, announced his support, which, he said, was what responsible opposition demanded. His was the sentiment of the Opposition Front Bench.

As *The Times's* editorial indicated, however, these were not ordinary times in parliament, where hallowed traditions were daily being challenged by an obstructionist coalition of Radicals and Irish Nationalists, whose chief goal was to delay the Crimes Bill by wreaking as much havoc as possible.

As soon as Childers sat down, therefore, the leader of the Radicals, the gadfly journalist Henry Labouchere, was on his feet, ready to challenge the comfortable, polite procedures which had come to distinguish parliament before the advent of

Home Rule. 'There was one sound rule in the House,' he said with a touch of his well-known sarcasm, 'which he trusted would always be followed at least in that part of the House where he sat [the back benches]. It was that whenever there was the slightest sign of a bargain or arrangement between the two Front Benches they ought invariably to upset it.'

With that Mr. Dillwyn of Swansea and Sir John Swinburne set about demolishing the goverment's case using arguments supported by the *Manchester Guardian* in an editorial of May 14. 'The necessity of making an exception in [Connaught's] case, which would admittedly not have been made in the case of any one less highly connected, suggests once more the anomaly and inconvenience of placing members of the Royal Family in posts of high command and responsibility in the services; and Mr. Dillwyn did well to call attention pointedly and strongly to this matter. . . . The opinion is widely held that it is not for the interests of the public service that Princes of the Blood, receiving as such allowances from the State, should hold offices of emolument or of responsibility. . . . Responsibility should be withheld from them, because in fact they cannot be made responsible.'

These arguments, by no means entirely without merit, did not succeed in stopping the bill, which passed its second reading by a comfortable 318 to 45 margin, but they did sting Queen Victoria, who was much angered by the whole business. She noted in her journal that the language of the debate was 'vulgar beyond all belief, but also showing great ignorance.' At the same time the Queen informed Lord Salisbury that she regretted 'more than ever' that the bill giving the Duke leave had been drawn for him alone and not for all officers similarly circumstanced, as he had therefore been needlessly exposed 'to every sort of insult' in a 'disgraceful' debate. There was not a word of gratitude for the fact that the government had postponed the Crimes Bill to handle this matter.

When deciding to do so, the Salisbury ministry had also concluded it would be best to take advantage of the break in the debate on the Irish measure to deal with the question of the jubilee supplies, too. Thus, as they thought, all parliamentary business on the subject might be dispensed with at once.

Given conditions in the House of Commons, a good deal of often anxious consideration went into the matter of how much money the government should request for the jubilee. On the one hand the Queen, more parsimonious than merely frugal, looked with growing horror on the prospect of paying all the expenses of the 'royal mob' expected to attend the event. She wanted the government to ask for some money to assist her. On March 26, therefore, she wrote the Prime Minister, 'She fears the expenses for the Jubilee will fall most heavily on the Queen & she hopes some small helps may be given in different ways.' Though the Queen presented the point rather delicately in this letter, she was to pursue it nonetheless with characteristic persistence.

Given the explosive behaviour of the Radicals and Irish Nationalists during this session and their scant reverence for things monarchical, it came as no surprise that they did what they could to embarrass the government and prune the appropriation. Labouchere especially enjoyed such imbroglios; earlier in the year he had delighted in leading his obstructionist band in a whimsical attempt to cut £10 from a post office vote for ten millions. He would take on the monarchy with even greater relish, not least because he had no possibility of winning. As he once told Captain Fred Burnaby, 'One must find some very solid institution to be able to attack it in comfort. If the love of Royalty were not so firmly established in the middle-class English breast, I should not dream of attacking it, for the institution might topple over, and then what should I do?'

In addition, there was Lord Randolph Churchill to consider. Since he had left the government because he thought its defence estimates were too high, officials were left to ponder whether he might not attack the vote of supplies if he judged it inflated. In at least one particular such an apprehension resulted in the budget being scaled down.

The budget had been drawn up by John Taylor of the Office of Works, basing his estimate of £20,000 on what had sufficed for the national thanksgiving in 1872. As on that occasion the money was to be used mainly by his department and the Lord Chamberlain for expenses concerned with the service at Westminster Abbey. Both the Queen and Goschen, the Chancellor of the Exchequer thought this amount 'enormous,' but their reasons for saying so were different. Anxious to divert some of the sum to her own jubilee expenses, Victoria on February 25 informed Goschen through Sir Henry Ponsonby that, 'the Queen observed she could not understand how £20,000 could be spent at West Abbey in preparing it for a brief Thanksgiving Service.'[1] It would be much more appropriate, she thought, (should it be impossible to increase the vote), if some of it could be earmarked for the Master of the Horse, for instance, so that he could provide adequate transport for the princely guests. Neither Goschen nor W. H. Smith, however, agreed with this idea. 'It is possible,' Ponsonby wrote to the Queen after meeting with them, 'they might ultimately get a vote for it—but there is no doubt it would be vehemently resisted and that disagreeable speeches would be made which would be most unpleasant for the Royal visitors.'

Goschen feared that the size of the appropriation, although too small to please the Queen, would attract such opposition in any event, for he knew that however reasonable and trim the final budget it was still likely to arouse the frenzied opposition of Labouchere's Radicals and the Nationalists. Therefore he stood firm against not only Victoria's continued prodding for 'small helps' but the Dean of Westminster's attempt to claim compensation for the fact that the service was being held in Westminster Abbey. Moreover, he was very much open to suggestions about how he could further reduce costs.

Only one significant part of the appropriation was not meant to be used in connection with the service at Westminster Abbey; this was a sum of £3,000 set aside for mounting four great displays of fireworks in the capital and illuminating government buildings. The Chancellor received a letter from John G. Gibson, Solicitor General for Ireland, warning him about what effect this part of the vote would have on areas of the country which would pay for the displays but not see them. Of course Labby would attack it on these grounds, Gibson wrote, but very likely Churchill would, too. 'I should not be surprised if Lord Randolph in his present mood of stern economist attacks vigorously the proposal.' Furthermore, Aretas Akers-Douglas, the government's Chief Whip in the House of Commons, had assured Gibson that many Tories from the provinces would act similarly.

His apprehensions confirmed, Goschen thereupon ordered that the fireworks and illuminations should be dropped from the budget. Despite having to pay £1,000 compensation to the firms already hired, £3,000 was saved, although certain members of the Unionist press like the *Daily Telegraph* (March 11) were outraged that the government should thus bow to some unruly elements of the opposition and deprive the people of a brilliant show.

This final reduction in the budget having been made, David Plunket, First Commissioner of Works, went before the House of Commons to ask for £17,000 in supplies. It was a very modest amount, indeed, compared with sums spent on other ceremonies during the reign. Although Plunket did not bother to say so, the cost to the public of royal pageantry had steadily been dropping. For the Queen's Coronation in 1838, for example, parliament had appropriated over £200,000. For the Duke of Wellington's funeral £55,000 of the £80,000 allotted was spent, while the Prince of Wales's marriage in 1863 had cost £25,000 and the national thanksgiving in 1872 just £17,300. It would no doubt have been sensible if Plunket had acquainted members with these facts and juxtaposed them to the sum of £230,000 lavished on the coronation of George IV, a monarch whom nobody much liked, but in all probability the First Commissioner did not know them. He might also have said that the decreasing amount spent by the state threw an ever larger burden of the cost onto the Queen's Privy Purse, especially when, as this year, many guests were expected.

Although Plunket did not cite these two key points, the nature of his request and his standing in the House of Commons were such that ordinarily there would have been little opposition. Even the Liberals respected him, and the *Daily News* had on February 9 congratulated Lord Salisbury for again including this 'most excellent First Commissioner' in his administration, though not without a passing dig: 'Mr. Plunket's position in the Government is ludicrously out of proportion to his talents and capacities. But if he prefers an easy and agreeable post to more ambitious, and also more arduous honours, that is his affair.'

On this occasion Plunket's speech was a moderate, rather dry effort with only one feature of any interest. Should members fail to vote the supplies, he hinted, there might be retribution. The appropriation was so barebone that if it were cut any further the Lord Chamberlain might have to reduce the number of guests who could attend. Unfortunately, said Plunket, spouses would probably be the first to be dropped, which was certain to cause difficulties since, as he noted, 'It has, I am aware, been a burning question with members of this House as to whether they will be allowed to bring their wives.' However, if the appropriation went through as it was, he was sure a satisfactory arrangement could be reached so that wives would be invited.

Such a threat was too much for Labouchere and as soon as Plunket sat down, the irreverent Radical was on his feet indignantly denouncing the 'wife bribe' made by the First Commissioner. Having so begun he carried on making sallies like this one:

'Speaking broadly, I think that, considering the atrocious want of taste in the proposals of the Right Hon. Gentleman, considering that the galleries will only be used one day . . . considering the many better ways in which this money could be expended, considering the reckless extravagance which characterizes everything with which the Lord Chamberlain and such people have to do . . . we owe it as a duty to the country and to ourselves, to protest against this expenditure.' Not wishing to do away with the celebration entirely, however, and recognizing the necessity for a 'dais for Her Majesty and those in attendance upon her, and a few special seats for the Corps Diplomatique,' he concluded by suggesting the Lord Chamberlain be given £2,000 or £3,000. 'Give us as good a show as you can for the money.'

Had the government Front Bench been content to leave well enough alone, Labouchere's remarks might have ended the debate, as many members were reluctant to attack the jubilee estimates so publicly. W. H. Smith, however, Leader of the House, felt impelled to rise and deliver a string of patriotic sentiments appropriate to the occasion. He could hardly have chosen a worse moment.

Many years later while commenting on this parliamentary session, Arthur Balfour, Chief Secretary for Ireland in 1887, wrote that although Smith was Leader of the House, Balfour himself actually did most of the work, Smith merely putting a few generalities in from time to time. Other Unionists, too, with less personal reason than the feline Mr. Balfour for spreading this opinion, found Smith an uninspiring, prosaic individual, fond of delivering platitudes and just the sort of mundane homilies which royal anniversaries then seemed to require.

The remarks on which he now launched were entirely predictable, centring on the unrivalled benefits accruing to England from the reign of Queen Victoria, a period 'which I believe will be memorable in the history of this great Empire, as a period in which certainly great advance has been made in the happiness and prosperity of all classes of the inhabitants of this great Empire.' Gathering steam as he clumsily proceeded from one congratulatory phrase to another, he approached the zenith of his rhetoric. 'Sir,' he said, 'there is a universal feeling of thankfulness and gratitude that we have been permitted to see the 50th year of a Reign during which the country has advanced in prosperity, has advanced in liberty ——. . . .'

As soon as the word liberty was out of his mouth, the chamber, which had been dealing for weeks with the Irish Crimes Bill and the subject of closure of debate, was filled with a volley of ironical cheers, catcalls and interjections which signalled an extension of debate and the existence of a good-sized body of opinion in the House which found Smith's unctuous sentiments affronting. Thus it was no less a person than the Leader of the House himself who proved responsible for giving the opponents of the vote of supplies the opening they needed to obstruct debate, the very thing the government had most desired to avoid. Sheepishly, in place of a grand rhetorical flourish, Smith was forced to beat a hasty retreat into a succession of practical facts about why the money was needed. 'I thought,' he said, 'I was fairly representing the views and the feelings of the great majority of the subjects of the Queen; but I will refrain from pursuing the topic.' The Irish Nationalists and their allies in expedience, the Radicals, did not feel obliged to desist from the subject, however.

Many gentlemen were anxious to follow Smith's speech. Sir Joseph Pease questioned whether the tenders accepted for work to be done in Westminster Abbey had in fact gone to those offering the lowest prices. 'I very much doubt whether we shall get value for the £17,000 proposed to be expended.'

Neither did Arthur Cremer, a Shoreditch Radical, who suggested that the costs of the ceremony be covered by having those who wanted to attend pay for their own seats. The most effective speeches against the vote came, however, not from English members but from the ranks of Irish Nationalists, who wondered what the jubilee of the Queen had to do with their troubled nation and why they should be asked to pay for any part of it. William Redmond, Nationalist member for Fermanagh, put it cogently:

'I do not at all feel surprised that hon. members who represent English constituencies should have a desire to celebrate the Jubilee of their Queen's reign, which has seen such an advance in the prosperity and greatness of England.' But what of Ireland? 'In Ireland today there are somewhere near 400,000 people in the workhouses or receiving out-door relief . . . and under these circumstances I think it is heartless in the extreme to expect that the people of Ireland will cooperate in a celebration of this kind which is to cost so enormous a sum of money.'

T. P. O'Connor of Liverpool put it more strongly. 'Why, Sir, if the right hon. gentlemen had proposed that on the 50th anniversary of the Queen we should have a day of humiliation and of general sorrow at the amount of destruction and desolution brought about by famine and by plague, and emigration and eviction in Ireland during this half-century, then we might not have grudged the £17,000 that is asked for.'

Dr. Tanner, the member for Cork, then got up to announce that in view of the English character of the celebration 'I venture to say none' of the Nationalist M.P.s would attend the service at Westminster Abbey, and that such being the case Ireland should not be forced to provide any funds for it. With that the question was put and the government triumphed by a vote of 208 to 84, a majority of 124.

Looking over an account of the debate on this issue the next day, Queen Victoria was struck by only one thing: its vulgarity. 'I will not dwell,' she wrote in her journal for May 13, 'on what is most disgraceful & better to be forgotten.'

Victoria was not alone in her appraisal of the debate or in missing the significance of the remarks made by Nationalist members. The *Standard*, an orthodox Conservative journal close to Lord Salisbury, concentrated solely on Labby's part in

1 Queen Victoria in the dress she wore at the Golden Jubilee ceremony

2 The Thanksgiving Service, Westminster Abbey, seen from the organ loft

3 (a) William Henry Smith, M.P. From the drawing by Spy

3 (b) The Hon. Spencer Ponsonby-Fane. From the drawing by Spy

4 (a) The Earl of Abergavenny.
From the drawing by Ape

4 (b) Sir John Richard Somers Vine.
From the drawing by Spy

5 (a) The Queen's Jubilee Drawing Room

5 (b) Queen Victoria unveils a statue of herself at Windsor, June 22, 1887

6 (a) The Royal Procession in Westminster Abbey

6 (b) A Mug from the Queen for Good Conduct

7 Jubilee Festivities: (*above*) Garden Party at Buckingham Palace, 1887; (*below*) Pageantry at Wakefield, Yorkshire

8 Queen Kapiolani of Hawaii (seated) with her sister-in-law, Princess Liliuokalani. The Queen is wearing her famous dress of peacock-feathers

the affair: 'Fifty years ago Mr. Labouchere's proposal . . . would have been regarded as a serious manifestation of disloyalty; now it is simply derided as a piece of impertinent buffoonery.'

By concentrating on Labouchere, however, a man whom the *Standard* had once called 'the recognized farceur of the House,' the paper, like the Queen, missed the point. Labby's opposition was blithe and self-serving; that of the Nationalists, however, was more significant because they had concluded that the jubilee pertained mostly to England and to Ireland not at all. Because it was an Anglo-Saxon celebration of intense self-congratulation, the Irish members felt no twinges of compunction about opposing the vote of supplies and absenting themselves from Westminster Abbey, although their Liberal allies thought such conduct unwise and irresponsible since it tainted them with the hint of disloyalty and called into question the wisdom of their relationship with Parnell's party.

Once the supplies had been voted and the Duke of Connaught secured his extraordinary leave, the ministry thought it had dealt with all jubilee matters needing the attention of parliament and could therefore get back to the provoking business of passing the Irish Crimes Bill. However, some members had yet another notion in mind.

Because the atmosphere in the House of Commons had become so tense and strained since the introduction of the Crimes Bill, the remarks made more personal and barbed, a body of opinion had grown up that some use should be made of the Queen's jubilee, an occasion above party, to ameliorate conditions and re-establish harmony within the Mother of Parliaments. The Venerable Frederic Farrar, Rector of St. Margaret's, Westminster, the House of Commons church, was particularly eager to see what could be done.

Farrar, a charismatic preacher and author of the children's classic, *Eric, Or Little By Little*, suggested that a special House of Commons thanksgiving service be held at his church, all members to be invited to attend, which by stressing the proper role of the Commons in the government of the nation might bring about better relations between those who served in the lower house.

When this idea was brought to the attention of the Cabinet,

the response was strong and automatic: the government, relieved that the process of passing the jubilee legislation had not been as difficult as many had feared, could not possibly consider such a proposal which would necessitate the approval of the House.

Farrar, however, was not to be put off. Instead of accepting the Cabinet's decision as final, he circulated a petition to M.P.s hoping to gather enough signatures to convince Lord Salisbury and his colleagues that the idea was not controversial and had such general support it would not be obstructed. In this he was finally successful and the Cabinet reversed its position. On May 7, a resolution was introduced into the Commons to permit such a thanksgiving, and, remarkably, no one opposed it. Neither the Irish nor Labouchere stood against it, although they could scarcely have been as interested as Farrar in restoring clublike repose to the chamber and curtailing the acidulous debates which had brought them such attention. Even so, Farrar was delighted with the result, though he had no way of knowing his intention was still to be frustrated.

Dr. Boyd Carpenter, Bishop of Ripon, was selected to preach the sermon on the day of the thanksgiving, May 22, when the House went in state to St. Margaret's. Given that he was a favourite of the Queen, having been before his elevation to the see of Ripon a canon of Windsor and a chaplain to Her Majesty, and given his Unionist inclinations, he was not an unexpected selection, though as it turned out he was an unfortunate one.

From the pulpit Boyd Carpenter delivered an address celebrating the progress of the reign and dwelling at length on those qualities of statesmanship he thought necessary if such greatness was to continue. It became clear as he spoke that he had Gladstone in mind when he drew up his remarks and that the GOM was the antithesis of what he admired. Running throughout the Bishop's address was a constant undercurrent of criticism against the former prime minister's activities and particularly for his adoption of Home Rule.

The congregation immediately understood what Boyd Carpenter was doing. As the Archbishop of Canterbury, who was present, noted in his diary: 'His description of a true statesman seemed framed to the very letter of what Gladstone is not; I saw members striving to see how Gl. took it.' The more Boyd Carpenter spoke, the worse it got. 'He shouldn't have done this,' Benson concluded, realizing, as Farrar must have done, that the healing purpose of this service had been blasted by the Bishop's behaviour.

Much anti-Home Rule opinion was frankly delighted by the course the Bishop of Ripon had taken. Both the *Standard* and the *Daily Telegraph* recommended portions of Boyd Carpenter's address to the Parnellites members, who had seen no need to attend the service.

Liberals chose to turn a blind eye to Boyd Carpenter's unfortunate behaviour and there was no question of opposing the resolution which followed in the House of Commons designed to authorize a public printing of the Bishop's address. On May 27 the *Daily News* even announced its regret when it was discovered that, as Boyd Carpenter had spoken extemporaneously, there was no copy of his remarks. The Bishop therefore wrote a new address, much more moderate, impartial (and dull), which was distributed under the title *Reverence: The Secret of Greatness*.

At this point, parliamentary business connected with the jubilee was for all intents and purposes over. Questions would be raised on the floor from time to time about what was happening in connection with the occasion: Sir John Swinburne asked the First Lord of the Admiralty in May, for instance, whether a special bill would have to be brought in to permit Prince Alfred, Duke of Edinburgh, to return home for the jubilee from his post as Commander-in-Chief of the Mediterranean Fleet. (No, said Lord George Hamilton, the prince had been given regular leave for about 10 days but would receive no pay while away.) Legislative business, however, was at an end, and the government could devote its full attention to the Crimes Bill which made its way through turbulent stages into law in mid-July.

As the ministry returned its attention to this issue, royal officials were left to get on with arranging the focus of the jubilee events, the one activity for which money had been especially voted: the thanksgiving service at Westminster Abbey.

CHAPTER THREE

CONFUSION IN THE ABBEY

IN THE absence of a central coordinating committee or general overseer, the work of directing the arrangements of the national thanksgiving at Westminster Abbey fell principally to the Lord Chamberlain's Department and the Queen's Private Secretary. Without a plan, an effective precedent or settled ideas about what should be done, the jubilee had to be handled as an impromptu business. What was needed more than anything was imagination, organizational skills, and the ability to improvise, but these were in short supply at the Court.

The Lord Chamberlain was Edward, first Earl of Lathom, who had since Lord Derby's premiership in 1866 held household office in every Conservative administration, advancing from the position of Lord-in-Waiting to Captain of the Yeomen of the Guard, finally becoming, in Lord Salisbury's first ministry, Lord Chamberlain.

At one time greater things had been prophesied for Lathom than arranging levees and drawing rooms, the chief tasks of the Lord Chamberlain. During Gladstone's great ministry, Lord Skelmersdale, as he then was, was appointed, at age 34, a Conservative Whip in the House of Lords. At that time *Vanity Fair* wrote, 'Well-favoured, of striking presence, and with equal manners, he has already, while yet a young man, become universally popular, and his popularity will secure for him sympathy and success when he shall venture to take a more public part in public affairs.'

Contented with his enviable lot in life, however, Skelmersdale lacked any burning desire to succeed in politics. Thus after a season or two marked as a promising young man deserving of attention, interest in him waned as he failed to realize these expectations. Henceforward the amiable if ineffectual peer was left to get on with his favourite interests: cricket and yeomanry, his significant political career at an early end. Perhaps because his 'personal popularity' [was] unalloyed by envy and jealousy,' he was advanced to be Earl of Lathom in 1880, there being no other evident reason for such a promotion. In 1886 he became a connection of the Prime Minister, when his second daughter, Lady Florence Bootle-Wilbraham, married the Reverend Lord William Cecil, Salisbury's second son. Lathom was much sought after by Society, whose distractions he preferred to his official duties. These he willingly left in the hands of his principal deputy, the Honourable Sir Spencer Ponsonby-Fane, Comptroller of the Lord Chamberlain's Department.

Born in 1824, a son of the fourth Earl of Bessborough, Ponsonby (as he then was) entered the Foreign Office in 1840 and at an early age became private secretary to three Foreign Ministers, Lords Palmerston, Granville and Clarendon. In 1857, he was appointed Comptroller of Accounts in the Lord Chamberlain's Office. Although a more substantial career might have been anticipated with such an excellent beginning, once ensconced in his office at St. James's Palace, Ponsonby aspired no higher and remained in his post for the rest of his life, 'the permanent authority on whom all Lords Chamberlain have relied, and the depository of ceremonial traditions to whom all men and women have referred for the settlement of the momentous questions involved in the etiquette of Royal presence,' as *Vanity Fair* put it. Wealthy as well as dutiful, he had taken the name Fane by royal licence in 1875 along with a large estate. Given Lord Lathom's priorities and disposition, Ponsonby-Fane necessarily took on the brunt of the department's work in arranging the jubilee.

Similarly hard working was Ponsonby-Fane's cousin, Sir Henry Ponsonby, Queen Victoria's Private Secretary, one of the most congenial and attractive figures among the personalities of the jubilee. Born in 1825, into an aristocratic, military family headed by the third Earl of Bessborough, Henry Frederick Ponsonby himself entered the army, advancing to the rank of Colonel in the Grenadier Guards. Having previously been an equerry to the Prince Consort, he had come to the attention of Queen Victoria, who in 1870 appointed him to be her private secretary upon the death of General Charles Grey. Thereafter he was closely connected with the Court for the remainder of his career, a succession of honours following his loyal service as a matter of course, even though he hated what his son termed their 'publicity, ostentation and not always well-merited distinctions'. He was gazetted a general in 1873, and made K.C.B. in 1879, and Privy Councillor in 1880. He was also made Keeper of Her Majesty's Privy Purse in 1878.

Ponsonby's approach to the duties of the private secretary was professional but somewhat lighthearted. Naturally inclined to a jaunty disposition, he could not help but see the humour in many of the situations with which he had to deal and which often lent themselves to satirical or comic treatment. His stuffier critics have felt obliged to fault this approach, suggesting that such levity was out of place in the unrelentingly seemly Court of the widowed Victoria. The truth is, however, that Ponsonby's admittedly somewhat schoolboyish humour and continuing good nature provided just the touch of relief that made the heavily respectable, dull ambience created by the Queen at all bearable.

To these two men, Sir Spencer Ponsonby-Fane and Sir Henry Ponsonby, now fell especial responsibility for the organization of the jubilee thanksgiving service. Given the circumstances, it was a precarious assignment.

The first drawback was the lack of effective precedent to provide guidance and inspiration. Although King George III had celebrated a golden jubilee in 1809, this event was of limited usefulness to royal officials in arranging that of Queen Victoria, because it had taken place in the midst of a great war at a time when many people were wondering if their sovereign was going irretrievably mad, as in fact he did the next year. For all intents and purposes, the forms of celebration for Victoria's jubilee had to be invented from scratch.

Royal officials, however loyal or dedicated, were not equipped to devise plans where precedent was lacking. Though all the permanent officials had long been in office, so few events had been staged since the death of the Prince Consort that their experience was decidedly limited; moreover even these had been of such spareness that they gave little indication how an occasion of magnitude and national importance should be mounted.

It is true there was an unwonted flurry of royal activity in 1886, when the Queen gave in to requests from Lord Salisbury

Confusion in the Abbey

to open Parliament in person (it was the last time she did so and the first since 1877) and to those of the Prince of Wales that she be present at the opening of the Colonial and Indian Exhibition in South Kensington, with which he had been prominently associated. Even so, the arrangement of these functions did little to alleviate the basic unpreparedness of responsible officials, who had not even had to deal with the state visit of a sovereign since Tsar Alexander II had come in 1874.

The situation, of course, would have been substantially altered had there been someone at hand to order events grandly and on a sound management basis reminiscent of Prince Albert. Lord Mount Edgcumbe's committee might have done so had the Prime Minister been prepared to support it. Even the Prince of Wales, as he later demonstrated at the time of the Diamond Jubilee, might have filled the bill had he been given the chance. As it was, however, he was heavily committed elsewhere, attempting to pump life into his faltering Imperial Institute scheme. There was no one else in the Royal Family able to take the lead, and unlike 1897 when Joseph Chamberlain stepped in to do so, Cabinet ministers were otherwise engaged and generally uninterested in the golden jubilee.

Unfortunately what either Sir Spencer Ponsonby-Fane or Sir Henry Ponsonby might do was distinctly limited by their circumstances. Both were aware of the liabilities facing the organizers of the jubilee, but both were the Queen's servants and obliged to follow her wishes in the matter, doing no more than she authorized or approved. Since what Victoria wanted for her jubilee approximated to the arrangements used in 1872, their options were curtailed from the start and the plans liable to be as strongly attacked and disapproved as those for the previous national thanksgiving had been. In the reckoning there was little enough to offset these difficulties. Nevertheless the officials were not entirely without assets, not the least of which was their familiarity with each other and good working relationships.

Ponsonby and Ponsonby-Fane were cousins whose friendly feelings and common outlook on life enabled them to communicate without formality in short, rapidly scrawled notes often more revealing because of their lack of self-consciousness than the careful phrasing of more studied documents. Both were hard-working and even-tempered. Thus, whereas Lord Lathom appeared anxious and fretful about the amount of preparation that had to be done, telling Madame Waddington, American-born wife of the French Ambassador, that 'no one could imagine how difficult it had been to arrange for the Jubilee ceremonial' and seemed stunned by the volume of correspondence involved, particularly pointing out one day when the Queen had sent him 42 telegrams alone, Ponsonby and Ponsonby-Fane took such matters very much in stride, being more likely to joke about their difficulties than to bewail them like the Lord Chamberlain. As the jubilee took form this proved an attribute they were fortunate to possess.

Although the occasion had been generally discussed from time to time from early 1886 and Ponsonby had first informed the Prime Minister on October 14 of the Queen's wish that the thanksgiving should be held at Westminster Abbey and arranged in semi, rather than full, state, it was not until April 2, 1887 that Salisbury officially informed Lord Lathom that his department in concert with the Office of Works and Public Buildings would be responsible for the matter.

Anticipating this order, an informal correspondence had already been opened between Ponsonby-Fane and the Dean of Westminster about the conditions under which the Dean and Chapter would relinquish the Abbey into the hands of the Office of Works. Ponsonby-Fane asked the Dean to supply the Lord Chamberlain with an estimate of the income the Abbey would lose when it was closed and also for a list of 'any claims for fees or other money charges, based on the precedents of Coronations or other occasions when the Abbey had been taken for Royal purposes.' Because the thanksgiving service was not to be a state occasion, however, coronations (which always were) did not constitute a precedent, a fact which seems not to have occurred to anyone in the Lord Chamberlain's Office, always unclear about the fundamental distinction between events arranged in state and semi-state.

Of course, by precedent, the jubilee as a significant national pageant should have been held in full state, just as the national thanksgiving in 1872 ought to have been. Yet the Queen's obstinacy forced matters to be revised. In the circumstances, therefore, the Dean would have had a case only had he been able to cite some payment by the Lord Chamberlain to the Dean of St. Paul's in 1872. There had, however, been no such payment. Nonetheless, Ponsonby-Fane's letter suggested that the Lord Chamberlain was willing to bargain, and there were good reasons why the Dean was willing to do so, too.

The Very Reverend George Granville Bradley, D.D., became Dean of Westminster in 1881, possibly because of a valuable friendship with his predecessor, the Very Reverend Arthur Stanley, an influential cleric close to the Queen. Bradley quickly discovered that the venerable edifice was in a state of acute disrepair and that funds to do much about it were lacking. He did what he could to improve matters, yet in 1886 *The Times* found 'the present condition of the Abbey is nothing less than deplorable. It is literally verging upon ruin, and there are no funds in the hands of the Dean and Chapter to meet the cost of necessary repairs.' Not surprisingly, Bradley regarded the jubilee as a windfall, and although he may have known Ponsonby-Fane had erred, he was not above taking advantage of that mistake to benefit the Abbey.

On March 29, therefore, Bradley wrote Ponsonby-Fane a rather high-blown letter about the immemorial rights of the Dean and Chapter. He reminded him that, following the precedent of coronations and royal funerals, all materials brought into the Abbey became the property of the Dean and Chapter. In return for these, however, the Dean would be glad to settle for financial compensation, the funds to be used for restoration of the Abbey's fabric and internal improvements. Ponsonby-Fane, having perused the Dean's case, thought it reasonable and cogent; so did H. W. Primrose, Secretary to the Office of Works, who wrote to the Comptroller of the Lord Chamberlain's Department, 'I am clearly of opinion that the claim of the Dean & Chapter cannot well be disputed and that the only thing to do is to make terms. I think we should get off cheap for . . . £1,000.'

In the event, someone seems to have caught the error about to be made; in any case, the bargain was not concluded, even though these two senior officials were quite prepared to accept the Dean's fallacious argument. Nonetheless, either because Ponsonby-Fane and Primrose had unnecessarily encouraged

Bradley's expectations or the government recognized that restoration funds for the Abbey were urgently needed, a compromise was worked out. The Dean was to be offered compensation for the loss of fees (mostly money paid to guides) for the period when the Abbey was closed to the public and a grant of £500 to cover unforseen contingencies. This was the most the government found itself able to propose, constrained as it was to keep the request for jubilee supplies as low as possible.

Perhaps a little abashed because of his previous letter, Ponsonby-Fane felt obliged to explain the reason for this decision to the Dean. 'I am permitted to tell you,' he wrote, 'that the matter has been thoroughly examined by Mr. Smith [the Leader of the House of Commons], the Chancellor of the Exchequer, and Mr. Jackson [Financial Secretary to the Treasury], and that they have satisfied themselves that the Parliamentary objections to recognizing *on this occasion* the claim of the Dean and Chapter to materials are so strong that it is most undesirable to raise such a question.' What Ponsonby-Fane meant, of course, and the Dean would have understood, is that Lord Salisbury expected trouble from the Irish Nationalists and obstruction-minded Radicals. However, if 'on this occasion' the Dean was prepared to give way, perhaps his full claim would be admitted next time.

Although Dr. Bradley could not pry any more money from the government for internal improvements, he could at least ensure that precautions were taken so that the erection of temporary structures in the Abbey did not result in further damage, for as the Dean was well aware, previous events had often led to extensive damage to both monuments and fabric. Fortunately, Bradley's insistence on protecting the Abbey fell in with a growing feeling in the nation that historic monuments and shrines ought to be preserved and maintained. The Society for the Protection of Ancient Buildings, for example, had been formed in 1877 to do just this. Five years later the first Ancient Monuments Act was passed.

Along with the Dean's good intentions in this regard, however, his resolve to protect the Abbey probably was also strengthened because he himself had recently been the target of sharp criticism about certain alterations he had made inside the edifice. At the same time he was corresponding with

Ponsonby-Fane about the terms under which the Abbey would be resigned to the Office of Works, Thackeray Turner, Secretary of the Society for the Protection of Ancient Buildings, was calling public attention to the situation. In an article in the *Daily News* of March 23, for instance, he had pointed out several doubtful 'improvements' ordered by the Dean.

To ensure that such criticism should not arise after the jubilee, Bradley asked that clauses designed to protect the Abbey be included in the contract between the Office of Works and the firm hired to build the special galleries. This was conceded. Even so, there were many who felt that it would have been more sensible to have mounted the event in the less-encumbered interior of St. Paul's than to have been forced to seek ways to protect the densely-monumented Abbey. However, as Queen Victoria adamantly refused to consider going anywhere else than to the altar where she had been crowned, no other course was possible.

While Bradley and Ponsonby-Fane were corresponding, John Taylor, one of the First Class Surveyors of the Office of Works, was holding a limited competition to determine which of four large London construction firms was to build the galleries inside the Abbey. Taylor was experienced in these matters, having in 1872 overseen the same task at St. Paul's. However, in deciding to have any competition at all, he immediately offended the directors of Perry and Company, the Office of Works' general contractors, who were further affronted when Taylor decided not to let them enter a bid, as he considered their offices were too far removed from the Abbey. Even though Perry and Company's management strongly protested at this decision, the contract was awarded to Mowlem and Company, who tendered a bid $17\frac{1}{2}$ per cent below the scheduled prices of the Office of Works. Later, however, Taylor managed to mollify the Perry organization somewhat by hiring them to build viewing stands along the route and setting up conveniences. As Labouchere later noted disapprovingly in his remarks on the vote of supplies, even before Parliament had considered the appropriation, Mowlem had moved into the Abbey, which from May 3 had been transformed into what the *Pall Mall Gazette* termed 'a sea of sawdust and sweepings'.

From the first there was much public uneasiness, possibly

prompted by the growing concern with protecting the national heritage. Reports generally containing a strong hint of disapproval appeared regularly in the metropolitan press about what what was being done. Some questioned whether the monuments and fabric could emerge from the ordeal unscathed. Others wondered whether a religious shrine should be turned into an auditorium. On May 27, for instance, the *Daily News* wrote, 'There is something decidedly dejecting in the interior of Westminster Abbey at the present time. Almost every trace of its sacred and historic character has disappeared . . . somehow it seems a terrible desecration.' Yet if any representative sample of the public was to be accommodated a good deal of construction had to take place.

An extensive series of temporary galleries, which went a long way toward disfiguring the building, was built. For instance, the problem of how some people were to get to their seats was solved by removing windows in the nave and erecting staircases to them from outside the Abbey. Queen's weather was assumed; no evidence exists that anyone ever considered the appalling alternative: hundreds of people sitting in makeshift galleries partially exposed to rainy blasts through the nave windows.

Probably the most poorly planned construction was at the great west door where the Queen was to alight from her carriage to enter the Abbey. Inside four tiers of galleries had been built which ran up about ninety feet to the vaulting. The Queen was to enter the building under this novel arrangement through a dark little passage ten feet high. Thus at the moment she stepped into the building, she would actually be under the feet of hundreds of her subjects. The most articulate and detailed critic of the arrangements generally and of this one specifically was Somers Clark, architect for St. Paul's Cathedral, who later wrote in *The Nineteenth Century and After*, 'It is needless to say that the dignity of the West End of the Church was absolutely done away with, whilst the danger to the lives of those who occupied the monstrous erection, with its inadequate stairs, was so great as to render the erection of such a pile of timber inexcusable.'

While the aesthetic disfigurement of the Abbey was, fortunately, temporary, the galleries often left a permanent mark, their considerable weight wreaking havoc with the Abbey's fragile and vulnerable fabric. Somers Clark wrote of this situation, 'When it was all over, the floor of the North Ambulatory had yielded considerably through the heavy beams and the porphyry and serpentine pavement of St. Edward's Chapel was badly damaged.'

Even though Mowlem and Company took more time than they had at first estimated to remove the temporary galleries and even giving them credit for general care, many still had reason for complaint. For Somers Clark, the clean-up operation constituted a sort of nightmare. He was present, for instance, when workmen found an ingenious way of replacing the surface scraped off the Abbey's walls when the scaffolding came down. 'Dirt from the London streets was collected,' he recalled with a low moan. 'A nice soup was made of it in buckets, and this was daubed on the wounded places with mops.'

Why this sensitive, evidently concerned eye-witness did not step forward at the time to protest at what was happening will probably never be known. However before the Abbey began to be prepared for the coronation of Edward VII in 1902, he did so in order to prevent something similar from taking place.

Whether any hint of such activities was brought to the attention of the Office of Works is doubtful. Probably, like the other officials involved in the arrangement of the jubilee, they had fallen prey to the rosy self-satisfaction that seemed to engulf the organizers in the aftermath of June 21. Thus the Office of Works expressed itself entirely satisfied with the job Mowlem and Company had done, H. W. Primrose writing to tell them it had met with the 'unqualified approval' of the Queen and public.

Before this point had been reached, however, there was still much to do in the Abbey. Once the galleries had been constructed, 350 men went hopping about on them to test their soundness, so that no visitor would be in danger on the day of the thanksgiving. Afterwards W. H. Smith was asked in the House of Commons what would have happened if this testing process had resulted in injuries to some of the men. A good Conservative and a large employer himself, Smith replied that the government would not have thought itself responsible to do anything. The Anglo-Catholic *Church Times* was then moved to remark,

'The process seems to be rather of an Irish complexion,' an insightful contemporary phrase indicating its oddness. Fortunately for those obliged to test them, however, the galleries were sound and when the workers had finished with them, the bare planks were turned over to the firm of Messrs. Banting for decorating. There was less than a fortnight left before jubilee day to complete the task.

The Bantings had already had a considerable career assisting in preparing royal ceremonial. At the time of the Duke of Wellington's funeral, their designs for the funeral car were discarded as unsatisfactory, but they had still been given the lavish budget of nearly £16,000 for the decoration of St. Paul's Cathedral. Later they had arranged the obsequies of the Duchess of Kent, the Queen's mother, of the Prince Consort, and of Lord Palmerston, the Prime Minister.

Primarily undertakers, they had had to solicit the Lord Chamberlain in 1872 for the chance to decorate St. Paul's for the national thanksgiving for the recovery of the Prince of Wales. Had the prince died instead, the firm would very likely have been commissioned as a matter of course to arrange the funeral. Nonetheless, their application succeeded, although they were allowed to spend only about £5,600, a sum which scarcely allowed for splendour. In its evaluation of their work, *The Times* wrote, 'Considering . . . that everything has had to be done quickly and with little thought . . . we need not find too much fault.' Fortunately for the Bantings, Ponsonby-Fane was much more enthusiastic, praising their 'zeal and intelligence,' an opinion which was probably responsible for getting them the contract to decorate Westminster Abbey in 1887 without their having to ask for it.

Unhappily for the company, although their usefulness had been recognized for more than royal funerals, they undertook the preparations for arranging the Abbey without some of the advantages they had enjoyed in 1872. At that time they had been able to re-use the plans and measurements drawn up for the Duke of Wellington's funeral, so that even though their time in St. Paul's was limited, much of their work could be undertaken beforehand. For the jubilee, the Bantings were at work in a new place where they were without experience.

The artistry of their effort was also adversely affected by the decision that the bulk of the decorations be done in the red of the Order of the Bath, with which the Abbey was associated. For reasons which may have something to do with the reaction to this decision, there is no indication in the records of who was responsible for selecting this colour, which in small amounts has both flair and vitality. In the large quantities which were necessary to cover the temporary galleries, however, it became an exhausting and even lurid optical assault. Somers Clark, who was an usher on jubilee day, called it 'detestable' and the overall effect was frequently likened to cascades of blood. Furthermore, the same colour was used for a carpet especially woven for the occasion, relieved by a pattern of white maltese crosses, which Somers Clark denounced as 'spotty and worrying,' dismissing the special decorations as a whole as 'incredibly mean and inartistic.'

Somers Clark's disapproval may have been somewhat excessive; certainly no one else who left an observation about the Abbey's decorations on jubilee day felt quite so indignant about them. Yet about the best that anyone could find to say was what the Scottish Widow's Fund and Life Assurance Society printed in a memorial book on the occasion: 'The change in the appearance of the Abbey was not after all so discordant as was expected.'

It was not entirely the Bantings' fault; not only were they allowed inadequate time in the Abbey and given no choice in the colour scheme, but they were handicapped by the shrinking budget allowed for pageantry, having to make do in 1887 for a much more important ceremony with £600 less than they had in 1872.

Their account might have been higher at the time of the jubilee, except that confusion in the Abbey due to the rush to finish on time resulted in muddled records of expenses being kept. In 1872, better organized, their accounts had been scrupulously recorded, and although one or two items submitted to the Lord Chamberlain's Department had been discounted, almost nothing was taken off their bill. In 1887, however, £350 was deducted because of careless record keeping concerning working time and confusion in the daily work vouchers. In the end they were paid only £5,000. This result naturally angered the Bantings, not only irritated because of the loss of profit but fearful if it had become generally known, their regular business would suffer. The latter consideration was by far the most important, so while they contented themselves with a fairly mild rejoiner about the items disallowed, they agreed to waive all claims if the Lord Chamberlain would issue the firm an official letter of approval for their efforts, which, as one of the Bantings wrote, 'will be a *Trophy* for all time.' Considering that the letter was well worth the £350 saved, Lord Lathom was glad to send it.

Bantings had incurred particular trouble by renovating the most ancient and venerable relic in the Abbey, the Coronation Chair which had been made in 1300 to enclose the Stone of Scone, symbol of Scottish sovereignty, and on which all English monarchs (except Edward V) had been crowned.

Early in their preparations one of the Bantings informed Ponsonby-Fane that the chair had a variety of defects. Not only was it much decayed and worn, but the entire back had been defaced by names, dates and initials carved in the wood. The firm therefore sent the Lord Chamberlain some suggestions for improving things: a little cleaning and polishing and the addition of some fringes, tassels and gold lace would probably be sufficient. The Lord Chamberlain authorized them to act in this sense.

Nothing more was heard of the matter until some months later when on June 9 at the tenth annual meeting of the Society for the Protection of Ancient Buildings, Frederic Harrison announced that the chair had been delivered over to 'tormentors and is being gilded and furnished by the court upholsterers.' He wanted the society to take action to stop any further tampering with the chair but could not arouse sufficient interest in the matter.

No more was heard about it until the jubilee service had been held at which time all the world could see what had been done. As a result, David Plunket, the First Commissioner of Works, was questioned in the House of Commons. Had the coronation chair been stained brown, he was asked? He said it had not. He assured members some apprehension had arisen from the fact that a few temporary pieces of tracery missing from the chair had been added, and that it was these and not the chair itself which had been stained.

These calm assurances did not end the matter, as *The Athenaeum* had eye-witness reports which contradicted Plunket's remarks. 'We shall scarcely be believed,' it wrote on June 25, 'when we say that the Coronation Chair, perhaps to most Englishmen the most precious of all the precious relics in the Abbey, was handed over to some barbarian to be smartened up, and he has daubed it the orthodox Wardour street brown and varnished it'. A week later, the same periodical revealed that it was the senior Mr. Banting himself who had given the order to stain the chair, and that as soon as the matter had been raised in parliament he had given another to have the stain scoured off. Again Plunket was questioned, and while he was forced to admit that when he had mentioned the matter before, he had been mistaken, he grumbled that the entire affair was the merest 'storm in a teacup.' Nevertheless, Charles Cox, a Fellow of the Society of Antiquarians, called for official action, demanding in a letter to the *Daily News* of July 8, that the Bantings should be rebuked and perhaps even Plunket himself. 'If sufficient stir is made about this outrage, it may happily result in the power being taken from the Office of Works to do similar harm in the future.' Instead of meeting such demands, the Lord Chamberlain, as already reported, granted the Bantings their trophy of approval.

While Mowlem and Banting were at work in the Abbey, others were puzzling over the problem of the building's protection and security. Given that the wooden galleries and special decorations constituted a fire hazard and that Londoners were on the alert to the dangers of Irish terrorists, both matters were necessarily of some significance.

To deal with the first of these considerations, additional fire insurance to the amount of £20,000 was placed on the fabric of the Abbey by the Sun Fire Office, although it is not clear how much this protection cost the Lord Chamberlain's Department. Four firemen, working in two shifts of twelve hours apiece, were stationed to watch the Abbey. Outside additional fire protection was provided by the famous Captain Eyre Massey Shaw, chief officer of the Metropolitan Fire Brigade, a popular figure immortalized in Gilbert and Sullivan's 1882 production of *Iolanthe*. His 'Brigade/with cold cascade,' two fire engines and crews, was placed in readiness in Dean's Yard, while a large floating fire engine with 100 men was at hand on the Thames for jubilee day. Once these arrangements were complete, Shaw, a man who knew 'the main/on which to draw,' wrote to Sir Francis Knollys, the Prince of Wales's Private Secretary, and offered his services for the entertainment of the princely guests, who might find the work of his department of interest. Such consideration did nothing to hurt his relations with the Court, and when he retired three years later it was with not only a pension but an unprecedented K.C.B.

Cloaked in more mystery was the work of those set to guard the Abbey against terrorist outrage. Although this duty was largely undertaken by the Special Forces Branch of the Metropolitan Police, the fact that the papers of this organization have very largely been destroyed (no doubt to protect informers and to shield its activities) makes it impossible to recreate in any detail what it was doing. Nonetheless an 1887 letter survives from William Jackson, Financial Secretary of the Treasury, to the Home Office demonstrating that more than £4,000 above the usual appropriation of about £20,000 had been spent between the autumn of 1886 and the beginning of 1887 employing police constables against Irish Fenians (very likely connected with the Plan of Campaign), thereby proving that much activity was suspected.

Although London had been singularly free from terrorist outrage for years, the virulent anti-Irish feeling in the capital gave rise to much conjecture about what groups like the dynamiting Clan-na-Gael might get up to for the jubilee. These fears increased after *The Times* in April published the notorious forged letter of Charles Piggott implicating Parnell in the brutal Phoenix Park murders of five years before. Otherwise reasonable individuals gave way to anxieties about conspiracy and impending violence which increased considerably after the Nationalist members in May announced they would boycott the Abbey on jubilee day. Finally on June 1, *The Times* published a lengthy article on 'The Dynamite Party, Past and Present,' which fed the tension.

In this article the Clan-na-Gael, a physical force terrorist group founded as early as 1867 and much publicized in the early 1880s, was portrayed as a resourceful and determined society with international organization, capable of amazing action. Nothing seemed to be beyond its reach and no calamity was to be thought impossible for such a group to contrive. 'It has resources, determination, and the power of acting with extraordinary secrecy. . . . It is beyond all question that this society has been at the bottom of all the explosions that have been caused or attempted since the spring of 1883.'

Fascinated and frightened, *The Times* hinted at the most daring schemes, so that imaginative readers were left to conjure up the stunning prospect of an attack of thrilling audacity on jubilee day, the prize being the destruction of the majesty of England, the Royal Family and the entire government of the empire. Here was a prospect which rivalled Guy Fawkes's legendary attempt at terrorism. Such articles led to many amateur sleuths sending the Lord Chamberlain's Office their ideas on how to foil the expected attacks. One advised that the police should take care to protect the Abbey's roofs, while another, in great detail, warned about an attack coming 'by means of a Subterranean approach from a considerable distance.'

Despite warnings from the press and suggestions from well meaning armchair detectives, London police found there was little effective work to be done within the Abbey. The temporary constructions had increased their difficulties considerably by creating hundreds of new hiding places. Even though six constables were constantly at hand during the work, security was not well maintained, largely through lack of co-operation between responsible officials.

Officials in both the Lord Chamberlain's Department and the Office of Works were not unmindful of the dangers which might mar the jubilee, but it was not their job to combat them. They fully expected that the police would make a last-minute search of the premises a few hours before the ceremony and that that would be sufficient. With constables at hand now and with six plain clothes detectives expected for the day itself, what else was necessary?

This being their general feeling, when Primrose of the Office of Works finally informed Sir Charles Warren, Commissioner of Police, that he should order a stoppage of all work for a few hours on June 20 so that a search of the Abbey could be made, he was put out to learn Warren felt such an operation would be almost useless. Warren explained to Ponsonby-Fane:

'The search in any case can only be of value to a small degree, as the Office of Works admit that there may be infernal machines concealed all over the Abbey which Police cannot search out, the spaces being closed up.'

Such doubts were not to be drawn to the attention of Queen Victoria, for they could only increase her nervousness about the event. Thus on June 13, the Home Secretary, Henry Matthews, informed the Queen that he had ordered a full search to be made of the Abbey. 'Mr. Matthews is happy to inform Your Majesty that the officers of the Metropolitan Police see no reason to apprehend anything like organized outrage; and the reports from America and Ireland are also reassuring.'[1] Far less sanguine than the Home Secretary, Warren nonetheless carried out his search after the Abbey had been cleared of workmen at noon on June 20. After his officers had finished, no person was allowed to enter the building, except ushers, musicians and the few workmen necessary to make finishing touches to the preparations.

Handicapped by the failure of other departments to work with them, the police concentrated their efforts outside the Abbey. Though the absence of records makes it impossible to suggest with any certainty what the Special Forces Branch was doing, some hint of their activities seems to have reached the press. On June 16 the *Manchester Guardian*, emanating from a county with a large Irish population, wrote that police authorities had full knowledge of a conspiracy intended for jubilee week and were taking action against the men who had been designated to carry it into effect.

It is impossible now to say whether the newspaper had any private information or not. If it had, it may have come from someone associated with the London police, which had only about nine months before succeed in regaining its autonomy for working against secret societies in the metropolis, after unhappily being part of a centralized effort under E. G. Jenkinson since 1882. There were thus good internal political reasons for the London police wishing to appear well in control of the situation. In any event, the *Daily Telegraph* on October 27 exposed in detail the frustrated summer plans of four members of the Clan-na-Gael who had contrived an outrage at the time the *Manchester Guardian* had originally suggested.

The *Daily Telegraph* story dealt with four Irish-Americans who had gathered in London directly following jubilee day bringing with them eighty pounds of dynamite. How the police became aware of what they were doing was never divulged, yet they were carrying on a close surveillance hoping to gain material against their leader, whose name was Melville. Unfortunately, the death of one of the other three men forced the police to move in prematurely. The two minor conspirators, Callan and Harkins, were arrested, but Melville escaped. When the trial of the two men took place in February, 1888, they were charged with unlawful possession of dynamite with malicious intent.

The prosecution alleged an association between Melville and two Irish Nationalist M.P.s, Messrs. Nolan and Stack. But without Melville, nothing more could be established than that they had met, and the prosecution was left to pursue its charges against Callan and Harkins. Each was sentenced to penal servitude for fifteen years.

When this result was announced, the Conservative and anti-Home Rule press was jubilant, although their joy would have been greater had the Nationalist M.P.s been implicated. Even so, not only had the police thwarted the Clan-na-Gael during the jubilee, but, more importantly, the activities of Melville and his gang had again demonstrated what every Unionist already knew, the falseness of Gladstone's chimerical 'Union of Hearts' with the Irish. 'It is,' the *Daily Telegraph* wrote on October 29, 'the most ironical of all possible commentaries on the patriot cry which passes muster with the Gladstonians for argument—the cry that the heart of the Irish race at home and abroad has been changed by Mr. Gladstone's desertion of the Unionist principles of a lifetime.'

Actually, however, it seems unlikely that either Nolan or Stack knew anything about what Melville was contemplating, much less that they supported his activities. Terrorism at that time could work to the advantage only of the Unionists, who would use it not merely to condemn the opposition but to promote the Crimes Bill then pending in the House of Commons. It seems more likely that the Unionist press would have imputed dastardly motives to Parnellite M.P.s than that these men, well aware of their party's position, would have directly aided the cause of physical force.

To be sure, such rational sentiments and the fine distinctions of the English political scene did not always impress those inclined to use terrorist methods, and it is illuminating that Melville and all his associates were Irish-Americans, always in the forefront of physical force activity. Even so, any dangers there may have been were probably exaggerated by the Unionist press which consistently attributed conspiracy to all Nationalists, wherever they were to be found. In such an atmosphere, Nationalist M.P.s' decision to boycott Westminster Abbey took on sinister implications. Certainly, scaremongers reasoned, they must have been advised what was going to happen and had hit on a plausible excuse to stay away. No wonder the Liberal *Daily News* was irritated when on June 20 it commented, 'They [the Nationalists] would have shown better sense and better judgment by attending. . . .'

The truth is that Parnell, only just recovered from a debilitating kidney ailment and looking like an emaciated grey ghost, was only too willing to appease the left wing of his movement by allowing his followers to vent their emotions in such a harmless (if public) fashion. Gladstone, of course, who delighted in reverence towards monarchy, did not agree with what Parnell was allowing, but saw nothing to be gained by opposing him.

After the Irish Nationalists had made their point, however, they were as concerned as everyone else that jubilee day should not be marred by outrage, especially since some of them privately determined to go to the Abbey to see the great show. Justin McCarthy, for instance, Nationalist M.P. for Newry, afterwards answered a telegram from his literary collaborator Mrs. Campbell-Praed with evident relief. 'I have just got your welcome telegram. So far then all is well. I fancy the real danger is over. No doubt there will be accidents in the night—people crushed perhaps in a sort of blood-tax on popular pageantry in a place like London, but that is not a calamity such as some people seem to have feared and almost anticipated.'

These were private feelings, however; publicly the Irish Nationalists' announced intention to boycott the Abbey service complicated the task of the Lord Chamberlain as he began to draw up lists of officials and representative individuals who should be invited. In Ireland, many of these were naturally members of Parnell's party. Lathom was thus uncertain how to deal with a situation which might be twisted to partisan purposes by the Nationalists. He therefore consulted A. J. Balfour, the new Chief Secretary for Ireland. Balfour, fully aware that the Nationalists were likely to lose as much sympathy in England as they might gain in Ireland by adopting a partisan course, sent the Lord Chamberlain a blithe reply. 'I am inclined to think that there can be no doubt that the Irish Mayors must be asked—just as if they were loyal subjects of H. Majesty—some may return insolent answers, but I see no harm in this, rather the reverse.'

Lathom took Balfour's advice, and sent invitations to the principal Irish mayors and sat back to await results. One by one the chief magistrates of Dublin, Cork, Limerick, Waterford and Kilkenny, all Parnellite controlled, returned answers officially rejecting places in the Abbey. As Balfour anticipated, the letters were not always couched in civil terms; the mayor of Cork, for instance, told the Lord Chamberlain that 'the Irish people were not prepared to dance in chains,' a ringing phrase of which his honour thought so well that he had it published in the *Cork Examiner* on May 24.

As soon as it became known that Nationalist office holders were following the lead of their parliamentary leadership, Irish Loyalists began applying for the seats, anxious that one of the three kingdoms should not be without a deputation on jubilee day. Neither Balfour nor Lathom were at all averse to rewarding with a ticket individuals whose interests had often suffered as a result of their faithfulness, and Lathom quickly decided upon a plan of 'dignified silence' to assist them. Since Loyalists could not officially occupy places declined by the mayors, they had to be given personal tickets. These the Lord Chamberlain distributed to ranking Loyalists wherever Parnellite officials had declined to participate.

This sensible way in which Lord Lathom dealt with Irish representation was regrettably nowhere else apparent as he dealt with other matters involving invitations. Instead, all too often the Lord Chamberlain obstinately relied upon faulty precedents established in 1872, although these usually raised more problems than they solved.

The national thanksgiving organized in 1872 had been the first significant time when the audience was made representative of the nation, an important development indicating the changing significance of these royal pageants. On that unprecedented occasion the Lord Chamberlain's Department did the best it could to bring about this result, acting as it did in so many matters on an *ad hoc* basis without effective guidelines. To assist him, Lord Sydney appointed representative individuals from groups hitherto not much regarded, nonconformist churches and workingmen.

In practice the organizational papers clearly show that the lists, especially those drawn up by his nonconformist aide, were subject to constant changes, for the Lord Chamberlain was so anxious to avoid further complaint about what he was doing that whoever sent a strong representation about not being included was very likely to be put on the list of those who should be. In the circumstances, therefore, when the jubilee invitations to Westminster Abbey had to be considered, little reliance should have been placed on the lists drawn up in 1872. But any precedent being better than none, officials considerably overvalued them.

In 1872 Lord Sydney had appointed Alfred Shepheard, Secretary of the Deputies of the Protestant Dissenters of the Three Denominations (Presbyterian, Independent and Baptist) to help draw up a suitable list of nonconformists to be invited. How the Lord Chamberlain determined upon Shepheard is not known, but once he had the job he set out to make sure his friends got most of the tickets.

In 1887, when Lord Lathom learned about Shepheard's previous work for the Lord Chamberlain's Department, he invited him again to handle invitations for the nonconformists. Reckoning that what had worked in 1872 would be acceptable for the jubilee, Shepheard used his old list with its heavy bias, omissions and inequities, all of which Lathom unfortunately accepted.

The more serious consequence was the effect of this decision on invitations to the established Church of Scotland. Following the 1872 precedent, Lathom granted this body, with which half the population of the northern kingdom was affiliated, a scant four tickets. At the same time, he allotted the Episcopal Church of Scotland, with which only about 2 per cent of the people was affiliated, ten places. By way of contrast, the established Church of England garnered fully 600 seats. When this result became known, W. J. Menzies, Agent of the Church of Scotland's General Assembly, complained to the Lord Chamberlain's Department. Ponsonby-Fane assured him, however, that the precedent in this case was quite clear, and as no complaint had been registered in 1872, no more tickets could now be given.

Despite Ponsonby-Fane's cool official tone, what he told Menzies was inaccurate and suggests that, not having bothered to go through the organizational papers of the previous event, he was relying on his imperfect memory. In fact, in 1872 the Moderator of the Church of Scotland had complained vociferously about the treatment his group had been accorded, a point Ponsonby-Fane could easily have established had he made even a cursory look through his papers.

Once Menzies had heard from Ponsonby-Fane, he set a number of prominent Scots and Scottish office holders to lobbying the Lord Chamberlain on behalf of the Church of Scotland. Within a short time, protests began arriving from such eminent individuals as the Earl of Hopetoun, Lord High Commissioner to the General Assembly; Lord Lothian, Secretary for Scotland; Sir James Fergusson, Under Secretary of State for Foreign Affairs; A. J. Balfour, late Secretary for Scotland; and Lord Balfour of Burleigh, a Scottish representative peer and Lord-in-Waiting.

Despite the calibre of these correspondents and the serious tone of their letters, Lord Latham merely let it grudgingly be known he would grant only a slight increase. One of the tickets so promised, he granted to the Reverend Robert Rainy, Principal of New College, Edinburgh, and one of the most significant figures in the dissenting Free Church of Scotland, but he did so only after Balfour of Burleigh made yet another representation. This departure from precedent evidently disturbed Lathom, lest it should lead to a surge of other requests, which would be difficult to consider. Balfour of Burleigh assured him, however, that 'you may rely on my doing all I can to keep things as quiet as possible.'

In the event, even though Lathom was forced to grant the Church of Scotland more tickets than Shepheard's schedule had allowed for, he never seems to have understood the importance of this group, a failure which became painfully evident on jubilee day itself, when its eminent delegation, arriving at Westminster Abbey, found itself indiscriminately placed among the nonconformist contingent rather than handled with the dignity befitting representatives of the state church of Scotland. Afterwards Herbert Story, a member of the delegation, sent a letter of outrage to Sir Fleetwood Edwards, an assistant to Sir Henry Ponsonby, complaining about what had happened. Edwards, blameless in the matter, passed the letter to Ponsonby-Fane, thus affording him a painfully clear indication of how ineptly the Lord Chamberlain's Department had handled the situation.

'These arrangements,' Story angrily wrote, 'were not what the National Church of Scotland, of which Her Majesty is a member, were entitled to expect, and they were regarded by all as a little less than insulting,' not least by the writer himself, who had been obliged because of insufficient space to sit on a step throughout the service, conspicuous and uncomfortable. The fact that Principal Rainy, from a hostile sect of Scottish Presbyterianism, was comfortably ensconced nearby, having had the good sense to arrive early, could only have rankled further. No wonder that the souvenir book printed by the Scottish Widows' Fund later in the year witheringly criticized the 'ignorance and obtuseness' of the Lord Chamberlain's Department for the way it had organized matters at the Abbey.

Not all groups had such difficulty. When Thomas Gregg, calling himself Bishop of Verulam and the Senior Bishop of the Reformed Church of England, applied to Shepheard for a ticket, he was refused, so referred his case to the Lord Chamberlain, suggesting that precedent could not apply to him, since in 1872 his group had not even been founded. A just man, Lathom found himself swayed by this argument and granted Gregg's request, a kindness which he must afterwards have regretted.

After the jubilee, the Very Reverend Randall Davidson, Dean of Windsor, informed Ponsonby-Fane that Gregg's newspaper, the *Reformed Church Record*, had announced that the man had been 'officially recognized' by the Court as Bishop of Verulam by virtue of his invitation. Davidson thought that the Lord Chamberlain should be made aware of Gregg's history and should issue a disclaimer. The newspaper, he said, was the organ 'of a strange little body of men . . . who are under the leadership of a certain Dr. Gregg who after a strange career in various places claims to have been consecrated a *Bishop* by an American Bishop who had been, as I understand, deposed from the ministry'. The Dean concluded, 'I could tell you more about this absurd little body by word of mouth but I w^d rather not write it.' As Davidson should have known, however, the Lord Chamberlain's Department used, as a simple matter of courtesy, whatever name or title was customarily borne by an individual. So Ponsonby-Fane explained to him that no question of recognition was involved, and the matter would be best left alone.

Distributing tickets to workingmen proved equally hazardous, largely because the Lord Chamberlain had misinterpreted the precedent from the previous national thanksgiving. In 1872, George Potter, lately President of the Trades Union Congress, had solicited from Lord Sydney the job of distributing tickets to workingmen and was appointed to do so. When, in 1887, Potter solicited for the job again, Lathom gave it to him, reasoning that a man who had discharged it efficiently the first time could do so again. But between 1872 and 1887 Potter's condition had significantly changed. In 1872 he had been at the peak of a career which had taken him from being an innovative labour journalist to becoming president of the recently-founded Trades Union Congress. By 1887, though, he had fallen from eminence. His position within the TUC had been so undermined by disputes that he had withdrawn to form a rival organization under his own control called the London Working Men's Association. It was a group anathematized by regular trade unionists; Sydney and Beatrice Webb called it 'a body of nondescript persons of no importance.'

Aware that his association with the Lord Chamberlain would be challenged by the current TUC leadership, and needing a boost for his own organization, Potter sent a general announcement of his appointment to the national press. At once, C. J. Drummond, an influential member of the TUC and a former member of the Royal Commission on Trade Depression, informed Lathom that Potter had no right to represent the working classes. 'He never at any time had their confidence to any extent, but for many years past has posed as a representative working man knowing full well that he has no right to do so.'

Lathom, never one willingly to change matters already arranged, may have disregarded Drummond's letter as politically motivated. 'Personally,' Drummond wrote, 'I have no object to serve but the Conservative cause of which party I am a humble member.' Was Potter, a strong Liberal and author of a laudatory biography of Gladstone, objectionable to Drummond on party grounds?

Possibly so reasoning, Lord Lathom ignored the major point of Drummond's letter, and gave Potter sixty tickets to distribute to working men, with the proviso that political considerations were to play no part in deciding who should be invited.

A bustling man anxious to consolidate his position, Potter asked Drummond to become a member of his selection committee. 'It was an honour I at once indignantly declined,' an enraged Drummond told Ponsonby-Fane. Potter urged that as Henry Broadhurst and George Howell, both Liberal M.P.s and former workingmen, would be associated with this effort, Drummond really ought to change his mind. Knowing both men himself, Drummond suspected that Potter was making improper use of their names to win his support. If Potter succeeded, he could then use the same argument with them, using Drummond's concurrence as a bargaining point. To stop this from happening, Drummond went off to the House of Commons, consulted Broadhurst and Howell, and had his worst suspicions confirmed. Again he wrote to Ponsonby-Fane, this time triumphantly declaring that neither he nor the two Liberal M.P.s could in any way be associated with Potter.

This letter finally alerted Ponsonby-Fane to the seriousness of the situation, and he asked George Potter to call on him at St. James's Palace. Potter probably had more than an inkling that all was not well, so, to give himself a bargaining position, he had a notice inserted in the national press for May 25 announcing that all workingmen wishing to be considered for a place in the Abbey should apply to him. On the same day, he went to see Ponsonby-Fane.

Sir Spencer was by now very irritated indeed; should Potter be dismissed, the newspaper paragraph would have to be contradicted, to the embarrassment of the Lord Chamberlain's Office. Their interview must have been rather heated, as Ponsonby-Fane reminded Potter he had promised to have no dealings with the press until authorized to do so, an understanding he supported by pulling out a memorandum of their previous conversation. Unabashed, Potter disputed the Comptroller's recollection of events, while apologizing profusely for any confusion he might unwittingly have caused. Poor Ponsonby-Fane had been outmanoeuvred by a crafty man whose vital interests were involved. Instead of compelling Potter to withdraw, he was forced by the threat of unsavoury publicity to buy him off with a bundle of twenty tickets, for distribution to his labouring friends. By a further singularly galling concession, Potter himself was to have another four.

Once Potter had been disposed of, Drummond was asked to chair the distribution committee; Broadhurst and Howell accepted his invitation to be members. Yet it was not quite the end of the irrepressible Potter; later he wrote asking the Lord Chamberlain for still more tickets. The Lord Chamberlain's response was a curt refusal.

No report of the Lord Chamberlain's difficulties with George Potter was ever published but there must have been rumours, since a certain Mr. Forbes MacBean wrote chiding the Lord Chamberlain for admitting workingmen at all and thus opening himself up to unnecessary troubles. 'Fifty years ago,' he concluded, 'it was not the fashion to admit the working class to state ceremonials,' and he saw no reason why that admirable state of affairs should ever have been changed.

Following the precedent of 1872, both the House of Commons and the House of Lords had set up Select Committees to deal with the proper representation of members at the ceremony, the Speaker being designated the official representative of the Commons, the Lord Chancellor that of the Lords. Even though large numbers of tickets were allotted to each body, not all members could attend. Those who were late in asking for a place, like the second Baron Monteagle, found themselves left out, a fact which so infuriated his lordship that he wrote indignantly to the Lord Chamberlain. Lathom, however, merely referred the angry peer back to his own house for consideration.

Lathom's troubles were increased by growing uncertainty about how many persons could be accommodated in the Abbey. The Office of Works found the number of monuments in the interior severely confused its reckoning. As pressure mounted outside from those eager to get a place, the Lord Chamberlain's Office was forced to consider desperate remedies. The first was to cut back the 20 inches of board originally allotted to each seat to 19 inches. But this was still not enough. The Honourable Edward Thesiger, an officer of the House of Lords who was handling the peers' ticket arrangements, reminded Ponsonby-Fane he was expected to fit 700 people into 510 places, a number, he added laconically, which 'I fear will be quite inadequate.' The Lord Chamberlain allotted him another hundred places and asked him to make do. So that he could, Thesiger persuaded the Law Lords to take their tickets from those given to the legal profession rather than from those meant for peers. When he tried to make a similar arrangement with the bench of bishops, requesting them to take their tickets from the clerical supply administered by the Dean of Westminster, the seemingly innocuous suggestion produced an immediate outcry. Thesiger, in his attempt to satisfy everyone, had innocently stumbled into a most sensitive area.

As the Reverend Montague Fowler, the Archbishop of Canterbury's chaplain, immediately informed him, the bishops had unanimously decided that those who had seats in the House of Lords would take their places in the Abbey as members of Parliament rather than as church officials. Their insistence had behind it a strong political point.

Since 1847 when the see of Manchester had been created, the number of bishops in the House of Lords had remained the same. Except for the five senior sees, each new bishop attained his place in Parliament through seniority only. Once the distinction between parliamentary and non-parliamentary bishops had been introduced, however, those who had seats felt that they should stress their parliamentary rights whenever possible. Their desire to do so increased in the wake of growing fears about disestablishment, a course which would have abolished the episcopal bench altogether, and which became a greater possibility as Gladstone grew equivocal on the issue. On an occasion as important as the jubilee, bishops felt they must attend in their parliamentary capacity rather than simply as clerics, and if their intransigence in the matter deprived Lord and Lady Monteagle of their places, that could not be helped.

The last group to be accommodated was the press, Arthur

Trendell, an official in the Art and Science Department of the South Kensington Museum, being put in charge of distributing 90 places. Matters had progressed from the days when Prince Albert had regarded members of the Fifth Estate with such suspicion; the journalists were accorded fairly good seats in the Abbey, and found Trendell attentive to their needs. The illustrated papers, so much a feature of the times, always worked on a close schedule so wanted their artists to be allowed inside the Abbey in advance to make preliminary sketches. These requests were granted, but sometimes with unfortunate results. Archbishop Benson, an important participant in the service, was irritated to see that one of the most important illustrated papers had featured a drawing of the thanksgiving which bore no relation to events. 'There is a very large picture in the *Illustrated London News*,' he wrote in his journal, 'wh is ridiculous—not representing any point whatever which occurred; and there were no bishops in lawn sleeves. It must have been drawn before the event.'

While both Trendell and Edward Peacock, President of the Press Club, wrote to thank Lathom for his help for journalists stationed inside the Abbey, less was done for reporters along the parade route. Sir Algernon Borthwick, proprietor of the *Morning Post* and a Conservative M.P., asked in Parliament what was being done to assist London representatives of provincial newspapers, doubt having arisen that Sir Charles Warren was supplying the assistance they needed. The Home Secretary, however, assured members his commissioner of police was doing everything in his power to help them. Despite this assurance, on jubilee day the *Daily Chronicle* found that press passes issued by Warren were not always honoured by police who often actually impeded journalists' work.

In the end, official delegations and representatives, clergy and members of the government took up most of the 10,000 tickets offered by the Lord Chamberlain's Department. Only two ways to get a place remained: one could try to buy a ticket, or, more safely, charm one from the Lord Chamberlain, who kept a stock of them for distribution to the 'General Public,' which meant in practice members of London Society.

Buying tickets was, of course, strictly illegal, since they were non-transferable. Nevertheless, attempts to do so were brought to the Lord Chamberlain's attention. Among the miscreants were one of the minor canons of Westminster, whose name was never divulged, and, more seriously, Charles Athill, Bluemantle Pursuivant in the College of Arms. When two tickets were discovered on offer for sale at the Civil Services Stores in the Haymarket for £100, Scotland Yard was asked to investigate. Athill's name was quickly detected and passed to both the Lord Chamberlain and the Earl Marshal. The fifteenth Duke of Norfolk called a special meeting of the College of Arms at which Athill was divested not only of his tickets but also of his right to participate in any further heraldic ceremonies until reinstated.

Bluemantle was contrite and wrote to the Earl Marshal suggesting that the sentence was too severe for the crime, detailing his reasons for thinking so; one was that Mrs. Athill, who had originally decided not to attend the service (thus prompting the attempted sale), was now 'keenly disappointed' that she could not do so. Luckily for Bluemantle, the Earl Marshal regarded his act as only an indiscretion and lifted his suspension later in the year. In 1889, Athill, by now rehabilitated, went on to become Richmond Herald.

Other individuals resorted to direct assaults on the Lord Chamberlain to gain their ends. While most of the correspondence was composed of ordinary begging letters, some showed flashes of creative inspiration. Mr. M. Ouseley, for instance, 'an actor fairly well known in my profession,' asked that the 'Court Jester of old ought to be revived, & what better time than now?' Not wanting merely a ticket (though he would have been contented by that), he asked to be allowed to appear in the Abbey 'dressed in the silken garb of an old English Court Jester.' Surely, Ouseley wrote, 'the reappearance of a Jester would help to swell' interest in the jubilee.

Sir Henry Vavasour, Bt. wrote to Lathom when he discovered that the baronets as an order would not be represented and suggested that the senior baronet of each creation—England, Scotland, Ireland and the United Kingdom—should be invited. Unlike most, Vavasour's suggestion was disinterested, since he himself would not be covered by it. Like his literary namesake Sir Vavasour Firebrace, Bt., in Disraeli's *Sybil*, he seems to have been motivated only by a compelling desire that his order should receive its proper recognition in the great pageant. Perhaps like Sir Vavasour, he was able to conjure up a romantic scene of splendid dignity for them. 'Picture us for a moment going down in Procession to Westminster ... in dark green costume—the appropriate dress of *equites aurati;* each not only with his badge, but with his collar of SS. ... In our hand the thumb ring and signet not forgotten, we hold our coronet of two balls'. Unfortunately for Vavasour, his suggestion found no favour with Lathom. Occasionally, however, a plea proved effective.

A certain Miss Gorham of Ursula Lodge, Foot's Cray, Kent wrote Lord Lathom: 'I learn that all classes of her Majesty's subjects are to be represented, but there is *one* class, to which I belong, which will assuredly be ignored unless I press the claim. I refer to that despised, useful, patient class of gentlewomen of small means, good education but *no* profession, called old maids. We cannot be represented by married ladies, or by gentlemen. We are debarred from many joys & privileges thro' no fault of our own. Are we also to be shut out of that earthly Paradise, the Abbey?'

Miss Gorham's letter evidently touched the heart of Lord Lathom for Ponsonby-Fane minuted on it, 'L.C. unable to resist the force of her argument.' Granted a ticket, Miss Gorham responded with a full heart and just a touch of the waspishness expected from an inhabitant of Ursula Lodge. 'I am most fully aware of the great privilege I am promised & flattered that for once a woman's argument is held to be logical.'

At last the vexing task of selecting the fortunate individuals who would be favoured with places in the Abbey was complete. But any satisfaction which Lord Lathom may have felt was soon dissipated. On June 20, *The Times* let it be known it was unimpressed by the sort of persons chosen to attend. At best, most of them were 'undistinguished', having attained their places not by merit but 'by dint of fear, favour, or affection.' Where were the eminent Victorians of the day, the poets, artists, and scientists? Unless they were in political life, they had generally been overlooked by the Lord Chamberlain. Such an omission, typical of the sterile Court, left the periodical *Nature* grumbling, 'England is not represented, but only England's paid officials and nobodies.'

CHAPTER FOUR

HOUSING 'THE ROYAL MOB'

OSTENSIBLY, THE princes who came for the jubilee were all part of a privileged caste set apart from the run of common humanity by blood and position, but comparatively equal to other members of their order. In practice, Victorian royalties were maddeningly conscious of often minute differences in rank and subtle personal distinctions which made the job of arranging their precedence a ticklish one at the best of times. When exotic cultural and racial differences were added, umbrage was virtually unavoidable. The way the jubilee royalties were handled, however, made it certain some would be affronted.

The last thing Queen Victoria wanted to grace her jubilee was a great mass of the 'royal mob,' not least because the government's failure to supply her demand for 'small helps' meant that all their expenses would fall on her privy purse. While she was reluctantly prepared to entertain her own relations and visiting European royalties not connected to her by blood, she let it be known her officials could not undertake to make or pay for the arrangements either of non-European or Indian princes or the heads of missions sent with congratulatory messages. As a result, several separate categories of guests emerged. Those to whom Victoria and her servants would attend were known as the 'Queen's guests' and constituted the elite of the jubilee visitors. Several steps behind in prestige were the non-European, so-called 'Oriental' princes, whose expenses were picked up, without enthusiasm, by the Foreign Office. Still further down were the heads of special diplomatic missions whose expenses were left to be met by their own governments, and finally the Indian princes, who were expected to fend for themselves in all respects.

Accommodating the Queen's guests was the responsibility

of Sir John Cowell, Master of the Household. Having, like so many officials at Court, begun with a military career, he later became governor to Princes Alfred and Leopold, taking on his present post, the duties of which Prince Albert had reformed in the 1840s, in 1866. No more than any other Court official, had he ever had to arrange anything remotely resembling the jubilee.

On paper, the options open to Cowell for housing the guests might have seemed considerable, Buckingham Palace heading a list of stately residences including Marlborough House, St. James's Palace, Clarence House and Kensington Palace. In practice, however, because of the Queen's long widowhood and the infrequency of foreign guests, none of these buildings was well equipped to handle visitors. Some of the royalties would therefore have to be put up in London hotels.

Since Cowell from the first did not know how many visitors he would have to house, he had no idea how many hotel suites to book. Members of the Queen's immediate family had been commanded to attend, but no one could tell how many other guests would be coming. No invitations were sent out to foreign courts; those who wanted to be represented simply informed their British diplomatic representatives, who in turn notified the Foreign Office, which told the Lord Chamberlain. As there was no central committee, it often took a long time before the Queen was informed who was coming. With this casual procedure in effect, officials lived in fear that the jubilee, like the recent ninetieth birthday celebration of the Emperor of Germany, would be swamped by guests. For this event, Prince Henry of Battenberg told Ponsonby, nine princes had been invited, but ninety had shown up.

Planning for the worst, Cowell advised Ponsonby-Fane in the spring of 1887 to take options on a number of suitably regal suites of rooms. Ponsonby-Fane was reluctant to do so unless the cost could somehow be reduced. He tried to get special consideration, but had little luck. On May 10, for instance, George Cooke, manager of the Buckingham Palace Hotel, informed him, 'In accordance with your wish, I have reconsidered the price named for the whole of the first floor. I regret to say that I cannot see my way to make any reduction. . . .' He did, however, make this concession, 'if the Royal Guests vacate the apartments by mid-day on the 27th of June (Monday) no additional charge will be made for the two extra days beyond the week.' With this, Cooke informed Sir Spencer that the terms named—£360 including 'special attendance, Lights, Bath, and Fires if necessary'—would have to do.

Reluctantly Ponsonby-Fane accepted Cooke's terms, also securing rooms at the Windsor, the Grand, the Victoria and the St. James's, perhaps hoping to appease those who would be placed at these hotels by the monarchical flavour of their names. Additionally, he secured the loan of the fifth Earl Spencer's London home, Spencer House. Spencer may have kindly surrendered it to regain the Queen's favour, which he had lost the year before when against her strenuous opposition he had joined Gladstone's Home Rule government as Lord President of the Council. Finally, Cowell's problems were further reduced when the first Marquess of Breadalbane, whose house, like Lord Spencer's, was conveniently near Buckingham Palace, asked the visiting Crown Prince of Sweden, who seems to have been a personal friend, to stay with him.

When Cowell faced the difficult task of allotting actual rooms, his job was lightened somewhat because the Queen had decided that relations could be housed together. Determined to have as many of her family as were without London residences near her in Buckingham Palace, the Queen had given her eldest daughter, the Princess Royal, and her husband, the Crown Prince of Germany, suites in the Palace along with their unmarried daughters. Their married daughter and her husband, the Hereditary Prince and Princess of Saxe Meiningen, were similarly accommodated; so were the Queen's widowed son-in-law, the Grand Duke of Hesse, and his two unmarried daughters; likewise the Connaughts, Prince and Princess Christian, the widowed Duchess of Albany, and the Battenbergs.

Prince Henry of Battenberg's place at Buckingham Palace may originally have been in doubt. One early accommodation list, which still exists, places his wife, the Queen's youngest daughter, at the Palace but consigns him to the Buckingham Palace Hotel. If such an odd arrangement was actually considered (it may only have been a slip of the pen, of course), it was probably due to Battenberg's equivocal princely status. He was, after all, merely the child of a morganatic marriage and was therefore not by birth a royal highness. He had the title by 1887, to be sure, but only because his mother-in-law had granted it to him on his marriage. It officially raised his rank in England, but if rumours were to be believed, neither at home nor abroad (where his new status often went unobserved) did it free him from snubs. Gadabout Henry Labouchere had written in *Truth* in April, 1886, for instance, 'The Prince of Wales has put his foot down in very decisive fashion to prevent Prince Henry of Battenberg from assuming a position at State functions to which he has no right.' If this gossip were true, then perhaps someone actually had suggested that husband and wife should be housed separately. In the end, however, they managed to stay together. The last member of the family to be accommodated in the Palace was the Queen's own brother-in-law the raffish and dissolute Duke of Saxe-Coburg and Gotha, as unlike his late, good brother as it was possible to be.

Joining this family assortment were European royalties of such high degree that protocol demanded their accommodation near the Queen, unless they had other relations in the English royal house with whom they might stay. Thus the King of Saxony, the King of the Belgians, the Crown Prince of Austria and the Crown Prince and Princess of Portugal all were lodged with the Queen. So was the Duke of Aosta, who had for a time been King of Spain, but now came as the representative of his brother, the King of Italy. Since these guests were taking up most of the available space in the Palace, it was decided that the representatives of the Spanish Queen-Regent, the Infanta Eulalia and her husband Prince Antoine d'Orleans, would be more comfortable at a hotel. The sensitive infantes, however, preferred to take their chances in the royal mob around the Queen rather than enjoy the delights of the Buckingham Palace Hotel; the hint sufficed to produce the desired result.

Other royal guests were farmed out to members of the English royal family to whom they were related, a sensible course designed to spare the Queen as much trouble as possible. Her reaction to a misunderstanding about whether she was to house the King of Denmark showed that her agitation was close to the surface. Upon learning that the King expected to stay at Buckingham Palace, the Queen wrote a jumbled letter to Ponsonby on March 22: 'She merely said she wd be vy much pleased if as she had heard he had expressed the intention of doing if he did come as he had been at her Coronation but she never meant to invite him & never dreamt of the Queen's coming as she cannot lodge them herself . . . what can have happened?' She went on: 'Altogether the Queen is appalled at the prospect of these endless visitors. The P of W who delights in such a mob of royalties wh quite kill the Queen will be vy happy & she owns she knows not how she ever can live through it all, especially in the summer when she dreads the heat so much & is always unable for anything.'[1]

When Count Falbe, the Danish Minister, learned of the Queen's distress, he was perplexed since it had already been arranged that his sovereign was to stay at Marlborough House with his daughter, the Princess of Wales. There they were to be joined by his son, the King of the Hellenes, and three nephews of the Waleses, the Duke of Sparta, Prince George of Greece and the Hereditary Grand Duke of Hesse. Other relations went elsewhere. The Edinburghs at Clarence House took in the Grand Duke and Grand Duchess Serge of Russia, representatives of the Tsar. The Duke of Edinburgh was the Grand Duchess's uncle, while his duchess was the Grand Duke's sister. Given the grandeur of the Russian imperial family, there was some doubt whether the dimensions of Clarence House would satisfy the Tsar's representatives, an official taking it upon himself to warn Ponsonby-Fane about how limited accommodation really was. If, however, the Russians felt unhappy there, no hint of their dissatisfaction has survived.

The Cambridge relations from Germany went to stay with the aged dowager duchess who had apartments in St. James's Palace. There her sister and brother-in-law, the Grand Duke and Duchess of Mecklenburg-Strelitz, were squeezed in with the Hereditary Grand Duke and Duchess. Finally, Princess Louise and her husband, the Marquess of Lorne, accommodated the Princess's cousin, the Princess of Leiningen, at Kensington Palace, which was in such a state of disrepair that no one else could be placed there.

Even after this massive dispersal of royalty to the Queen's residences, Cowell still had to make use of all the reserved hotel suites. The most important royalties not yet taken care of, headed in rank by Prince and Princess Louis of Battenberg, who had difficulty deciding whether to come, were placed in the Buckingham Palace Hotel, where six suites of apartments rented in March cost the Queen £350 a week. Meals did not have to be paid for, as the royalties always dined at Buckingham Palace. As *Punch* put it, it was a case of 'sleep out, and take meals in the house.'

Once all these arrangements had been made, one troublesome individual still remained to be dealt with. This was Prince William of Prussia, the Queen's twenty-eight-year-old grandson, who came with his wife, Princess Augusta, and whom Victoria had marked for special treatment.

In the year 1887, the Court of Berlin was more than ever rent by intrigue and conspiracy. The reigning Emperor, William I, though hearty, was ninety years old so could not be expected to live much longer. It was questionable, however, whether his son and heir, Victoria's son-in-law Prince Frederick, would be able to succeed to the German throne. For some time, he had been known to be ill with what was diagnosed in November as malignant cancer of the throat. Throughout the jubilee summer, he was slowly, agonizingly dying. Indeed it was an open secret that he was coming to England as much to see his controversial physician Dr. Morrell Mackenzie as to attend the celebration of the Queen's jubilee. Inevitably, therefore, much attention was centred on the next heir, Prince Frederick's eldest child, Prince William. Increasingly lionized, the prince, who was without inner control, gave way to galloping hubris and swaggering arrogance. Encouraged in his delusions of grandeur by self-seeking members of the Court and even by the Emperor himself, William by the spring of 1887 was wondering what should be done if his sickly father proved unable to attend the jubilee. Accordingly, the prince began intriguing with the Emperor to see whether he might not displace his father.

Just how Sir Henry Ponsonby became aware of what was going on is not clear, although he may have been informed through correspondence with Col. L. V. Swaine, military attaché in Berlin. In any event, Swaine on June 3 wrote him that, 'It is the old story. No. 3 wants to gain his spurs & play a big part which the wife of no. 2 don't seem to see.'² Since the Emperor was only too happy to gratify his headstrong grandson by designating him the personal representative of the Crown, Ponsonby was forced to suggest to Lord Lathom the need to upgrade William's English attendant. As a mere grandson, he had been assigned one of the Queen's equerries, but now that the Emperor had intervened, Ponsonby told Lathom that Prince William would need a 'big man' in attendance, one of the Lords-in-Waiting.

The Queen was furious when she discovered what was going on. On June 9, she wrote a scorching letter to Lord Salisbury informing him (somewhat inconsequently) that, 'There is *no special representative* of the Emperor. If the C Pce cannot go to W Abbey his place as son-in-law will be vacant and Pce Wm remains his *son as before*.' At the end of her letter, she was outspoken about her grandson's wayward behaviour. 'Wm,' she wrote, 'is rash & inconsiderate.' In no circumstances would she ever consent to his having a Lord-in-Waiting to dance attendance upon him; men of such rank were reserved for reigning sovereigns alone. William would have to make do with an equerry as previously arranged.

William's behaviour had already put the Queen out severely; his attempt to supplant his father simply capped her irritation. Already he had angered her by proposing to bring over an extravagantly large suite; she had personally reduced it to manageable size.

The root of the difficulty was, of course, William's 'disgraceful' conduct to his parents, a theme to which the Queen returned again and again and which was echoed by other members of her family as well. On June 18, for instance, Princess Alexandra, who never missed a chance to say ill of a Prussian, wrote to the Queen, 'I have no words to say what I think of that horrid William of Prussia's behaviour towards his Parents.'³

The Queen determined to teach William a lesson by exiling him and his wife to Spencer House where, removed from all her other guests, he would have time enough and reason to contemplate the effects of his continuing selfishness and unnatural pride. Moreover, she resolved to treat him with the barest civility when they met, not with the exuberant affection which 'Gan Gan' liked to display towards her grandchildren. Her icy correctness had its effect on Prince William; years later when, as an ex-Emperor, he came to write his memoirs, he still remembered the 'exquisite coolness' and 'bare courtesy' with which he had been received. Characteristically, however, he got his own back, alone among the royal guests, by recording a number of instances of organizational ineptitude which he had encountered at the time.

Unless royalties were assigned to hotels, Cowell's responsibilities did not end when he had found them accommodation. He also had to make what had been assigned habitable, not always easy in view of the long disuse of some of the rooms. Cowell was assisted in this job by Mr. Heather, an official in the furniture division.

On June 8, less than a week before the first guests were to arrive, Heather notified Ponsonby-Fane that Sir Philip Cunliffe-Owen, who had an instinct for knowing where money was to be made, had offered to sell a set of 'French furniture' for £100 for the decoration of rooms. Even though it was 'plainer in style than I hoped, still it is genuine.' Heather therefore advised getting it, because it 'would be useful to us for some rooms that will be occupied by Royal Guests & which at present have only chintz covered furniture in them.' Knowing how long it took the Lord Chamberlain's Department to settle its bills, Cunliffe-Owen asked for his money at once, advancing a plausible story about having paid for the furniture out of his own pocket. Ponsonby-Fane promptly settled his account.

At last, with the plainer-than-hoped-for furniture in place, and the numerous royalties marked for suitable, if nicely differentiated, accommodation, all was ready for the arrival of the guests. At this late moment, the British Ambassador in Berlin telegraphed to Lord Salisbury that the Hereditary Duke of Anhalt, representing the reigning Duke, had decided to come. At the thought of having to reconsider every detail of protocol and precedence, the Queen reacted snappishly. 'Certainly not,' she telegraphed to Ponsonby. 'He should be stopped. It upsets everything which has been arranged with so much trouble.'

To avoid hurt feelings and perhaps a diplomatic incident, the Queen allowed herself to be soothed by the Duke of Cambridge, who assured his cousin that he would take it upon himself to find the prince rooms and a carriage. With this understanding, the Hereditary Prince, little aware of how nearly he was kept at home, was allowed to attend the jubilee.

The non-European princes were handled with much less courtesy.

In the spring of 1887, Arthur Nicolson, Secretary of the British Legation in Teheran, informed the Foreign Secretary that the Shah of Persia wished to send a representative to the jubilee. Because this was the first intimation that any non-European prince would be coming, Lord Salisbury laid the matter before the Queen. His recommendation of what Victoria should do seems no longer to exist, but it is likely he advised her to treat the Persian prince as any other, being aware of the hazards of any distinction which could be interpreted as invidious. Furthermore Persia at that moment was strategically significant territory where important negotiations were taking place about building railways. As the British were eager to strengthen the defences of Persia to stop Tsarist encroachments from the north, it seemed wise to handle this representative with 'hospitality & distinction,' as Salisbury later informed subordinates in the Foreign Office. Besides, as the Persian representative to the coronation of Tsar Alexander III had been the sovereign's personal guest, nothing less would do in London.

Why did Queen Victoria reject such a compelling case? It was certainly not because she was racist, as many other European royalties undoubtedly were. As Empress of India, she took pride in her good relations with Asian notables. Rather, the significant reason seems to have been money. Had only one non-European prince decided to come, she would probably have taken him in, but there was no telling how many more would follow, and with the government unwilling to meet their expenses, the Queen saw no reason for extending herself. Perhaps she reasoned that if she stood firm, the government would change its mind and make her a grant.

Having presented his position and been rebuffed, Lord Salisbury asked his counterpart in the India Office, the first Viscount Cross, for assistance, rather than return himself to face the Queen. Cross boldly carried the attack right to Victoria's dinner table itself, the Queen afterwards noting in her journal for March 17, 'Ld Cross talked a good deal about Persia & the necessity for conciliating the Shah.'[4]

When this tactic also failed to produce the desired result, Salisbury and Cross, regarding Persia as being in the sphere of Britain's Indian Empire, agreed to divide the prince's expenses between them. He thus became a guest of the state, as did the princely representatives from Hawaii, Siam and Japan, who later announced that they, too, would be coming. £88 a week for up to a month was to be allotted for their expenses.

To highlight their different status, these princes, who were not of course invited to stay in any of the Queen's residences, were housed apart from the other royalties; the Foreign Office put them up at the Alexandra, a comfortable hotel off Hyde Park but less imposing than the Buckingham Palace or the St. James's. There they went without courtesy of guards snapping to attention each time they went in or out, a slight about which Prince Komatsu of Japan complained, reminding the Foreign Office that such attentions had not been neglected during his recent visit to Berlin. Guards were promptly put into position.

Each of the visiting 'oriental' princes, as officials called them, found some particular grounds to be affronted. Komatsu, a member of the Japanese imperial family, was at first surprised and then irritated by the laughter which greeted him each time he exercised the royal privilege of driving through Horse Guards. Finally, his coachman discovered that the guards sniggered because his ivory pass made out in the name of the Mikado reminded them of Gilbert and Sullivan's 1885 success. It was promptly altered.

More serious were the snubs inflicted on the Hessan es Sultaneh of Persia, the Shah's representative. The Hessan was a first cousin of his sovereign, and had been chosen because no one else seemed suitable. According to an unsigned extract from a Foreign Office document still existing in the Queen's papers (very probably written by Arthur Nicolson), 'There was a good deal of difficulty as to whom to send. The Shah won't let any of his sons go. His brothers are poor creatures, with the exception of one who is in disgrace somewhat. There are only three ministers who could go; and they so successfully intrigued against each other that the Shah would not send any, so they had to fall back on a Prince.'[5] According to the extract, the one finally selected ought to have done well enough, for 'He is a young man of about 30; speaks a little French, and is a presentable youth.'

When he arrived in London, the Persian prince found things little less complicated than they had been in Teheran, his arrangements constantly dogged by petty factionalism and oriental intrigue. The English attendant upon the Hessan, for instance, told the head of the Treaty Department in the Foreign Office, J. H. Bergne, that he had been instructed, although he did not say by whom, to make sure his charge arrived slightly later at Buckingham Palace than other royalties so that the prince would not be able to participate in the procession in to dinner. He had reluctantly obeyed this suggestion, because 'the European Princes [have] objected to go in procession with the orientals.' The alternative might be unseemly, with rank-conscious royalties elbowing and jostling one another for pride of place. The Hessan es Sultaneh was so affronted that he threatened to leave the country at once. Fearing perhaps that the railway negotiations were threatened, Lord Salisbury had personally to right matters and soothe the injured pride of the Shah's cousin. He therefore paid special attention to the prince at a garden party he gave at Hatfield House and no doubt asked the Queen, who was also present, to do likewise: mollified, the Persian decided to stay on. Privately, Salisbury was furious about these unnecessary problems, blaming the Lord Chamberlain's Department. As he wrote to Lady John Manners, an old friend, 'The Chamberlain's office declined to recognize the Persian, Siamese and Japanese Princes as anything else but blacks and treated them accordingly.' The person who suffered most from such treatment, however, was one Salisbury didn't even mention, Queen Kapiolani of Hawaii, the most deeply insulted of all the guests.

As the wife of a reigning monarch, Kapiolani ranked above all but a handful of the royalties at the jubilee. Because of her ebony skin, however, and the supposedly trifling importance of her realm, no one felt she deserved much consideration. No one, that is, except Lord Salisbury, who thought she might.

1887 was an important year in the history of Hawaii. King Kalakaua was involved in a strenuous attempt to increase the powers of the crown by attempting to find a way to realize his long-time dream of annexing Samoa and trying to diminish the power of the elected popular assembly in Honolulu, which tended to be controlled by foreigners, especially Americans. As a result of the king's schemes, many Americans resident in what were also known as the Sandwich Islands began to consider counter-measures designed to contain the monarchy and looked to their homeland for support. Thus while Kalakaua cast his eyes on Samoa, others were considering how Hawaii could itself best be annexed. Following the traditional Anglophile policy of his house, Kalakaua looked to Britain to sustain his islands' independence. Complicating the situation was the fact that in 1887 the Hawaiian-American Reciprocity Treaty, under which each nation was permitted to export its goods freely to the other, was up for renewal. It was essential for the Hawaiian economy that the United States should reconfirm the pact, but the Americans were demanding as their price for doing so the cession of Pearl Harbor, a key strategic factor in the Pacific which, in American hands, would virtually assure later takeover of the islands as a whole.

Since there would be no place for the royal house if the Americans gained their way, Kalakaua determined to play on English fears of United States expansionism in an effort to shore up his throne. The Jubilee served as a convenient excuse for him to send a mission to London headed by his queen and including Colonel Curtis Iaukea, the King's Chamberlain, who was sent to do the business. As it sailed from Honolulu to San Francisco whence the Queen's party was to cross the United States, Lord Salisbury was following developments, telling the German Ambassador in London, 'We must keep a sharp watch on American fingers.'

Salisbury's recognition that Queen Kapiolani was coming for no idle purpose did not enable him to protect her from snubs and irritants. To begin with, the Queen arrived in England far too early to be allowed to proceed to London, where officials had no time to deal with her. It was therefore arranged that she and her travelling companion, Princess Liliuokalani, Kalakaua's niece and Heiress Apparent to the throne, should spend some days in Norfolk, staying on his estate with a gentleman named Stewart. Nothing in the records indicates how or why he was selected for this honour.

Her Hawaiian Majesty could not, however, be kept buried in the country forever, and on Tuesday, June 7, she and her party took up residence at the Alexandra Hotel, which her servant James McGuire correctly characterized as 'not a large Hotel, but more of a family Hotel.' As soon as Kapiolani arrived, she was pained to discover that Queen Victoria had not assigned a Lord-in-Waiting to be in attendance as protocol demanded. Indeed, no member of the Court was on hand to greet her. Rather, she discovered that Mr. R. F. Synge, an official of the Treaty Department, who had been raised to the temporary rank of second secretary for the occasion, was to wait upon her. This could, however, be only on a part-time basis, since later he was also to be in attendance on all the other oriental princes.

Gregarious by nature, the Queen did not let such disturbances spoil her holiday, and so accepted a series of invitations from such metropolitan notables as the Archbishop of Canterbury, the Duke of Westminster, Lord Rosebery, the Bishop of London and Sir Julian Goldsmid. Everywhere her striking appearance aroused much interest, some of it malign. One rumour, first published by *The Times* in the summer of 1886, was that Kalakaua's kingdom was up for sale on the open market. Another recalled a recent volcanic eruption when the King's sister was supposed to have thrown herself into a fiery cone to appease the enraged fire goddess who lived within. Many people found her regal ways ludicrously presumptuous. The rather derisive curiosity with which Kapiolani was regarded knew no boundaries of class. Sir Francis Grenfell said she provided the humour for the occasion, while the radical newspaper *Reynolds's* scoffed that she had given 'a regal position to Darktown.' That her precedence should have been difficult to arrange *vis à vis* other royalties was therefore no surprise. To be sure, Queen Victoria treated Kapiolani almost as an equal: at least she allowed her cheek to be brushed by the lips of the mahogany lady and returned the favour, as protocol demanded two queens should do. She could not, however, bring herself to call Kapiolani 'my sister,' as she did with her European counterparts. Instead, having kissed the Queen of Hawaii, she let matters take their course.

Luncheon on jubilee day, for instance, was declared a family occasion, so that particularly Kapiolani could be kept away, a ruse which seems not to have been communicated to Sir Henry Ponsonby, who promptly added her name to the guest list when he noticed it was missing. On June 18, Princess Beatrice took it off again, informing him, 'Queen Kapiolani is not to be invited as it is impossible to place her properly.'[6] What Beatrice meant, of course, was that the Europeans became livid whenever they had to give her precedence. In the absence of an internationally accepted standard of protocol, it was easier to leave her out.

The lack of any such standard bedevilled every aspect of dealing with the visiting royalties, officials arguing interminably about precedence and who was responsible. Although no one in the Foreign Office liked to admit as much, it seemed to fall to the Treaty Department to advise the Queen on the matter. Reluctant to make mistakes, Foreign Office officials delayed until finally the Lord Chamberlain's Department was forced into undertaking a task for which it was not prepared. The result was a continuing succession of varying lists, altered again and again.

Thus at one time, the King of the Hellenes was given precedence over the King of Denmark based on their respective dates of succession to the throne. When the Prince of Wales learned about this arrangement, he was appalled, and had Ponsonby write to Synge of the Treaty Department. 'The P of Wales says that you cannot put a son before a father.' Instead the Prince suggested that the age of the kingdom should be used as the operative factor. Later, this notion was also dropped and a commonsense solution adopted: Christian IX of Denmark was given precedence over his son George I of the Hellenes, while the King of the Belgians and the King of Saxony followed, based on the years of their accession to the throne.

But the squabbles were far from over and as Princess Beatrice's letter to Ponsonby three days before the jubilee shows, the difficulties regarding Queen Kapiolani's proper place were never solved. The other Asiatic princes suffered as well. Naturally, no one wanted to admit responsibility: Ponsonby-Fane minuted that 'The F.O. have all along shirked this, but I maintain it is for them to advise the Queen as to Foreign precedence—no one else can.' Mr. Bergne of the Treaty Department stoutly maintained the reverse. 'It is too bad of the Lord Chamberlain's Office to cast the blame on the F.O.' Ultimately, of course, it was up to the Queen herself to arrange her guests, for no one was more aware of the nuances of their standing than she. Unfortunately, with her advisors at loggerheads and unable to forget that some of the royalties were not her guests, Victoria was not as helpful as she might have been. No widely acceptable general protocol list was ever drawn up. As a result on jubilee day, the guests had to be despatched to the Abbey in a series of carriage processions rather than in one unified parade.

Although the troubles of the Master of the Horse thus were considerable, they seemed never to bother the head of the department. William John Arthur Charles James Cavendish-Bentinck, sixth Duke of Portland, was not yet 30 at the time of the jubilee. Once a favourite of Benjamin Disraeli's, Portland (who had succeeded to his great patrimony in 1879 at the age of 22), with his youth, bland good looks and dashing equine verve may have reminded the aged Prime Minister of his character the Duke of St. James. St. James, 'fortune's favourite,' is the protagonist of Disraeli's novel *The Young Duke*, in which, 'stamped at the mint of fashion as a sovereign of the brightest die,' he fulfills the opulent, romanticized role Disraeli thought suitable for such an epitome of the nobility.

Still a bachelor at the time of the jubilee, very rich and very eligible, young Portland considered he had better things to do with himself than worry overmuch about how the vexatious processional arrangements were coming along. Indeed in the organizational papers, there seems no evidence that he considered them at all. Instead they were left to Colonel George Ashley Maude.

Born in 1817, Maude was the oldest of the permanent officials concerned with the jubilee. Having first had the almost obligatory military career (which included service in the Crimea) pre-requisite to Court service, Maude had been since 1859 secretary to the Master of the Horse and superintendent of the royal stables as well as Crown Equerry. Thus in 1887, he was the individual charged not only with finding enough carriages to accommodate all the guests on jubilee day but also during the remainder of their stay in London. Given the modest number of vehicles which sufficed for Victoria's ordinary purposes, this was a sufficiently difficult task, but it was made much worse by the Queen's refusal to allow any of the gorgeous state coaches to be used.

As the Queen must have known from what had taken place in 1872, this arrangement pleased no one but herself. Indeed the outcry, once the plans leaked out, was considerable. Even the *Standard*, the most orthodox Conservative journal, joined in the complaints, writing on June 10, 'It is our duty to say, at once, and in the plainest of language, that the Procession designed for Jubilee Day . . . is utterly inadequate, mean, pinched, and narrow, and appears to be dictated by a parsimonious spirit unworthy of a rich and powerful state.' That the parsimonious spirit in charge was the Queen herself, of course, made matters difficult to change, but there was constant pressure to do so. When on June 9, the *Daily News* reported that Messrs. Thorne Brothers, royal coach builders, had returned the Coronation coach to Buckingham Palace newly refurbished with 300 books of gold leaf, many were prepared to take it as a sign that the Queen was about to change her mind and comply with the expressed wishes of her subjects. There was thus pleasurable relief when an 'official' announcement was published in all the leading metropolitan newspapers on June 13 that the Queen would go to Westminster Abbey in state. But as this was immediately denied by the Lord Chamberlain's Department, disappointment merely increased.

Realising that such continuing criticism might at any moment force the Queen to order a pageant in keeping with the public's wishes, Maude found himself in a state of constant uncertainty, only exacerbated by one alteration after another as more and more princes announced they were coming. Months before, writing to Sir Henry Ponsonby about carriage arrangements, he had made plain how matters should be dealt with. 'I see no difficulty either way,' he wrote in January. 'Only let us know and don't alter afterwards. If we listen to everybody's opinion it will never be settled.' In the event, of course, this sensible advice went unheeded.

Splitting princes up into separate processions did not, of course, decrease anybody's work. Maude still had as many carriages to locate, and the difficult problem of precedence, impossible to arrange generally, was little easier for the smaller groups. As Ponsonby informed his assistant, Fleetwood Edwards, 'The carriage containing the Siamese, Persian & Japanese will be rather a heterogeneous collection as none can speak the others' language and all claim the precedence & right to sit forward.'[7] The Indians proved equally difficult, though characteristically Ponsonby made light of the situation. As he wrote to Ponsonby-Fane, 'There are to be councils today as to whether Ram Bux goes before or after Snooks Khan and if wrong—then perish India!' Neither Maude nor the Indian princes themselves, however, found the problem of what should be done with the maharajahs as amusing as Ponsonby did, though Maude's problems at least would have lessened had someone thought to mount these splendid subjects rather than lock them away in carriages which all too often had the look of common London cabs. That such a solution would also have pleased the crowds along the parade route makes it the more strange that it was never brought up.

Even when the precedence of the Asians and the Indian princes had been arranged, there still remained the problem of Queen Kapiolani. As the jubilee approached, this became more difficult to arrange because Lord Salisbury seems to have decided it would be unwise to give her too much consideration, lest this suggested to the United States that he intended to help King Kalakaua. Although it is difficult to tell what was in his mind, he seems already to have concluded that it was more important to bolster Anglo-American relations by winking at what the United States was intending to do than to sustain Hawaiian independence. In any event, he joined the ranks of those who poked fun at the lady, though in his case he did so privately. After the jubilee was over, he wrote Lady John Manners a letter which made his feelings about Kapiolani clear. 'The whole Court was never tired of lavishing honours on the Black Queen of Hawaii—who looks exactly like Lady Rosebery stained walnut. The Queen kissed her—and after that we all had to be very civil to her.'

In fact as Salisbury well knew, whatever civilities Kapiolani received, she had to fight for, which was particularly evident when it came to the matter of her escort on jubilee day. Queen Victoria, of course, desired to keep the procession as simple as possible. Originally, therefore, she had contemplated a parade made up only of herself, a few outriders and some members of the Indian cavalry which the Queen had especially ordered to remind people that she was an Empress, too. From the surviving records, it is not even clear that Victoria intended any foreign royalties to process with her. Mounting public criticism of the arrangements ultimately forced them to be changed, Victoria allowing a cortege of the princes of her house to be added and a grander parade made up of three separate carriage processions.

At first, the Queen assigned her own procession a field officer's escort of the Household Cavalry and the Indian cavalry. The Kings' Procession was given the same escort, which remained constant even when Victoria added the cortege of princes to her own array. The procession headed by the Duchess of Teck and that of the oriental princes was each assigned a captain's escort of cavalry, the usual escort provided for the Queen when she appeared in public on non-state occasions. Queen Kapiolani let it be known that while such an escort might be sufficient for the Queen's cousin Mary of Teck and the Asians, it was not enough for the Queen Consort of Hawaii. If she did not receive something more suitable, she would not participate.

Who made the decision to assign Kapiolani a mere captain's escort does not emerge in the record. It was not, however, Sir Henry Ponsonby, who on June 3 had informed Fleetwood Edwards that he presumed she should have a royal escort, because 'She is most particular about being treated as a Queen, and her English Suite are very punctilious.'[8] Since no one wanted a public incident, Kapiolani succeeded in securing the same escort as her sister of England. On jubilee day, her servant James McGuire noted in his homey way the presence outside the Alexandra Hotel of an escort made up of '60 life guards on fine black horses, dressed in scarlet jackets & white pantaloons with a steel helmet.' As the Queen of Hawaii entered her carriage, this hard won contingent drew its swords and saluted.

Throughout these intricate manoeuvrings, Colonel Maude had attempted without much success to keep his work intact. As the Queen made fundamental changes in the processional arrangements and as new guests announced themselves and had to be fitted in, his frustrations increased. 'If the Queen of the Sandwich Islands is not an invited guest of the Queen,' he wrote sharply to Ponsonby, 'I don't see why H.M. should be called upon to supply a carriage. But if the Queen thinks she ought to have a carriage . . . it should be a dress carriage and we have not got one. . . . I should have thought the F. Office might have taken care of her altogether.'[9] Maude certainly had good reason to be irritated, but things would have been even worse for the crown equerry if it had been decided that the string of special diplomats in town for the jubilee should also be included in the procession. This, however, the Queen would not consider.

The first hint that foreign governments might want to send special missions to congratulate the Queen on her jubilee was sent to Ponsonby by Salisbury's aide Eric Barrington at the Foreign Office in November, 1886. The Chinese had begun to ask whether such missions 'would be agreeable to the Queen.' When Ponsonby laid the matter before Victoria, her response was illuminating. 'The Queen concludes this *shd* be, but trembles at the result. It should be made clear that the *Queen* is put to *no* expense.'[10]

In this instance, Lord Salisbury seems to have accepted the Queen's decision without demur. However, he saw no reason why the Foreign Office should assume any responsibility in the matter. The jubilee missions were to have no part in the processions, no carriages were to be assigned for their use, and their arrangements were their own concern. But when the Turkish Ambassador wrote to inquire about what role they were to have in the jubilee, it is not surprising that the Foreign Office did not relish having to tell him the news. Through his private secretary, therefore, Salisbury asked a favour of Lord Lathom. 'It wd be almost out of the question for the F.O. . . . to write to the Turkish Ambassador on this matter, as some of the answers might not look well on paper.' Would Lathom do so instead? He did, but he grumbled about it.

Only five nations despatched special, non-princely envoys. Nine others, however, were represented by the usual head of the London mission, who had been given authorization to present congratulations to the Queen. They were received *en masse* at Buckingham Palace on June 20, not merely in order to spare the Queen fatigue, or to prevent the diplomats not so honoured from taking umbrage, but because this was Lord

Salisbury's way of letting people know that there had been no special communication between Victoria and the one jubilee envoy who aroused considerable interest, Monsignor Ruffo Scilla, despatched from the Vatican on the orders of Pope Leo IX.

Scilla's mission was potentially most important. From time to time in the nineteenth century, the possibility of establishing formal diplomatic relations between England and the Vatican had been contemplated. Indeed, in 1848 Parliament had even passed legislation enabling the Queen to enter into such relations, though the House of Lords added the proviso that no ecclesiastic could be sent. By 1887, however, this law no longer existed, as the Statute Law Revision Committee had secured its repeal some years before, after the Italian government in 1871 had laid down a guarantee of the Vatican's right to receive foreign envoys.

Given the position of the Church of Rome in Ireland, it was inevitable that informal discussions would be held now and again on matters of mutual interest. The last such meetings had occurred during Gladstone's second ministry, when George Errington was sent to see what he could do about keeping Roman Catholic clergy from assisting the Land League. Now that the Plan of Campaign had intensified the land war, A. J. Balfour, Irish Secretary, thought it advisable to consider the matter of formal relations.

Recognizing the Vatican, however, was a touchy business at best, for it was certain to arouse vehement opposition from those who feared the pernicious influence of abominable popery. Salisbury was soon given an indication of how such people would react when Henry J. Atkinson, an obscure Tory M.P. from Boston, wrote to him, after hearing lobby gossip that the Prime Minister might be contemplating such a step. 'There are *many* who put Protestantism before general politics, especially *nonconformists*,' Atkinson warned sternly, hinting that he was among them. Serendipity, however, suggested a way of finessing such difficulties, for not only was Victoria celebrating a jubilee in 1887, but so was his holiness, who in the autumn would pass his fiftieth year in the priesthood. Mutual congratulatory missions would be very much in order. Once having determined upon this course, however, both Salisbury and the Pope proceeded with caution. Indeed, it soon became clear that Leo IX considered that simply despatching an envoy was sufficient to begin with. At least that is how the Foreign Office evaluated his appointment of Ruffo Scilla.

Scilla was the titular Archbishop of Petra *in partibus infidelis* and the newly-appointed nuncio to the Bavarian Court at Munich. According to the British *chargé d'affaires* in Rome, he was an 'ideal monsignore,' rich, good looking and a man of the world, who, in the opinion of the Duke of Norfolk, who also sent Salisbury an evaluation, was all the more worthy of consideration because he did not take snuff. However amiable and with what polished manners, Scilla was, however, a lightweight, for as Norfolk candidly informed Lord Salisbury, 'Monsignor Ruffo Scilla is not looked upon as a man of great ability and people wonder why the Pope is sending him to Munich.'

Leo IX had chosen Scilla with care, however, meaning that his envoy should make a good impression in London but not (it seems) undertake any serious discussions. Therefore, although Norfolk took the trouble to discover that Scilla's views on Ireland were 'sound,' Salisbury seems never to have asked Scilla for them. Indeed, the Prime Minister went out of his way to avoid a private meeting with the papal envoy, and made certain that their conversation was very general when at last he was forced to have one. Thus Scilla found when he reached London he had nothing to do but amuse himself; manfully resolving to make the best of this situation, he accepted all the social invitations he could. Coming upon Scilla at a Foreign Office entertainment, the Archbishop of Canterbury was irritated to find him being lionized by the crowd, scandalized that many were curtseying 'as to a royal person.' He was only able to calm himself by remembering that at the 'last reception Buffalo Bill was the lion.'

The fact that Ruffo Scilla was not allowed to broach the subject of Ireland with the Prime Minister by no means impeded speculation about what might be brewing. Opinion particularly looked to Victoria's reception of the papal envoy for a clue as to what Salisbury intended, so the Prime Minister had to be most careful about the protocol of his visit.

The precedence of Roman Catholic ecclesiastics was not defined in England, although after the disestablishment of the

Church of Ireland during Gladstone's first ministry, bishops and archbishops of the Church of Rome were permitted to take on the official standing previously enjoyed by the establishment. The only other clue available to Lord Salisbury was a recent one: in 1884 in the arrangement of the Royal Commission on Housing, Cardinal Manning, as a prince of the church, was placed directly after the Prince of Wales, who was also serving. Unfortunately, this precedent was not useful to Salisbury because Scilla's rank was not cardinal, but nuncio. By regulations stemming from the Congress of Vienna in 1815, a nuncio was bound to claim precedence over all other diplomats. Naturally no British government had ever recognized this claim. The niceties of diplomatic usage, however, did not prevent either officials or indeed the Queen from referring to Scilla as a nuncio, but he could not be received as such by Lord Salisbury, who was forced to seek another basis on which to deal with him.

Asked to assist in the matter, J. G. Kennedy, the chargé in Rome, found it difficult to discover from the 'wily prelates' in the Vatican precisely what Ruffo Scilla should be called, informing Bergne of the Treaty Department that he was 'an Envoy Extraordinary as far as England is concerned.'[11] Fortunately for Salisbury the conundrum was solved by deciding to recognize Scilla on the basis of his personal rank rather than any of his clerical positions, for the papal envoy also happened to be head of the Neapolitan princely family of Ruffo Scilla. As far as his presentation to the Queen was concerned, it was thought best to rank the diplomats according to the dates their commissions were signed, thus giving the Vatican's representative an inconspicuous twelfth place. These arrangements allowed Sir James Fergusson, Under Secretary at the Foreign Office, to assure anxious members of the House of Commons on at least two occasions that Ruffo Scilla had come to England on only a congratulatory mission which was absolutely without diplomatic or political significance.

One of those who felt unsatisfied by such assurances was none other than Henry Cardinal Manning, the highest ranking Roman Catholic prelate in the kingdom. Manning's mistrust stemmed from the fact that his leading rival among English Catholics, the Duke of Norfolk, had had a hand in bringing the papal envoy to London. Norfolk was anxious to diminish Manning's influence and thought that the establishment of a Vatican mission in the capital could undercut him. Expecting such a mission to be headed by his kinsman, Cardinal Howard, he anticipated a considerable boost in his own influence. Salisbury was not averse to assisting Norfolk in this instance, because Manning was known to have strong Home Rule sympathies, while the Earl Marshal was the staunchest of Unionists.

Throughout the visit of the papal envoy, therefore, Manning was in a morose, splenetic humour, prone to raging spasms of anger. As his biographer Edmund Purcell later noted, during this period he saw his eminence 'in an almost uncontrollable outburst of indignation' lashing out against 'the intriguers who are planning and scheming for Diplomatic Relations.' Still worse, Manning made these feelings known publicly. He boycotted all the jubilee events and, though invited, even chose not to attend the Abbey service. Instead, he organized a competing, strictly Roman Catholic affair in the pro-Cathedral in Westminster at the same hour as the national thanksgiving. Naturally, as Manning had intended, Ruffo Scilla was forced to forgo the great national pageant. This considerably irritated Queen Victoria, and she asked Lord Salisbury to assure the papal envoy that she felt Manning had not acted at all 'nicely' in the matter.

In fact, as Manning gradually became aware (in part through a gentlemanly letter Norfolk sent him), the chances for diplomatic relations were almost daily diminishing. Salisbury hoped that his government's coercion policy would succeed in making Ireland quiet without the need for any concessions to be made to the Vatican, and was therefore playing for time; having indicated his willingness to have a papal envoy at the Queen's jubilee and to send a British mission to Rome for that of the Pope, he sat back to await developments.

By the time the Duke of Norfolk was despatched to Rome in the autumn, it was now the Vatican which wished to speed up events, sensing that the British government's attitude was shifting and afraid that too much coyness would allow a good opening to slip by. Leo IX himself indicated to Norfolk that the conduct of the clergy needed to be corrected, but informed the

British envoy that he hesitated to do anything publicly. Perhaps the Pope hoped Salisbury would move towards formalizing relations, if he offered the lure of disciplining fractious clergy as the *quid pro quo*.

Salisbury did not rise to the bait. Instead he set Norfolk and his assistant, Ross of Bladensburg, to work on the Pope to initiate a move which would prove his *bona fides;* a simple matter of disciplining priests was not to be thought equal to the weighty consideration of full diplomatic relations. It was a plausible approach, and the Vatican accepted it. As a result, a certain Monsignor Persico was sent to Ireland to investigate the state of the country and the activities of the Roman clergy. Although his final report contained some views favourable to the Nationalist position, these generally went unnoticed because his findings resulted in the proclamation of a papal rescript condemning the Plan of Campaign and the boycotting of landlords, forbidding clergy to take part in such activities. As was only to be expected, Parnellites were as outraged as Unionists were jubilant at this outcome.

Any hopes the Vatican may have cherished that its intervention in Irish affairs would move the Salisbury government closer to instituting diplomatic relations, were entirely disappointed. Pleased though Unionists may have been about the papal rescript, its publication had no demonstrable effect on Roman Catholic clergy, who remained as prominent in Nationalist affairs as ever. As a result, Salisbury may have reasoned that there was no point in making concessions to the Vatican (principally in the area of educational policy), because the Pope's influence was obviously diminutive in Irish internal affairs. Thus the immediate prospect of Anglo-Vatican relations dimmed considerably. In the event, they were not finally established until the period of the First World War.

* * *

The final group of notables to attend the jubilee was made up of feudatories of the Empress of India. Princes though they were, they were the guests neither of the Queen nor of the state. Like the foreign missions, they invited themselves and were left to make their own arrangements. Having traversed half the globe to offer their good wishes to their sovereign, they were understandably disappointed about the insignificant part they were to play in her jubilee, and eager to spot any lapse from civility which would allow them to say so. That neither the India Office nor the Lord Chamberlain's Department took any interest in the maharajahs made it likely, however, that there would be difficulties.

Just how Indian princes should be handled was no new problem, but it was no nearer to solution in 1887 than before. In 1884, the Royal Commission organizing the Colonial and Indian Exhibition had tried to regularize the precedence of maharajahs included among the commissioners. But the problem had proved too difficult to resolve, and the Indians were simply grouped together and placed after the English commissioners. No decision was ever attempted about what kind of precedence they were entitled to outside India. In view of the Queen's extended mourning and the distance between London and her Indian possessions, the issue of how Indian princes stood in relation to European royalty and the British aristocracy seldom arose. The jubilee was bound to bring it to the fore, and very probably with unfortunate results, since one of the most important Indian princes was due to attend.

The Maharajah Holkar of Indore was, in the words of *The Times*, 'in a European sense a ruling Prince,' reigning over a land area and population larger than those of many German princelings. He also had full treaty powers under the Raj. On June 2, therefore, the newspaper urged the government to make certain he was received with full honours and continued to be treated appropriately throughout the jubilee.

Unfortunately the India Office entirely ignored this good advice, lumping the visiting maharajahs together as 'chiefs,' disregarding the many and significant distinctions in their rank, although these had been fully set out in time for the jubilee by Lieutenant-Colonel A. W. Roberts of the Indian Army in a helpful book entitled *The Imperial Indian Peerage and Almanack*. Why such treatment was accorded to Holkar, the most important of the group, may have had something to do with the fact that the Viceroy, the first Marquess of Dufferin and Ava, passionately disliked him. As soon as Lord Dufferin discovered the Maharajah of Indore was coming to the jubilee, he informed the Queen that he was 'a coarse Mahratta with bad manners and vicious tastes, supplemented by a perfect knowledge of English and a pince-nez.' The Viceroy told Victoria that such an unsatisfactory personage should be given no encouragement. Undoubtedly some hint of Dufferin's opinion got to the India Office. But Holkar was not a man who would meekly accept treatment he regarded as unsatisfactory. Punctilious about his rank, as the *Times of India* recalled at his accession in 1886, he was also noted for 'eccentric conduct and overbearing temper.' All that was needed to set this powder keg afire was the match.

The pinpricks began as soon as the Indians arrived in London. No attendants had been assigned to them by either the Queen or the India Office. They were given four wheelers for the jubilee procession, thus assuring that the Indians who would be noted on the great day would be those who made up a cavalry escort around the Queen rather than themselves. When they arrived at Westminster Abbey, they were not allowed to make a flourish by marching to their seats by way of the main aisle but were escorted to them privately. Like the major oriental princes, they were not asked to luncheon on jubilee day.

Even worse, on the one occasion they were especially presented to the Queen, the Lord Chamberlain's Department bungled the arrangements. Only some of the maharajahs were told that this would be the suitable moment to present the Queen-Empress with their gifts. When they were ushered into the royal presence at Windsor, the Maharaj Sir Pertab Singh, brother and representative of the Maharajah of Jodhpore, had not brought his gift. A quick-thinking man, when it came time for him to be brought forward, he simply took a costly golden ornament encrusted with gems from his turban and laid it at Victoria's feet. The Duke of Connaught, who was present, advised her to wear it at dinner that evening to make up for the lapse. The Queen did so.

Some of the maharajahs were also piqued that the wife of a disloyal former Indian ruler received nearly as much consideration as themselves, the Maharani Duleep Singh and her sons having been placed among them on jubilee day, although her husband's current activities prevented his family from being part of the Indian procession.

For many years, Duleep Singh, the last Maharajah of the

Punjab, had been an exotic housepet of Victoria's, always treated with respect and deference by the Royal Family, and conspicuous at such ceremonies as the Prince of Wales's wedding, where he headed the procession of princely guests into St. George's Chapel. In his older age, however, such hollow marks of honour palled, and he longed again for the substance of power. In early 1887, he therefore fled from his comfortable exile, setting out for adventure. By March, he was in Moscow, where he had taken up residence under the improbable name of Patrick Casey and was spinning plans to secure the aid of the Russian government to pass through Afghanistan and move toward Lahore, where he dreamt of fomenting rebellion and regaining his throne. The situation was such that the British Ambassador felt obliged to inform the Russian Foreign Minister that Duleep Singh 'was in a state of rebellion to the Empress of India,' his former friend and patron of nearly forty years.

As the jubilee took shape, the India Office had its eye on the matter. Towards the end of May, for instance, Lord Cross sent a dispatch marked 'secret & confidential' to the Viceroy, informing him that the Maharajah of Kashmir had been giving Duleep Singh financial assistance. He asked Lord Dufferin to report on the feeling of the Sikh army and population towards Duleep Singh, so that he could gauge how much support their former ruler might command. Despite these signs of sedition, which had already attracted press attention, Queen Victoria still approved the invitation of the Maharani Duleep Singh and her sons to Westminster Abbey.

Had certain members of the diplomatic corps had their way, there would have been even more irritants to the Indians, for as Madame Waddington, the wife of the French Ambassador, noted, her husband and his colleagues did not approve of the maharajahs being given precedence over the ambassadors and worked to reverse the situation. Their failure may account for Madame's descriptions of the Indian princes as 'barbarians' with 'false faces' and for the fact that when they were compelled to mix the occasions were charged with ugly tension.

As these aggravations accumulated, Holkar brought matters to a head, after having been forced to walk about 150 yards from his rented carriage, drawn by only a pair instead of four horses, to the royal reviewing stand at Buckingham Palace, to watch the volunteers' march past. The last straw of irritation came when the Lord Chamberlain's carriage sped by the now very angry maharajah enveloping him in a choking cloud of dust. Although it had been announced that Holkar would be spending the summer in England, he now gave public notice that he had had enough and immediately left for India.

As soon as he arrived home, he gave a provocative interview to the *Times of India*, which on August 16 published a number of his complaints about slights and rudeness to which he had been subjected by unnamed 'Court officials.' When word of this interview reached London, there was predictable outrage that Holkar should have so far breached decorum as to have mentioned the matter publicly. Furthermore, the *Standard* of August 23 especially took him to task for his criticisms, as he himself had admitted that both the Queen and Lord Cross had treated him properly. Really, what more did the man expect?

Unfortunately, the matter did not end with this exchange. In October, an anonymous writer subsequently identified by the *Times of India* as Sir Lepel Griffin, British Resident in Indore and the official who had accompanied Holkar to London, published an article in the *Asiatic Quarterly Review*. Its most constructive suggestion was that Indian princes of full treaty powers, of whom Holkar of course was one, should be given the same precedence in England as German princes, for their relation to the Queen-Empress was the same as German princelings had to their Kaiser. Griffin cited as his reason for advocating this course the slights to which the Maharajah of Indore had been subjected during his recent visit.

This article further intensified the severe dislike many officials already felt towards Holkar and Griffin. Just how strong it was can be gathered from a very frank letter Lord Dufferin had already sent to the Prince of Wales in September. 'I am not surprised at the impression made upon your Royal Highness by Holkar. He is a low born, ill-conditioned Mahratta and objectionable from every point of view. I also quite concur in your Royal Highness's opinion about Sir Lepel Griffin . . . the real misfortune is that Sir Lepel Griffin should be an Indian public servant. In spite of his talents, which, however, are much less than either he himself or the general public imagines, the conviction that he is both an unsafe and an untrustworthy instrument has been forcing itself upon my convictions lately with redoubled force.' The Viceroy then concluded, 'the truth is that he is a vain, silly, self-conceited snob, with a dash of flashy cleverness and some literary ability.' Given Lord Dufferin's candour in this matter, it followed that he asked the Prince of Wales 'to consider what I have said about Sir Lepel Griffin as very confidential.'[12]

Sir Lepel's main point about the need to regulate the precedence of Indian princes was not a foolish one. When a certain Mr. D. Boulgar sent Sir Henry Ponsonby a copy of the magazine in November, Ponsonby quickly answered him in a forthright manner intended to dispel the idea that he and his associates might have been the unnamed 'Court officials' at fault. 'I may remark that I and the Court officials pressed most earnestly that these Princes should have a greater amount of show but the Indian officials objected and it was only owing to our persistence that we secured a procession of Indians and a Cavalry escort at all. I only mention this to show you that I think we occidentals were more *alert* to the necessity of the Indian pageant than the orientals—I mean Indian officials.'[13]

As far as the royal officials closest to Victoria were concerned, her private secretary, officials in the Lord Chamberlain's Office, the Master of the Household and the permanent secretary of the Master of the Horse's Department, their work was largely at an end. Though it had been marked by a series of embarrassing incidents and by constant uncertainty about procedure, only a few hints as to their problems seeped out to the public. Dogged by difficulties as they had been, officials at least had the satisfaction of knowing that their problems were not generally known.

It was quite otherwise with the three major jubilee commemorative schemes, the Church House, Imperial Institute and Women's Jubilee Offering, which not only suffered from acute organizational problems but did so in the full glare of intense publicity.

CHAPTER FIVE

PAVED WITH GOOD INTENTIONS

BECAUSE A golden jubilee is a rare event, there was a rush of proposals to commemorate it. A host of schemes mainly of civic betterment were dusted off or conceived for the occasion and placed before the public, which was solicited for funds for these 'jubilee' memorials. As projects mushroomed, officials at the highest reaches of the Court found themselves with grave reservations about that was happening. Sir Francis Knollys, the Prince of Wales's private secretary, growled to Sir Henry Ponsonby that 'there are 100 schemes in the air of different sorts and they increase daily.'[1] Ponsonby himself was dismayed because with so many at hand 'the good intentions of the suggesters may be frittered away in separate objects.'[2] More ominously, *The Times* towards the end of 1886 inveighed against the self-seeking, idiosyncratic nature of most of these proposals: 'The occasion of the Jubilee seems to have given the signal for an outpouring of collective selfishness and greediness beyond all previous experience. In the happy fact that Her Majesty has reigned fifty brilliant years all the institutions and projectors of the Kingdom have discovered an excuse for assaults upon the pockets of the Queen's subjects.' What was needed were projects of national, not local interest, which would suitably commemorate an unprecedented event in the nation's long history, the first reigning queen to rule for fifty years.

Three such schemes were placed before the country, with generally unhappy results. The first was brought forward by Harvey Goodwin, Bishop of Carlisle, who proposed that the established church should erect on the occasion of the jubilee a central meeting place in London for the Anglican convocation.

As Goodwin knew, this idea had been discussed in Anglican church circles ever since convocation was re-established in 1853.

Serious efforts to get such a scheme launched were made in 1867 and again in 1876 by members who thought it *infra dig.* for high officials of the church to go begging for a meeting place every time they wanted to convene convocation. The last attempt had come in 1884, when Horatio, third Earl Nelson, drew up a detailed scheme for what he christened 'Church House.' To erect it, he suggested forming a public company with dividend-paying shares. It was his idea that once these shares had been repurchased by the company the finished building could be turned over to the church as a gift. Nelson's scheme was an elaborate one with provision not only for quarters in Westminster for the Convocation of Canterbury but also for accommodation for church societies, hotel rooms and a restaurant.

Lord Nelson submitted his prospectus to Archbishop Benson of Canterbury, whose approval was necessary before the proposal was made public. Unfortunately for Nelson, while the Archbishop very much wanted a church house to be built, he was not eager to see it begun under Nelson's auspices and doubted the wisdom of inaugurating the project under the auspices of a public company. He resolved, therefore, to squash Nelson's scheme.

Unwilling to affront an influential member of the laity, however, Benson assured Nelson of his general support but noted his inability to commit himself at the moment on the particulars. Having thus lulled Lord Nelson, he appointed the Rev. Sir James Philipps chairman of a special committee to investigate the question of a church house in the hope that some more suitable proposal would be brought forward. After much backstage manoeuvring with Phillips at one time thinking he could combine a church house with Sion College, which had a new site on the Embankment, Benson found himself at the eleventh hour faced with only Nelson's scheme. At this moment significant opposition arose.

A. J. B. Beresford-Hope, an influential churchman and Tory M.P. for Cambridge University, told the gratified Archbishop that he opposed the church house proposal, since he found the union with convocation of a club, reading room and restaurant 'a stride towards disestablishment.' Philipps, informed of Beresford-Hope's timely opposition, got him to submit an alternative recommendation to the committee. His response was to present a far simpler plan. 'I want to kill Lord Nelson's absurd Noah's Ark,' he wrote to Benson, '& merely provide two rooms for the two houses of Convocation to meet in with the most moderate lobby accommodation.' To increase his differences with Nelson, he advocated that Lambeth and not Westminster be used for the site. To Benson's intense satisfaction, such stark divergence in views between two leading Anglican laymen made it impossible for the committee to deal with the issue. So for the time being, it was shelved.

On July 15, 1886, the Bishop of Carlisle revived it by writing to *The Times*. Unlike Nelson's, Bishop Goodwin's proposal was not a detailed one. He simply suggested that 'a more distinct habitation' for the Church of England be constructed. A few days later this letter was followed by the announcement of a general committee to implement the proposal, Archbishop Benson's name heading a distinguished list which also included the Archbishop of York and the Dukes of Westminster, Buccleuch and Buckingham. The absence of specific details may have been an advantage: Beresford-Hope soon announced his support, which was supplemented by that of at least two former members of Lord Nelson's committee. Indeed, in its opening days, the scheme gained strength; both *The Times* and the *Church Times* gave it their powerful support. Only Lord Nelson, perhaps still smarting from his earlier treatment, was silent.

Unfortunately, the seemingly satisfactory position of the church house proposal was deceptive. 1886 was by no means a prosperous year in England, it was another time of hardship in the years between 1873 and 1896 which earned the title of 'The Great Depression.' During this period, a general downward trend in agricultural prices severely blighted the land and straitened the circumstances of those dependent upon it. Because clerical income was still largely based upon tithes from agricultural produce, bad times in the countryside necessarily meant bad times for most of the clergy, who were left to make up their shrinking incomes by application to one of about 225 relief societies.

Only two of these, however, had fairly substantial funds: Queen Anne's Bounty and the Ecclesiastical Commission.

Because of its peculiar eligibility requirements (applicants had to hold country livings with a small population and an annual income of £200 or less), the Bounty was restricted in what it might do, while the Ecclesiastical Commission had for a variety of reasons been forced to cut back the size and number of its allocations. Normally granting far more than the Bounty, it had for the first time in 1886, at a moment of acute clerical distress, distributed less. Given this situation, it was not surprising that disagreement arose over Archbishop Benson's desire to commemorate the jubilee with a church house scheme. Surely a clerical distress fund would be more suitable and timely?

Had Benson consulted with a wider variety of opinion than the grandest members of the laity before announcing his general committee, he would have heard this sentiment frequently expressed. Indeed, his failure to do so invites speculation that he may have known the views of the grass roots and deliberately chosen to get his notion before the public first, before opposition could be organized. In any event, the Archbishop soon found that his selection of the church house proposal was a grave mistake.

The first hint of opposition came from a quarter unlikely to influence supporters of the church house: the Radical newspapers *Truth* and the *Pall Mall Gazette*. More seriously, the fact that the Archbishop of Canterbury was himself heading the general committee did not deter lesser churchmen from announcing rival proposals. On July 15, 1886, Archdeacon Norris of Bristol wrote to *The Times* to suggest that completion of the endowments for the bishoprics of Wakefield and Bristol, sees already approved by Parliament but inadequately funded, would also make a suitable commemoration. His letter was followed by a rash of critical correspondence charging him with the kind of frittering Sir Henry Ponsonby feared, but the Archdeacon replied that he saw no reason why one worthy project should pre-empt the presentation of others equally desirable. He was determined to carry on and in the end did so successfully.

More seriously still, advocates of a clerical distress fund began to make themselves heard, hoping Archbishop Benson might abandon his scheme and adopt theirs, or at least bless a dual arrangement whereby both proposals could go forward. During the summer, Benson gained some months' respite by announcing that the question of the church house would be taken up at a special meeting at Lambeth in October, leading the more sanguine to expect the Archbishop to announce a satisfactory compromise.

On October 15, however, the Archbishop of Canterbury completely disappointed all who felt it unwise to think of bricks and mortar when large numbers of clerics had been forced to the edge of genteel poverty. Benson, however, adamantly refused to accept any alteration in his original plan or any amendment which would permit a clerical distress fund to co-exist with the church house. Such a fund, though worthy of consideration, was, he maintained, not a suitable jubilee project. What was needed instead was something which would permanently commemorate the greatness of the church and its place in the Queen's reign. This the church house was marvellously equipped to do, and the Archbishop was therefore determined to have it.

Stung by Benson's intransigence, opponents of the church house determined to make their feelings as public as possible. They were aided by the *Standard*, perhaps the newspaper closest to the government, which after the Lambeth conference, decided that it would force Benson to change his mind. On October 22, it urged him in the strongest terms to drop the church house scheme and make the clerical distress fund the jubilee project of the establishment. This brought in a flood of correspondence, mostly from clergymen, each letter more critical than the last, of Archbishop Benson's proposal. 'A Churchman,' for instance, wrote, 'With the anticipation of great distress amongst the working classes during the approaching winter, with the acknowledged distress amongst the working clergy from the inability of the farming classes to pay their rent and the many glebe lands that are lying waste for want of a tenant, is it not utter folly to talk of an enormous sum being raised and spent in erecting a "Church House". . . ?' By the beginning of November, swamped by such mail, the *Standard* was exulting that the Archbishop's plan was 'moribund.' On October 29, to add to Benson's problems, the *Church Times*, which had hitherto been in support, announced its opposition.

Although in private the Archbishop gave way to bouts of depression, he resolved to have still another great public meeting to rally support. At this point, it must be asked why Benson simply didn't abandon his proposal and with as much grace as possible gratify its opponents by advocating clerical relief? Part of the reason, of course, is that it is difficult for a prideful and determined man to admit he has erred, especially when that man is the highest ranking figure in an organization. Additionally, Benson was committed to the church house because its construction would assist him in centralizing the administration of the established church and thus augment his own power as its leader. This development of archiepiscopal potency, which had been the hallmark of Benson's tenure as Archbishop of Canterbury, was not, of course, welcomed by many other prelates, particularly those from the north of England, who knew that their own powers would be diminished if Benson had his way and succeeded in amalgamating the Convocations of Canterbury and York, a very likely possibility once the church house was built. Despite the fact that it was the Bishop of Carlisle who was cleverly used to suggest the proposal, many northern prelates naturally found themselves in the forefront of those advocating a clerical distress fund, which was undoubtedly needed and safely eleemosynary. Determined to continue his centralizing tendencies, Benson dug in and arranged with the Lord Mayor of London for a public meeting at the Mansion House on December 10, at which, it was announced, both he and Frederick Temple, Bishop of London, would present their views.

On the day of the meeting, the Bishop of London was indisposed. Unable to appear in person, he sent a letter with his opinions strongly set out. Unfortunately, it contained no hint of what the church house scheme would encompass, and unwisely concentrated on denigrating the clerical relief fund as totally inappropriate for a jubilee memorial. Gathering momentum, the Bishop of London appealed to the fears and even to the cupidity of rich clergymen, who were urged to reject such a fund, lest its inability to afford relief to all needy clerics lead to suggestions for a general redistribution of clerical income. Patience, Temple counselled, was what was needed. In thirty years, the greater efficiency which a church house could bring to affairs of the establishment would be of more assistance in raising clerical incomes than any immediate relief fund. No press report indicates how the audience reacted to Temple's remarkably obtuse letter, but one can imagine with what bitter incredulity it must have been received in many provincial rectories. Thirty years indeed!

Temple's letter, which Benson seems not to have realised constituted a severe liability, was not an auspicious introduction to the Archbishop's remarks, which, in their turn, did nothing to improve matters. He neither attempted to appease supporters of a clerical relief fund nor to present a detailed prospectus of his own proposal. Instead, he adopted a new line of reasoning: 'I do truly and really believe in my own heart,' he said, 'that we shall help the Imperial Institute by building the Church House.' Just how this wonderful result was to be brought about, the Archbishop never explained, but he had two very good reasons for wanting to link his scheme to the Prince of Wales's. In the first place, there had been a good deal of criticism from organizers of the Imperial Institute that the church house proposal, to which the Queen as head of the church was obliged to give some sanction, was providing disturbing competition. Benson meant not only to indicate that there was room for both but that their purposes were complementary. Should he succeed in getting this point of view across, those who donated to the Imperial Institute might also be induced to contribute to the church house.

These arguments did not dispose the *Standard* to change its position. The Mansion House meeting, it wrote, was a failure, hinting that the Archbishop would shortly be obliged to withdraw his proposal. With less grasp of what was happening, *The Times* urged the Archbishop to make the details of his scheme public as soon as possible—advice which should have been offered before the meeting, not after.

As Benson opened his diary for the new year, he headed its first page 'A Drear Beginning' and noted the 'strong opposition & wide apathy' which were stalling the progress of the church house. Well might Benson lament; only £13,000 had been collected in six months, an embarrassingly small amount of which about a third had been contributed by only nine people. Moreover, his nod towards the Imperial Institute had done him no good; not only were its organizers still affronted by the competition of his plan, but the Prince of Wales's much publicized scheme was itself foundering and in no position to bolster Benson's faltering campaign.

* * *

Like the church house, the Imperial Institute was not a new idea at the time of the jubilee. Its roots go back to an 1873 memorandum which the first Earl of Kimberley, Colonial Secretary, sent to colonial governments soliciting their views on the establishment of a colonial museum; it had previously been suggested that some of the exhibition facilities erected in South Kensington might be turned into a permanent colonial museum. Though Gladstone's ministry fell before the results were in, the fourth Earl of Carnarvon, Disraeli's Colonial Secretary, did not drop the idea but appointed a committee under Hugh Childers, a Liberal M.P., to look into its feasibility. Ultimately its members urged Carnarvon to establish a joint colonial and Indian museum, its anticipated cost of £100,000 to be paid jointly by the Colonial Office and colonial and Indian governments.

The Commissioners for the Exhibition of 1851 at once stepped forward and offered to give the museum a site in South Kensington, a proposal which caused the government promptly to drop its commitment for financial assistance. Though the South Kensington site was most agreeable to the Queen because of its association with Prince Albert, who had himself been primarily responsible for the Great Exhibition, it unfortunately met with almost unqualified opposition from the business and commercial communities, who considered South Kensington too far from the City of London to be useful.

These sentiments particularly outraged members of the Court, who held Dr. John Forbes-Watson, who was maniacally dedicated to securing a spot on the Thames Embankment, responsible for the opposition. 'I believe you rather admire Dr. W's energy & independence; I am not sure I don't also,' Sir Francis Knollys wrote to Sir Henry Ponsonby at one point, 'but still it is inconvenient & he ought to be "squashed".'[3] In the event, Lord Carnarvon had no choice but to put the matter aside for later resolution. If one thing was clear from what had happened, however, it was that no South Kensington site was likely to gain widespread approval.

This lesson seems not to have impressed the Prince of Wales, however, for when in 1884 he wrote to the fifteenth Earl of Derby, Colonial Secretary, about his wish that the Colonial and Indian Exhibition scheduled to open in 1886 should be followed with a permanent colonial museum, he suggested that it be built on the South Kensington site of the Colonial and Indian Exhibition, which *Punch* had re-named the 'Colinderies.' To finance it, the Prince suggested that the Colonial Office should solicit funds from the colonies, but he wanted it strictly understood that control of the venture was to remain in his hands.

Senior Colonial Office personnel perusing this letter knew that it might well be possible to finesse the matter of the South Kensington site, but only if the Prince could be made to draw up a full prospectus, including detailed financial and managerial information. If this were done, perhaps the colonial governments could be swung around to approve. It was, however, widely suspected that a group of the Prince's cronies commonly called the 'South Kensington Gang' would strive to keep the scheme as vague as possible, because they knew that publicizing their own expectations and involvement would ensure their eventual exclusion. As the Honourable Robert Meade, Assistant Under Secretary of the Colonial Office, wrote in a most perceptive memorandum, 'The Prince is very much in the hands of Sir P. C. Owen and it is conceivable that he may be led to embark on a costly scheme on the assurance of support from a few colonies hoping that others will follow. The result might easily be a gt disaster & the govt would then find their hands forced & would have to provide large sums or consent to leave H.R.H. in the lurch.' Meade himself doubted whether any appeal to the colonies would succeed and told the Colonial Secretary the Prince should not be 'placed in the position of a suppliant who will not take a negative answer.' Lord Derby agreed with this intelligent advice and advised the Prince of Wales nothing could be done without a detailed prospectus.

The Prince made no attempt to act on Derby's sensible counsel for two more years, thus showing he had no intention of meeting the wishes of the Colonial Office. Instead, he authorized Sir Philip Cunliffe-Owen, Director of the South Kensington Museum and a leading member of the 'South

Kensington Gang,' to float his true purpose and see what the reaction might be. At a public meeting held at the Colinderies in June, 1886, therefore, Cunliffe-Owen let it be known that instead of constructing a serious utilitarian institution, the Prince wanted the Colonial and Indian Exhibition to continue on a permanent basis, a scheme which would, not so incidentally, secure for members of the 'Gang' lucrative executive positions and contracts which they were loath to lose.

Cunliffe-Owen's announcement, as any sensible person could have told the Prince of Wales, brought forth no support. Indeed on June 15, the *Standard* declared that it would not do. There had been some educational exhibits at the Colinderies and a booth for the distribution of emigration material, but its overall purpose had hardly been serious. As the newspaper later wrote, 'It was pleasant enough but where did the instruction come in? . . . The Colonial Exhibition, like its predecessors, has been successful as a place of entertainment, and in no other capacity.' Other newspapers like the *Illustrated London News* agreed with the *Standard* that if any permanent colonial and Indian institution was to be considered, it had better have a significant purpose. The *Pall Mall Gazette* on June 22 began publishing a multipart series by Charles H. Lepper designed to show how this might be achieved.

All this good advice had no effect on the Prince of Wales, who, with his essentially trivial mind, had no desire to do anything but perpetuate the profitable amusement park which had conferred so many benefits on friends such as Cunliffe-Owen, his nephew Edward, and John Somers Vine, City Agent for the South Kensington Exhibitions, the leading members of the 'South Kensington Gang'. What was more, he had every intention of using his mother's good name to bring this about.

On August 9, Sir Henry Ponsonby gave the Queen a draft letter which the Prince of Wales proposed to send to the Lord Mayor of London to make the launching of a permanent colonial exhibition the chief commemoration of the jubilee. Having perused it, Ponsonby thought the fact that 'Your Majesty's name is a good deal brought forward' made the letter into 'almost a public expression of the Sovereign's opinion,' and that therefore Lord Salisbury would have to give his approval before it was dispatched. When Ponsonby informed the Prince of Wales that the Queen had agreed to its being submitted to Lord Salisbury, the Prince was most put out, fearing that he would lose his control (and his friends their places) if the government became involved. As a result, Sir Francis Knollys, the Prince's private secretary, wrote to Ponsonby on August 10 that 'it must be clearly understood that if he is to be at the head and have the management of the proposed undertaking, that it must be entirely under his control and that he is not to be interfered with or hampered in any way by the Government. He must take his stand on his letter to the Lord Mayor and if it is not sent . . . he wishes at once to withdraw his name from the affair.'[4]

Ponsonby was somewhat startled by the insistent tone of this letter. As he responded to Knollys, the matter was clear; the letter the Prince wanted to send was in the nature of a public command and had, therefore, to be approved by the Prime Minister. The Marlborough House contingent did not agree, arguing on the spurious grounds that since the Queen was not directly quoted this left the Prince free to do what he wanted. The real crux of the matter, however, was contained in a petulant paragraph Sir Francis Knollys sent to Ponsonby. 'The govt of the day (Liberal or Conservative, they are both the same) are very fond of talking of the Prince of Wales's position when it suits their purposes to do so, but they take very good care to keep all matters of importance from him as much as possible. Why therefore shd he consult their wishes?'[5]

In the event, the Prince had no choice but to alter the letter he was intending to send to the Lord Mayor, conveniently forgetting his threat to drop out. Still, it was indisputably clear in the final result how the Queen felt about the proposed institution. 'I have ascertained,' the Prince wrote, 'that a public memorial which would illustrate the progress her Empire has made during her Reign would be more gratifying to Her Majesty than any personal or private tribute; and that the form which the Queen would most wish such a memorial should take would be an institution illustrative of the Arts, Manufactures and Commerce of Her Majesty's Colonial and Indian Empire to be created on the site of the present Exhibition, a site made sacred to the Queen as being so intimately associated with the labours of the Prince Consort.'

Once this letter was generally agreed to, Sir Charles Tupper, once prime minister of Nova Scotia and at the time Canadian High Commissioner in London, was dispatched to Canada to see what he could do about securing the support of this most important of the colonies. As soon as its government had agreed to a grant—£20,000—it was decided that the Prince's letter could be published; in addition to what Canada was to give, an additional £16,000 had also been donated by the time the letter appeared on September 20.

Although the Prince's letter in no way included the information Lord Derby had previously told him would be necessary, being utterly devoid of administrative details, all the major metropolitan newspapers including the *Daily News*, *Daily Telegraph*, *Standard* and *The Times* loyally endorsed the proposal. There were, however, dissidents even at this early stage. The usually docile ladies' magazine *Court Journal* joined the more predictably opposed *Pall Mall Gazette* and *Truth*, in which Labouchere advised that the site be dismissed from consideration, the 'South Kensington Gang's' ties to the operation be severed and the account books from the previous exhibitions be audited, before any new undertaking was contemplated. As events soon proved, these comments were highly perceptive.

The generally affirmative responses which the Prince's letter elicited were due more to courtesy than to commitment; all eagerly awaited a prospectus or substantial outline. Indeed, it was expected that the Mansion House meeting to be held on September 27 had been called to place these details before an audience of the leading commercial figures in the City of London. But when the meeting took place, the Lord Mayor had embarrassingly to admit that no details had been settled and that he had no idea when to expect a prospectus.

Indications poured in from the colonies during the next few weeks that the Imperial Institute would soon be in serious trouble, especially if the Prince persisted in trying to revive the Colinderies in connection with the jubilee commemoration. A Reuters telegram on October 7 alerted Sir Henry Ponsonby to how poorly this notion was being received in Melbourne: 'Good deal uncertainty prevails at present regarding matter establishment permanent Institute being mixed up with suggested Colonial Exhibition.'⁶ Ponsonby translated this into a form fit for the Queen: 'The Proposed Institution for Your Majesty's Jubilee is receiving strong support from some colonies,' he wrote, 'while others ask for more information.'⁷ In reality, things were much more serious.

This became clear, when those opposing the Kensington scheme announced the establishment of a fund under the auspices of the London Chamber of Commerce to set up a City commercial museum catering to the needs of businessmen. Such an idea had been on ice since the beginning of the year, its sponsors hoping that the Prince would adopt their leading ideas in his own proposals. When it became obvious that he had no intention of doing so, they independently made their plan public. At once the Imperial Institute's supporters panicked, realizing that this new proposal could completely undercut their hopes. A deal was therefore promptly put through whereby 30 per cent of the City's collection for the Imperial Institute would be devoted to the commercial museum. On this basis, Kenric Murray, secretary of the Chamber of Commerce, wrote to *The Times* on October 27 urging support for the Prince of Wales's proposal.

Though criticism was now becoming intense, the Prince made no answer. His public silence was deceptive, because he was frantically manoeuvring backstage to arrange a satisfactory formula which would allow him to use the one ace in his hand without committing him (as he thought) to specific details. He meant, of course, to draw in the Queen if he could.

Poor Ponsonby! He was well aware what the Prince wanted to do and how 'dear Bertie's' anger was likely, in the event of failure, to focus itself on him; but his first obligation was to the Queen. Having spoken with Lord Salisbury, on October 19 he wrote to Queen Victoria, 'while thinking that the expression of Your Majesty's approval might be repeated everywhere by word of mouth, he is strongly of opinion that no official publication of Your Majesty's views should be made as it is a scheme which involves a great amount of controversy and therefore it would not be right that the Queen's name should be introduced officially.'⁸

But official acknowledgement that the Queen endorsed the Imperial Institute was what the Prince of Wales needed; the mere fact that she was known to favour it was not enough. Increasingly frustrated, the Prince raged against Lord Salisbury, whom he blamed for his problems. On October 22, Sir Francis Knollys wrote to Ponsonby, 'It is obvious that Lord Salisbury means to "crab" the Prince's scheme, and to do what he can to throw cold water upon it. HRH sees this himself & is incensed at it. If all the Prime Ministers who ever existed tried to make out it would be unconstitutional, inexpedient or undesirable for the Queen to allow it to appear in public that she approved of the plan, they would not convince me.'[9]

This letter struck Ponsonby as unusually perverse, if only because the Queen's support for the Imperial Institute was universally known. 'But you want more,' Ponsonby wrote to Knollys in exasperation. 'What exactly is the nature of your desire? For you say you don't want an official & authoritative declaration with the advice of Ministers? But every such public announcement by the Sovereign must be with the consent of her responsible advisers. The Prince of Wales told me the best thing would be if Lord Salisbury would announce the Queen's approval at the Mansion House. This he will not do.'[10]

How could Salisbury possibly do so, when the scheme was entirely undeveloped and seemed unlikely to prove a financial success? On November 2 the Prime Minister wrote to Ponsonby, 'it would not be for the Queen's dignity to take, formally & officially, under her patronage, a project 1. which at present has received no definite shape & may mean anything from a lecture room to a tea garden & 2. which at present no confident hope of pecuniary success.' The next day Ponsonby informed Knollys that the Queen 'scarcely thinks it would be proper' for her to take part in opening the Imperial Institute, and therefore could not do so.[11] The Prince's attempt to involve the Queen in promoting the Imperial Institute had now been effectively stymied, though Sir Francis Knollys continued to bombard Sir Henry Ponsonby with letters. One of these gave a good indication what the Prince was about.

On November 5, Knollys wrote, 'I don't suppose that there are 500 people in England who would give a farthing towards the Institution for itself, but there are thousands who would come forward with subscriptions as a mark of loyalty and a feeling of sentiment on account of the Queen if they thought that by so doing they would please H.M.—we want a "lift" just now from the *Queen*. . . .'[12] It all went for naught.

To add to the gloom at Marlborough House the *Daily News* now chose this moment to withdraw its previous support from the proposal. On November 2, it made a stinging attack on the exclusivity which was marring the project and said that if it was to have any chance of success, the Prince of Wales would have immediately to appoint a representative committee to draw up a detailed prospectus. Three days later, the Prince bowed to the inevitable by announcing that Lords Carnarvon, Revelstoke, Herschell and Rothschild; Sir Lyon Playfair, Sir Henry James, Sir Frederick Leighton; and Messrs Goschen, Fowler, Holland and Ritchie had answered his call to serve. Kenric Murray from the London Chamber of Commerce was also included among the members. Even the appointment of this committee, however, did little to advance matters; the *Standard* complained that it was too little, too late.

As soon as the committee set to work, its members realized they had a problem in the Prince of Wales, who fought a rearguard effort to keep the final result as similar to the entertaining Colinderies as possible. Though its members included a good many of his friends, the Prince made no headway. Indeed, one of the committee's first actions was to drop the embarrassing idea of re-opening the Colonial and Indian Exhibition. It was also decided to include the United Kingdom in the proposal, an idea first mooted by the *Daily News*. Finally, the first Baron Herschell was appointed head of a prospectus subcommittee which included Lord Carnarvon, the eminent scientist Sir Lyon Playfair and J. H. Tritton, President of the London Chamber of Commerce.

Though *The Times* on December 17 wrote a despairing article on how unlikely the Imperial Institute was to succeed unless detailed information about it was given, no such information was included when the prospectus was released on December 24. Ignoring matters of finance, organization and administration, the members of the Herschell committee contented themselves with a broad general description of what was intended and a few more specific suggestions: a hall for the discussion of colonial questions, a bureau to disseminate emigration information, and an arrangement permanently affiliating the contemplated

City commercial museum with the Imperial Institute. (It was the kiss of death as far as the City venture was concerned, for it was never built.)

Examining the prospectus a few days before it was published, Sir Henry Ponsonby characterized it for the Queen in this way: 'This plan proposed that the Imperial Institute should be the central working point of almost all Institutions, Home, Colonial and Indian that are not governmental.'[13] Its scope came as a complete surprise to Victoria, who sensibly told Ponsonby 'she thinks the scheme is too large & *too* many things are proposed . . . the Queen thought it was to be a sort of museum with occasional exhibitions of Indian & Colonial manufactures but did not know so many things were intended.'[14]

When Ponsonby brought the Queen's objections to the attention of her son, Bertie's reply was extraordinarily blithe. According to Ponsonby 'His Royal Highness said that probably half these objects would not be taken up. But it was necessary to give ample power to include them all if necessity arose and unless the scheme was made wide enough to attract the Home Towns as well as the Colonies they would each start some petty plan of its own.'[15] On this basis the Queen went along; when shortly afterwards the prospectus was published both *The Times* and *Standard* reaffirmed their support, though with many reservations about the South Kensington site and the 'Gang' members still associated with the enterprise.

There was now for the first time real optimism about the future of the Imperial Institute and its chances for success. Sir Henry Ponsonby, for instance, felt that the prospectus outlined 'a grand scheme [which] ought to enlist general support.'[16] Hoping to take advantage of such sentiments, the Prince announced that two great public meetings would be held at Marlborough House and the Mansion House to promote the proposal. *The Times* commented that these would be the perfect occasions to clear up the many doubts which still remained.

The Prince did not accept this sensible advice; his remarks at Marlborough House were embarrassingly slight, merely assuring his listeners that the Institute would be useful in providing improved technical education; he did not bother to say how.

Had the afternoon session of the Mansion House meeting

been as unproductive as the one in the morning, the Imperial Institute would have probably been doomed. Just when its prospects seemed beyond hope, Professor T. H. Huxley got up and made a rivetting speech in favour of the proposal. Huxley, the renowned scientific provocateur, vividly discoursed on the competitive war going on between industrial nations, a war in which England was lagging and in which she would continue to fall behind, unless something were done to bolster her position. What Huxley had in mind was the marriage of science and industry, a marriage to be consummated by the Imperial Institute, which, he said, was 'the first formal recognition of this great fact—that our people were becoming alive to the necessity for organization and discipline of knowledge.' Huxley demanded support for the Imperial Institute to help revive English industry and assist in the well-being of the nation. To establish such an undertaking would be the highest form of patriotism.

While the overall effect of the meetings was poor Huxley's endorsement towered over everything. It was widely assumed he could not have come to such a conclusion unless he was in possession of private information or was himself collaborating with the Prince to bring about such a result. Nothing could in fact have been further from the truth, although the Prince of Wales was so thrilled by Professor Huxley's unexpected remarks he had them printed on handbills and widely distributed.

Just why Huxley had decided to make such a ringing declaration of support for the Imperial Institute is not clear; perhaps he hoped his intervention would move the organizers in a serious direction. When, only a few days after his speech, he was warned that the Prince had no such approach in mind, Huxley was stricken by grave after-thoughts. In a letter to his friend the philosopher Herbert Spencer, he wrote that the Imperial Institute was 'flat as a pancake' and he 'greatly doubted' whether any good would come of it.

On January 20 Huxley wrote to *The Times* effectively withdrawing his support. 'I do not presume to say that such a plan is demonstrably contained in the documents before the public. Perhaps I have only read it in to them.' Not content with these remarks, he concluded by commenting that as the

Imperial Institute now stood it could not possibly do what he wanted it to but would simply involve 'huge working expenses, the potentiality of endless squabbles, and, apparently, the cheapening of the honour of knighthood,' taking a swipe at the awards garnered by the 'South Kensington Gang'—most recently by the newly-knighted Sir John Somers Vine.

Huxley's denunciation of the Imperial Institute constituted the *coup de grace* for the whole project. A writer in the *Pall Mall Gazette* exulted about this 'nastiest stab yet given to the Jumbo of the Jubilee.' Huxley's letter did not, however, persuade the Prince of Wales to let the professor go. Instead, a carefully edited version of Huxley's letter to *The Times* was added to his Mansion House remarks and distributed as promotional material, compelling Huxley to write to *The Times* on two more occasions in February to emphasize his dissatisfaction with the South Kensington scheme.

What a sorry state the jubilee was now in! The Mount Edgcumbe committee was groping for something to do; officials had only the haziest idea about what kind of event they were to create; the Queen was adamantly opposed to a ceremony in full state; the church house proposal was moribund, and the Imperial Institute beset on all sides with difficulties. And if all this trouble was not sufficient, the scheme which was supposed to be diverting attention from this confused and unhappy situation was itself engulfed by a storm of controversy which was only adding to the general malaise.

* * *

The Women's Jubilee Offering had been announced to the public on December 20, a movement of 'girls of all classes, grades and ages' to present the Queen with a personal jubilee offering, a token of their affection and loyalty. It was not self-seeking, not a proposal resurrected from a troubled past, by no means political. It was therefore almost rapturously received as the one thing needed to set a suitable tone for the jubilee. How could such an inspiration fail?

Seemingly the idea of Caroline Elizabeth, wife of the ambitious social reformer Sir James McGarel Hogg, the question of a women's jubilee memorial to the Queen first crops up in August, 1886. Lady Hogg wanted a national movement organized to collect money to buy the Queen a personal present. The great question, of course, was what could possibly be given to the woman who had everything? Sir Henry Ponsonby told Sir James that both 'a new cloister beyond Westminster Abbey' and a statue of the Queen had already been suggested to Victoria but that a reproduction of a Glasgow statue of the Prince Consort by Baron Marochetti 'found most favour in her eyes.'[17] Without batting an eye, Hogg informed Ponsonby that he thought the Queen's idea would do nicely, although 'Lady Hogg also thought that perhaps a superior kind of alms house for widows and spinsters might be given with the statue . . . as this would meet the approval of many who think utility and the good of the poor should be as much as possible combined with such commemorations.'[18] This good advice was not regarded. Instead more attention was paid to selecting an organizing committee, which finally contained a host of fashionable ladies headed by Alice, Countess of Strafford. Lady Hogg and Emily Charlotte, Countess of Cork and Orrery were also officers.

To gratify the Queen, the committee (whose most indefatigable member was Lady Cork) decided that no object was to be specified for the funds collected, thus leaving the Queen free to choose whatever she wanted. The Queen's desire for a copy of the Marochetti statue of Prince Albert infuriated her son. On December 8, Sir Francis Knollys addressed a strong letter to Ponsonby, advising him that such a selection would be 'very much out of place' as a jubilee memorial; 'there are quite enough statues of the Prince Consort in existence,' he said; besides, such a mode of spending the subscription would be 'very unpopular.' The Prince of Wales, of course, wanted the money applied to the Imperial Institute. In the same letter, Knollys exploded to Ponsonby about 'that d——d fellow Leo Rothschild' who was advocating a hospital endowment scheme as a jubilee commemoration. 'It is really too bad of the Rothschilds who (some of them) are asked to Sandringham and the others to Marlborough House & with whom H.R.H. frequently dines, to run a plan of their own against his, and I have sent them H.R.H.'s opinion on the subject.'[19]

In a further letter, Knollys, a bulldog of a man, enlarged on the Prince's feelings: 'He only thinks that to erect a Statue of one who will have been dead for 25 years is not quite an appropriate memorial for the purpose of celebrating a *joyful* event in the life of a living person. . . . People have had almost enough of the Prince Consort, and another Statue of him would provoke remarks which if the Queen knew they were made would pain her. Nobody admires the Prince Consort more than I do. . . .'[20]

Ponsonby felt bound to get the Queen's opinion on how to respond: the result was a decided snub both for her son and for his private secretary. On December 9, Ponsonby reminded Knollys that the Queen had discussed the matter previously with the Prince, who 'seemed to approve of it, at any rate he did not object to it.' Even if he did, however, the Queen meant to have the statue, and 'she would be deeply disappointed if any other turn were given to this movement.'

The fact that the Prince of Wales and Sir Francis Knollys were quite right to suggest that the statue would be decidedly unpopular complicated the organizing committee's task. Led by Lady Cork, they again advised the Queen that no public mention should be made of what she intended to do with the money; the women's offering should simply come as a free gift to Victoria to do with as she wanted. Perhaps prodded by Lady Cork, *The Times* on December 21 suggested that the Queen follow this course, not even announcing her intentions on the day the money was given to her. Victoria, however, was a plainspoken woman for whom this disingenuous course had no appeal. On December 20, she told Ponsonby that 'it ought to be known' what the object of the women's offering was to be.[21]

When Ponsonby so informed Lady Cork, her response was candid. 'Between ourselves,' she wrote, 'if the Statue is publicly mentioned at this moment we have no more chance of obtaining the money for it, than of getting the moon out of the sky.'[22] She suggested instead a waiting game, until enough was collected to cover the cost of the statue. Victoria was against this, so on January 3 Ponsonby informed Lady Cork that the Queen's wish in the matter should be made known as soon as possible in case subscribers 'dislike being invited to join in contributing to a mysterious object.' Besides, 'the Queen would much dislike being presented with a sum of money.'[23]

What was to be done? To mention that the Queen wanted

yet another statue of her late husband was to ensure failure. To avoid doing so, however, was to run counter to the Queen's own admirable wish that subscribers should give money only for an object which they approved. For more than a month, the committee stalled for time, searching for a way out of their dilemma, hoping that enough money would be subscribed to solve their difficulties. Unfortunately, however, the press got wind of the Queen's intention to use the money for another statue of the Prince Consort; there was immediate consternation. 'Depend upon it', one correspondent wrote to the *Daily News*, 'the report will be traced to an unscrupulous Socialist, glad to make the throne unpopular, if only for a few weeks.' Contributions dried to a trickle.

With the project coming to a standstill, Sir Henry Ponsonby apparently suggested to the Queen that some other idea might be substituted for the statue for she wrote to him that 'The Queen is much hurt & annoyed. The Statue has been her wish for above 20 years & she wd have gtly valued it—but what other personal gift they want the Queen cannot imagine. An institution will not be a personal present to her & they must not pretend it is.'[24]

Irish women, incensed by the idea of the statue, withdrew from the scheme in mid-February and formed their own committee headed by Lady Londonderry, wife of the Lord Lieutenant. Much English opinion was equally unenthusiastic. The Queen, increasingly dismayed by the situation, showed signs of becoming intransigent and confusing things still further. She had not only set her heart on the statue but had expected to use the surplus to pay for a picture of her entire family. She was thus doubly put out. Indeed, she was so irritated that at one point it seemed she might give the entire surplus to the Imperial Institute, an especially extreme course considering her casual interest in the Prince of Wales's jubilee project. At other times, she thundered about abandoning the whole thing. 'If the Queen is not to receive a *real* present or a memento, she wd rather accept nothing & thinks this vy unkind & *again* like profiting of an occasion to get what they want.'[25] Poor Ponsonby! He bore the brunt of the Queen's anger. Finally on February 16, he told Lady Strafford, 'I am afraid we are coming to a crisis in the affairs of the W.J.O.'[26]

At this point cooler heads prevailed. The real leadership of the committee began to assert itself; Major Tully, the Hon. Secretary, informed Ponsonby that he must no longer deal with Lady Cork (Ponsonby told the Queen she was energetic but quarrelsome), but with the Countess of Strafford. Shortly afterwards, Lady Strafford (supported by Tully) presented a compromise plan to correct matters: the statue would be retained as the object of the fund, but it would also be announced that any and all surplus was to be spent on a charitable object. Thus 'the temporary misunderstanding can be got over,' Tully told Ponsonby.[27] Although this plan later caused problems, the Queen went along with it on February 24, though not without a final, pungent word on the matter. 'The Queen has no objection to Ldy Strafford's proposal but considers it *no present to her*, tho' she will value the statue *vy* much.'[28]

By March more than the £10,000 needed for the statue had been collected. Despite this, critical comment rumbled on in the press. A provincial collector wrote to the *Daily News:* 'The hard times have tried the temper of the women of the working classes severely and the idea that their hard-earned pence are to swell a fund to be devoted to no useful end is quite repugnant to them.'

* * *

Thus, as spring approached, every aspect of the jubilee was in turmoil, marred by mismanagement, disorganization and, very often by selfishness and obstinacy. Well might the *Court Journal* complain on February 19, 'We await, and are really in want of, some signal movement to set the Jubilee right, and to give it a tone of due dignity and of practical aim; for upon the while, it is a very straggling and weak movement. . . .' Further depression resulted from the increasing mendicancy of prominent promoters, who did not know when to stop.

In February the church house fund stood at about £16,500, while the Imperial Institute appeal had garnered £50,000. As the *Pall Mall Gazette* sneered upon learning this figure, 'A paltry £50,000, not half as much as could be raised in a week in London alone for any project that really compelled the sympathies of all classes.' Despite the lack of support for their proposals, neither the Archbishop of Canterbury nor the Prince of Wales had any intention of giving way. Instead, they started making even more extreme attempts to prise money from an uninterested public.

In February, Archbishop Benson told his general committee that he was 'quite unshaken by anything that had passed,' and afterwards, he and the Bishop of London called on the clergy of Dr. Temple's metropolitan diocese to contribute to the church house and to press their parishioners to do so as well. On that same day, the *Standard*, always vociferously opposed to the scheme, wrote: 'Obstinate men never willingly admit that they have blundered, until the fact is beyond all dispute. It is enough to say that the scheme has fallen stillborn as we were sure that it would.' Next day, it pointed out that London clergy were now forced to choose whether to gratify the Archbishop of Canterbury and Bishop of London by contributing to the church house or follow their own wishes and abstain from doing so, thus affronting their superiors.

A few days after the letter to the London clergy had been sent, the lower house of the Convocation of York passed a resolution urging the establishment of a jubilee fund for augmenting the stipends of poorer benefices. At this point, its advocates still believed their scheme could be offered in tandem with the Archbishop's. Labouchere rightly commented in *Truth* that the resolution 'amounts to a condemnation of the improvident and uncalled-for project of the Bishops.'

Perhaps Archbishop Benson had been informed in advance that this resolution was going to be offered, or perhaps by that time he had simply had enough. In any event, two days before the Convocation of York acted, he had privately written to the Registrar of the Sons of the Clergy, the oldest church institution engaged in combating clerical poverty, proposing that it should receive and distribute funds to alleviate clerical distress. On February 21, this proposal was made public; by the summer it had proved so popular that more than £50,000 had been collected. It undoubtedly would have done far better had Benson adopted it in the summer of 1886, though he never admitted as much; indeed, writing to a friend in March, he said, 'If ever that [augmentation of benefices] or even a Distress Fund, had been proposed at first as a Jubilee Memorial, it would have seen infinitely more vehement opposition than the Church House. . . .'

Despite the announcement of what came to be called 'Queen Victoria's Bounty Fund,' Benson had not withdrawn his scheme. Instead, pushed out of the way, its connection with the jubilee for all intents and purposes severed, it still continued to exist, though its financial situation was never other than bleak. By November, 1888 only £32,000 had been collected. Nonetheless the executive committee under Benson's direction began the often trying task of purchasing lots in Dean's Yard, Westminster, where it was planned to build the church house.

The later story of the church house lies beyond this history. Suffice it to say that although Sir Arthur Blomfield, an eminent clerical architect and son of a bishop of London, was given the commission to begin work on the building in late 1889, it took more than half a century before the complex was completed, by which time scarcely a soul remembered that it had been begun as a commemoration of Queen Victoria's golden jubilee. Always handicapped by severe financial problems, the church house never achieved the grandiose goals prophesied by Archbishop Benson, either in domestic or international Anglican affairs; in fact, it ended up looking very much like the barebone proposal advocated by A.J.B. Beresford-Hope in 1884. Still pursued by a fateful nemesis, Church House was damaged in a blitz attack not long after it had been completed, six people being killed.

* * *

No more than Archbishop Benson did the Prince of Wales know when to withdraw gracefully. Instead, as the Under Secretary of the Colonial Office had perceptively forecast some years before, Bertie blundered into 'the position of a suppliant who will not take a negative answer'; it was acutely embarrassing for those who had to respond to his wheedling advances.

His most concerted attack was launched on the Queen, for the Prince seems to have had no scruple about invoking her name and her office to overcome criticism. The fact that Lord Salisbury and Sir Henry Ponsonby were both opposed to any direct intervention on the part of Queen Victoria was a setback for the Prince, but only a temporary one.

Once the Queen had given her blessing to the prospectus published in December, the Prince renewed his attempt to gain her explicit public approval. At last in January, a formula was found which satisfied both the Prime Minister and the Prince. The Queen, perhaps gratified by the Prince's present of a jubilee inkstand, was pleased to concur. In the middle of January, Ponsonby was directed to send a letter for publication to the Mayor of Bradford. 'I hasten to reply to assure you that the proposal of the Prince of Wales to unite all classes of the Queen's subjects from all parts of her dominions in raising the Imperial Institute as a tribute to Her Majesty on the occasion of the Jubilee of her reign is specially pleasing to the Queen.' Whatever prospects the Prince had meant this letter to open, its effect on the progress of the Imperial Institute was nil.

The Prince of Wales, however, always had an immense capacity for disregarding the disagreeable when it so suited him. The fact that Ponsonby's letter containing the Queen's opinion on the Imperial Institute had fallen completely flat only made him resolve to try all the harder elsewhere. He therefore had begging letters sent to all the cities and towns in the kingdom, asking municipal authorities to assist the Imperial Institute. Because this was the heir to the throne seeking their help, responsible individuals generally gave it. Usually, therefore, two jubilee funds were set up, one for the Imperial Institute, the other for some local project. While press releases drew attention to how many such collections were taking place, the overall effect was paltry.

Then, like the Archbishop of Canterbury, the Prince of Wales went on to ever more extreme action. He asked his cousin, the Duke of Cambridge, to send letters to officers commanding military districts and also made arrangements to have the fleet at Portsmouth solicited for funds, the names of contributors to be sent to the Queen. He asked the Viceroy of India to organize collection efforts in the subcontinent and requested that his brother, Prince Arthur, obtain subscriptions from the troops under his command.

As was to be expected, these constant pesterings for funds drew much adverse comment. The *Daily News* lashed out against the 'Jubilee Poll Tax', while the *Pall Mall Gazette* dubbed the Prince of Wales the 'Beggar General in Ordinary for the Imperial Institute.' Officials such as Lord Dufferin sought reasons for excusing themselves from participation.

The Viceroy wrote to his sovereign that the Indians were reluctant to contribute money to any institution outside their country, which would bring them no direct benefit. 'Moreover,' he wrote, 'for some time the shape which the Institute was ultimately to assume was so uncertain, and its objects were so vague that it would have been very difficult to explain in sufficiently precise terms its meaning and uses to the public at large.'[29] The Prince complained to his brother, the Duke of Connaught, that 'Dufferin has not only been lukewarm but has virtually discouraged the movement in India wh is a shame.'[30]

Nor would the Colonial Office give the Prince any assistance; he had failed to follow its well-considered advice, and had also neglected to invite any representative from the Colonial Office to join his organizing committee. This meant there could be no official approach to the colonies, still less any Colonial Office endorsement of the scheme. Thus, no more than £80,000 was collected from the colonies on which the sun never set.

Fast running out of alternatives, the Prince had yet one golden expedient, where his name and position would work wonders: the Indian feudatories of the Queen-Empress. Early in 1887, therefore, he sent Sir Roper Lethbridge, Conservative M.P. for North Kensington, former Press Commissioner of India and a member of the 'South Kensington Gang,' on a special mission to collect contributions from princes. It is perhaps significant that many of those who contributed found themselves on either the Indian jubilee honours list published in February (the celebration in the Raj was held early on account of the searing summer heat), or that released in England in June. The names included the Gaikwar of Baroda, the Rajah of Rutlam and the unsatisfactory and much-deplored Maharajah of Indore. In addition, a sizeable contribution from the Nizam of Hyderabad, the greatest of Indian princes, preceded the decoration of his all-powerful chief minister, the Nawab Salar Jung. In any event, Lethbridge's efforts considerably offset the Viceroy's foot-dragging and the minimal help offered by his administration, so that in the final accounting India contributed some £100,000 to a project which had never aroused any enthusiasm. Indeed as *The Times of India* put it in March, opposition had been general. 'The idea has proved a failure, if not altogether a fiasco. . . . India . . . is a poor—very poor—

country; and we strongly object to any celebration of the fiftieth year of Her Majesty's most glorious reign . . . that shall be coupled with a demand—for in the East Emperors cannot request or solicit—for subscriptions for an institution, of which not one in a million will ever see the real object, and which not one in a hundred thousand can possibly comprehend.'

As gloomy February passed into gloomy March, a general feeling began to arise that the jubilee had been stunted enough by projects and schemes in which there was little interest and about which antagonism was widespread. It was now time, past time, to get on with it, and the Prince ought to recognize as much by removing his obstructive proposal. As he showed absolutely no signs of taking the hint, however, the *Financial News*, a major newspaper in the City of London, decided to publish a series on the various exhibitions held at South Kensington and the 'Gang' who had done so well out of them. As these were the men whom the Prince had selected for positions of leadership in the Imperial Institute, such articles were bound to be damaging.

On March 10, the *Financial News*' first article dealt with the inadequate accounting procedures of the 'Fisheries' Exhibition of 1883 and the 'Healtheries' of 1884. Why was it, the newspaper wondered, that despite its physical plant and other equipment contributed by the first exhibition, the expenses of the second were so much higher? It was impossible to tell from the accounts which had so far been released.

Subsequent articles were lengthy, fact-filled and much more embarrassing. One concentrated on how Sir John Somers Vine, City Agent for the exhibitions and already designated assistant secretary and sub-director of the Imperial Institute, had approved both contracts and concessions for firms in which he held stock or by which he had formerly been employed. Another discussed a concession Somers Vine had granted to Sir Edward Watkin, Liberal Unionist M.P., railway tycoon and 'Gang' affiliate, designed to bring working men to the exhibitions via Watkin's rail lines. This article came at a particularly unfortunate moment for Watkin, since he had just been taken to court by an irate stockholder for having attempted to give a large corporate contribution to the Institute.

A further article gave embarrassing details of the generous

perquisites received by those connected with the exhibitions; it was alleged that Sir Philip Cunliffe-Owen, for instance, had received 'testimonials' from various exhibitors worth £30,000. There were also unpleasant details about the misuse of the franking privilege, the doubtful distribution of passes and free admissions, and how Somers Vine made good personal use of exhibition property and personnel.

The eight articles in the *Financial News* between March 10 and April 14 threw devastating light on the Prince's cronies and the management of the exhibitions with which he had been so closely connected. Though no explicit wrongdoing was alleged and no charges were ever pressed, friends of the Prince, in whom he had repeatedly voiced confidence, were plainly shown to be designing men of questionable business standards. Promotional types, floating one notion after another, the members of the 'South Kensington Gang' looked and acted as if they had stepped out of the pages of Anthony Trollope's classic indictment of Victorian jobbery and loose business ethics, *The Way We Live Now*. No wonder then that the *Pall Mall Gazette* wrote on March 26, 'The Prince of Wales is at this moment perhaps in one of the most uncomfortable positions which he has ever occupied . . . The Prince has done himself considerable harm by allowing the clique of officials who surrounded him at South Kensington to abuse the patience of the public and create suspicions of dishonesty.'

It needed strong measures to remove the taint of opportunism from the Imperial Institute and its organizers. Unfortunately, the Prince of Wales did little to dispel it. His only concession was to sever the connection of Sir Philip Cunliffe-Owen from the Institute, a heavy blow for the man who had expected to be the Institute's first director. Otherwise, nothing published by the *Financial News* was disputed and no attempt made to answer its charges.

As the series drew to a close, it was announced that there would be yet another great public meeting in favour of the Imperial Institute. The Prince himself would take the chair; the main speech was to be given by Sir Frederick Abel, long associated with many scientific projects and now Secretary of the Imperial Institute. If ever there was a need for candour, for specific information and for direct responses to the many questions about the project, this was the moment. For months, the Prince had disregarded common sense and thoughtful advice, trying to circumvent public opinion by invoking his mother's name and prestige. But he had not been successful. At the end of April, when he took the chair at the meeting, the public still rightly expected a serious and utilitarian institution run by experts, not some variation on the amusing "Colinderies" run by the Prince's glib business associates who held their own interests highest. Again, however, this meeting disappointed expectations.

Abel dispelled no suspicions, supplied no facts, gave no substantial indication that the Institute would ever serve a useful purpose. Instead, he offered what were by now the usual platitudes, stringing out a staggering variety of projects which the Institute might undertake. Its activities, he said, would link up with every aspect of commerce, industry and education throughout the United Kingdom and the empire.

Even the most loyal were no longer prepared to give credence to such blatant hyperbole. The *Standard* dismissed Abel's speech as 'wide of the mark,' while *The Times*, ever hesitant about publishing words offensive to royal personages, gently fluttered: 'As we read Sir Frederick Abel's list of various works which the Institute is to perform or to aid others in performing, we are almost tempted to ask whether there is anything which it is not to do.' *Punch*, in rollicking doggerel, suggested what Abel should have done:

> Sir Frederick told them all 'what's what'
> In the Institute Imperial
> But the Public do want to know who's who
> Which is far more material.

It was too late for good advice, however; after the April meeting the public was prepared to hear no more about the Imperial Institute, and until the Queen laid the foundation stone on July 4, for Bertie had wheedled and wheedled until he had secured this favour, too, virtually nothing was heard of it. Even then, however, the *Pall Mall Gazette* was at pains to point out that the crowds who turned out along the route came only to see their jubilee sovereign, not because they had any interest in the project itself.

Despite such apathy, the Imperial Institute, like the church house, continued to exist, although plagued by financial problems (only about £360,000 had finally been collected) and by vagueness about what it was supposed to do. Both created problems for Thomas Collcutt, the architect; he had to revise his designs as the committee changed its mind about the Institute's activities. And as the *Standard* reported, he may have sacrificed a knighthood, because he would not consider removing a costly tower from his plan. Nonetheless in May, 1893, the building was completed and opened by the Queen. Its first exhibition was of the Duke and Duchess of York's wedding presents, a choice which led the *Manchester Guardian* to complain that, 'it seems to be a simple perpetuation of the amusing Colonial and Indian Exhibition.'

The principal difference between the two was that, unlike the Colinderies, the Imperial Institute could not pay its way; by the end of 1898, its trustees could no longer maintain the pretence of financial solvency, not even after the daily concerts in the Institute's gardens had been abolished to save money. Thus, just as the Colonial Office had predicted so many years before, the government had to be asked to intervene and set matters right. After many other expedients had been attempted, the Imperial Institute was wound up in 1901, and the building transferred to the Board of Trade. Finally in 1956, having been found unsatisfactory for use by the Colonial Office and the Ministry of Education, it was destroyed to make way for the Imperial College of Science and Technology, the sort of place T. H. Huxley had probably had in mind, when he first advocated that the Imperial Institute should be a place 'for the improvement of industrial knowledge and an industrial university.' Only the central or Queen's Tower was left standing, the feature which may have deprived Collcutt of getting a handle to his name. It still stands today, a forgotten relic celebrating royal obstinacy and obtuseness.

But what of the Women's Jubilee Offering?

As soon as Queen Victoria, interested only in the statue of the Prince Consort, reluctantly concurred in the plan to donate any surplus funds to charity, someone had to decide what beneficiary would be acceptable. Sir William Jenner, the well-known physician who was connected with the Court, told

Ponsonby that while London opinion favoured a hospital for women, he himself leaned toward 'a fund for supplying female emigrants with comforts,' because it would please both England and the colonies. 'Sir Henry Ponsonby rather doubts it,' the private secretary told the Queen drily.[31] Lord Salisbury, utterly out of character, asked if £3,000 might be used to supply the London fireworks his Chancellor of the Exchequer had cut from the jubilee budget. Ponsonby gravely told him he did not think the expenditure appropriate but that it was up to the ladies' committee to make the final determination. Was the Prime Minister put out by this response? Not a bit, Ponsonby told the Queen, 'he had only made the suggestion because urged by the Prince of Wales. . . .'[32]

Although Ponsonby raised the idea of appointing a small committee of ladies, including Florence Nightingale, to advise the Queen on how to spend the funds, it was apparently Victoria herself who determined that the women's executive committee should itself submit three ideas from which she could make a final choice. After confusing matters in June by voting to give the surplus absolutely to the Queen (which, Ponsonby patiently explained to Major Tully, reversed the decision members had taken in February), the committee eventually suggested three ideas: pensions for distressed women, some scheme of self-aided insurance, and nurses. Of the three, nursing had the most support; Ponsonby himself told the Queen he could scarcely speak objectively about the other two, because he favoured this one, which would 'be a monument of the Jubilee offering to endure under the Queen's control.'[33] In the end, this was the course adopted and about £75,000 went to the Queen Victoria Jubilee Institute for Nurses, a project to aid the sick poor in their own homes. Although the Queen herself was never very interested in the new Institute, feeling it had been forced upon her by the well-meaning, she had sharp advice for those who were to organize it. She told Ponsonby, 'The Queen has no objection but there must be men on the committee to get on. A group of women is most useless.'[34]

If she was unconcerned about how the bulk of the money was to be spent, Victoria was nonetheless most interested in what would be done with lesser amounts. In June, she hinted to Ponsonby that as so much had been collected for the charitable object, she felt some money might be spent on a jewel for herself. 'If a small additional portion of the surplus cd be taken for a jewel for the Queen to be able to wear as a *gift* from the women she wd gtly *value* it. She knows many wish this.'[35]

Many did, indeed, and as soon as the Queen's desire became known, the fashionable aristocrats on the committee began discussing how the Queen's wish could be satisfied. One of them, the Countess of Effingham, told the Dowager Duchess of Roxburgh that the industrious Lady Hogg had located a '*unique* single row of Pearls' which could be purchased for just £15,000. 'Oh how delightful it would be to know that our beloved Queen was wearing it as a token of the love for her women subjects.'[36]

The trustees of the offering, however, felt that the committee had bound itself in February to devote *all* the surplus to a charitable object, and that as this intention had been publicized and people had given accordingly, it could not now be altered. The Marchioness of Hertford roundly disputed this opinion. In July, she informed Ponsonby that, 'As far as Warwickshire is concerned, the money by my desire was collected to be "given as a Free Gift to Her Majesty". . . .' After disparaging Lady Cork, who had forced the troublesome resolution through in February 'against the wish of half the Executive Committee, who did not wish the Queen to be tied down in any way,' she concluded with a flourish, 'What the Dss of Marlbro' tells us of the Queen's wishes is *quite* sufficient for us.' As Lady Salisbury told Ponsonby, 'The pearl necklace affair is likely to be as serious as poor Marie Antoinette's . . . was!' cattily adding that 'Lady Cork & her friends are miracles of bad management.'[37]

While this provoking affair was still pending, the Queen had also to direct her attention to how J. E. Boehm, the sculptor selected by the committee, was rendering the designs, first created by the deceased Marochetti, of the equestrian statue of Prince Albert. At the beginning of August, Boehm, who had been responsible for the unsatisfactory effigy of the Queen on the jubilee coinage, informed Ponsonby that 'some parts' of the horse needed changing due to the increased size ordered by Victoria. Would the Queen object?

Immediately scenting danger as she knew that 'Boehm grtly *underrates* & deprecates Marochetti,' she informed Ponsonby that 'the Queen must insist on the attitude of the horse & above all on the excellent likeness of the dear Prince being in *no* way altered. In fact the fear of *this* made the Queen *dislike* Boehm being selected to do this & she *still* fears it.'[38]

In the end the Queen fared somewhat more satisfactorily with Boehm, whose work when unveiled on Smith's Lawn, Windsor in May, 1890, entirely met her expectations, than in the matter of the personal ornament. In late January, 1888, after a memorandum had been drawn up of the legal difficulties involved in presenting the Queen with the 'trinket' she desired, Major Tully submitted an idea which he hoped would set matters right: perhaps the Queen would accept the first badge of the jubilee nurses set in diamonds 'when Your Majesty has decided upon it.'[39] Because such an ornament might be said to be connected with the main object of the fund, the trustees would probably allow it. The Queen, however, wanted real jewelry, nothing less. After a time, during which Victoria tenaciously hung to the idea, it was finally decided to set aside £4,000 and get her the personal ornament she desired.

* * *

The part played by the Queen in the affairs of the Women's Jubilee Offering, where the larger, public aspect held almost no interest for her, was very like the part she played in the golden jubilee as a whole. To Victoria the occasion was entirely personal, an event taking place solely because of her and meant solely to honour her long service. She therefore felt her wishes should be pre-eminent and her notions catered to in all aspects of the celebrations. In resolutely maintaining this personal focus, the Queen missed the larger importance of the event in the life of the nation whose people all had their own ideas about how it should be celebrated. Since these were usually substantially different from the Queen's own highly idiosyncratic views, clashes were inevitable. Paradoxically, however, they had little effect upon the jubilee, even though the Queen never fulfilled public expectations about what she should do.

CHAPTER SIX

STATE OR SEMI-STATE?

ALTHOUGH THERE had been random discussion throughout 1886 about how the Queen's golden jubilee should be marked, it was not until October 14 that Sir Henry Ponsonby sent a hurriedly scrawled note to the Prime Minister informing him that Victoria would celebrate the event next June by returning to Westminster Abbey to the altar where she had been crowned. In selecting June 21, 1887, as the date, Victoria had chosen to follow royal rather than biblical precedent in the celebration of jubilees; King George III had had his at the end of his fiftieth year on the throne, instead of at the end of the forty-ninth as laid down in the twenty-fifth chapter of the book of Leviticus. His granddaughter decided to follow his example. Ponsonby also told Lord Salisbury that arrangements were to be handled in semi- rather than full-state.

Salisbury could have spared himself much later trouble had he advised the Queen that what she wanted was unlikely to prove generally acceptable. There is no evidence that the Prime Minister ever considered doing so, however, possibly because he was not in a position to pay for any added pomp and circumstance. Being unable to pay the piper, he felt unable to call the tune. He therefore took the path of least resistance and simply acquiesced in the arrangements desired by the Queen.

By doing so, Salisbury may have gratified Victoria and freed himself from a blast of royal indignation. But he did not serve the interests of the crown. The selection of Westminster Abbey over St. Paul's may have been perfectly understandable in sentimental terms, but as Gladstone had realized in 1872, it was open to grave practical objections. At the time of the national thanksgiving for the recovery of the Prince of Wales, he, in his capacity as Prime Minister, had informed the Queen that the less encumbered interior of St. Paul's, permitting the invitation of more guests, and its location, which allowed for a more suitable processional route to be drawn up, constituted compelling reasons for the selection of the metropolitan cathedral. With the development of the historical preservation movement in the intervening years, a further reason against using Westminster Abbey had also emerged, for it seemed impossible to accommodate large numbers of people there without damaging the Abbey's fabric and many monuments.

As soon as the Queen's choice of the Abbey became known, paragraphs criticising it were published, but with little effect; certainly the jubilee organizers seem never to have contemplated shifting the thanksgiving service to St. Paul's. As for the Queen herself, having once made up her mind, she saw no reason to change it. Nonetheless, after the jubilee was over, officials in the Office of Works informed the First Commissioner that better arrangements could have been made at St. Paul's.

The second matter, that of semi-state, was more serious, and here Lord Salisbury, like Gladstone before him, should have made some dignified objection. Unfortunately, the Prime Minister seems not to have cared much whether the Queen went in an open carriage or a coach, whether she wore a bonnet or a crown. Yet as the Tory newspaper the *Standard* editorialized on June 10, when the matter had fully burst into the open, just what the Queen decided to do for jubilee day was a most important point. 'No expense should be spared,' it wrote, 'to make it clear to the multitude that the Crown represents the wealth, the strength and the material progress of the Empire.'

Prince Albert, of course, understood that in large part the monarchy gained the loyal affection of its subjects by its apt representation of their exaggerated self-esteem. For an event that was simultaneously the marking of a golden jubilee on the throne and fifty years of brilliant national progress and international influence, the full panoply of monarchic pomp was not only suitable but indispensable. What a heavy irony it was then that the reason for Victoria's unending aversion to the use of such accoutrements was the demise of the prince who knew better than any how necessary they were to the continued well-being of the throne.

The immediate result of the Queen's decision was that the organization of the event fell to the Lord Chamberlain's

Department rather than to the Earl Marshal and College of Arms, who would have been eligible to participate only if the jubilee were arranged in full-state. Indeed, it was the fact that the Duke of Norfolk and his assistants had been cut out of the proceedings, which first alerted public opinion to the prospect of a diminished pageant. Unfortunately, however, the Duke's private circumstances would in any case have made it difficult for him to be closely involved since his wife was taken so seriously ill that Norfolk in February felt obliged to decline to serve as Under Secretary of the Colonies. The Duchess's condition grew worse and she died shortly before the jubilee, an event which would no doubt have precluded the Duke from taking any part in its organization. Had a ceremony in full-state been intended, the Earl Marshal would probably have had to appoint a deputy to act for himself, a procedure which had not been used during Queen Victoria's reign, but was common enough beforehand, when the Roman Catholic Dukes of Norfolk had not been permitted to exercise their hereditary prerogative for the Defenders of the Faith.

Such technicalities, however, were of no interest either to the press or to the numerous public which concerned itself about the jubilee arrangements. What was important was that people get 'gilding for their money,' as the second Viscount Halifax, once Groom of the Bedchamber to the Prince of Wales and President of the English Church Union, put it. Lord Rosebery complained that a bonnet would not suffice as the symbol of empire. As such sections of public opinion gradually began gently but firmly letting the Queen know that she had better order more suitable arrangements, Victoria, who was nervous about the whole business in any event, could at last stand it no longer. In March, therefore, a particularly provoking month, she exploded to Ponsonby: 'The Queen hopes he will speak strongly to the Ministers saying she will not be teazed & bullied abt the Jubilee & wh seems to be considered only for the *people* & their *convenience* & amusement while the Queen is to do the public and newspapers bidding. She will do *nothing* if this goes on.'[1]

What was it that the public and newspapers wanted from their Queen?

Oddly enough, while criticism was always strong against the

State or Semi-State?

amount of pomp approved by Victoria, no one ever stepped forward with a blueprint about how to improve the jubilee, no one that is except the self-proclaimed 'Lord' George Sanger, who placed his circus at the disposal of the Lord Chamberlain. Sanger offered to mount an historical procession representing the monarchs of England dressed in faithful period costume beginning with William the Conqueror and ending with the reigning sovereign herself. He also proposed that eight triumphal cars be included and a troop of circus animals, elephants, lions and tigers. Lord Lathom was presumably appalled by Sanger's inspiration, which he curtly declined to consider.

Just what ought to be done instead, however, was left unspecified. Indeed, not until the *Daily News* announced on June 9 that Messrs. Thorne Brothers, royal coachbuilders, had returned the newly regilded state coach to Buckingham Palace was there any public hint as to what critics expected.

The opportune return of the Gold State Coach led to joyful anticipation that this most gorgeous equipage in the mews was to be utilized on jubilee day. Built for King George III in 1762, it had then been called 'the most superb and expensive of any ever built in the Kingdom,' a lustrous description which had in no way lost its validity over the years. It was, it is, a great and showy thing with a framework composed of eight exotic palms which branch out to support the roof. Four of these palms, arising from the heads of lions, stand at the corners of the vehicle, heavy with trophies symbolizing Britain's great victory in the Seven Years War, only recently concluded when the coach was built.

But the vehicle is rich in other diverting features, too: gilt muscularities at its front blowing notes of triumph through conches which announce the approach of the Monarch of the Ocean ensconced within; gilded creatures at its rear bearing imperial fasces topped with tridents; stunning allegorical panels by Cipriani on the sides, front and back, all surmounted by an expanse of golden roof at the centre of which stand three cherubs representing the three kingdoms of the realm, in their upraised hands the Sceptre, Sword of State and Ensign of Knighthood. Above it all these genii resolutely hold the Crown.

To accompany such a splendid coach, there are, of course, equally splendid accoutrements: for its postillions, scarlet and gold jackets, wigs and black caps; for the eight famous cream horses which would pull it, the richly-worked state harness heavy with gilt ormolu; for the coachman, a magnificent scarlet and gold frock coat, pink silk stockings, gold buckled shoes and a wig and tricorne hat decorated with ostrich feathers.

All this resplendent finery, used only for coronations and in the early part of the Queen's reign for the state opening of Parliament, had not been seen on the streets of London since the death of Prince Albert. Gladstone had hoped against hope that the Queen would order it up in 1872. It was generally thought fitting that she should do so to mark the occasion of her golden jubilee.

Instead, it became known that the Queen had asked for an open carriage, which proved to be the semi-state postillion landau, a vehicle built to carry Victoria to the laying of the foundation stone of St. Thomas's Hospital in 1866. By this order, eight horses were reduced to six; pink stockings and tricornes gave way to more prosaic red frock coats and black top hats; and the gilt state harness to less gaudy strappings. Moreover, since no one else could outshine the Queen, grand vehicles such as the Irish State Coach and the state landaus were taken out of the procession. At least the Queen was pleased, however; in her landau, she could whirl along the route at the brisk pace she liked, not slowed by the lumbering gold coach.

Unfortunately, the Queen's own pleasure did nothing to mitigate many people's disappointment concerning the arrangements. Several major metropolitan newspapers in the first days of June bluntly stated their views. On June 7 the *Daily News* wrote, 'When the Queen went to St. Paul's [in 1872], it was generally felt that the Royal Cortege was unworthy of the occasion, and out of keeping with the costly and tremendous efforts the public had brought forth in decorating the route. . . . If it is worthwhile getting up a procession at all, it is worthwhile getting up a good one.' Three days later the *Standard*, of all newspapers, put the matter more baldly, 'It is our duty to say, at once, and in the plainest of language, that the Procession designed for Jubilee Day . . . is utterly inadequate, mean, pinched and narrow, and appears to be dictated by a parsimonious spirit unworthy of a rich and powerful State.' The next day, the *Pall Mall Gazette* was characteristically blunt about the procession, 'It promises to be a very shabby and tenth-rate affair.'

These frank opinions had no effect on Queen Victoria, however, other than making her even testier. Furthermore, she was determined that in the procession she would not be forced to wear any of the exaggerated costumes of monarchy or to carry any of its weighty symbols of sovereignty. Thus although her 'favourite son,' Prince Arthur, told his mother she must look 'smart' for the occasion and the Princess of Wales was deputized to present the family's case for a more regal appearance, Victoria obstinately dispensed with the robes of purple velvet, the sceptre and orb and the Crown of State, with all of which this jubilee monarch might have been expected to adorn herself.

As far as Princess Alexandra's own attempt to change matters went, she told Ponsonby after a harrowing interview with the Queen, 'I never was so snubbed'. No one else fared any better, and the only person who seems to have been at all pleased that the Queen could not be included to change her mind was Victoria's cousin Princess Mary, Duchess of Teck. When the newspapers on June 13 printed the unauthorized announcement that the jubilee was to be celebrated in full state, Lady Geraldine Somerset, Lady-in-Waiting to Princess Mary's mother, the Duchess of Cambridge, immediately wrote to Ponsonby-Fane to determine the accuracy of the paragraph and to ask whether the style of dress for June 21 would now be different. Given the Duchess's great girth, she had been thrown into consternation at the thought of having to alter her apparel. Even before Ponsonby-Fane had had the opportunity to quiet her fears, however, the rumour was officially contradicted, thus killing all hopes that the Queen would respond to the demands for a more striking pageant, but sparing Princess Mary the need to consult again with her dressmaker.

The Queen's determination to have her own way with the jubilee tended to produce adverse effects on most aspects of its arrangement. Even the actual date of celebration became a subject of dispute.

Queen Victoria had succeeded her uncle, King William IV, on June 20, 1837. Because she wanted to wait until the full fifty years of her reign had passed before marking its golden jubilee, Victoria ordered it to be celebrated on Tuesday, June 21. Before the date was finalized (but long after it was first proposed), Lord Salisbury asked Victoria to shift it to Monday, June 20, 'a very convenient holiday for all working men, on account of its coming next to Sunday,' the Prime Minister wrote.[2] Despite support for such a change both from members of the House of Commons and the *Daily News*, the Queen greeted the suggestion coldly.

As Ponsonby informed Salisbury on March 24, not only could the Queen not bear 'making the anniversary of her uncle's death a day of rejoicing,' but since she could not travel on Sunday (and would not consider coming up any earlier than she had to), the idea was quite impossible. 'She will readily undertake to do all she has promised to do but cannot add further fatigues to those which she fears will tax her strength to the uttermost.'[3] Thus the Queen's rooted dislike of her capital and of Buckingham Palace deprived working men of a long weekend's holiday.

More vexing was the matter of the processional route. The Queen wanted not only the minimum of state, but the shortest route possible. Learning nothing from 1872, when pressure had forced her to have the original route reordered, Victoria again authorized a short course. The route to the Abbey would take her from Constitution Hill to Hyde Park Corner, Piccadilly, Waterloo Place, Charing Cross, Whitehall and Parliament Street. She would return via Horse Guards, St. James's Park and the Mall, the quickest way back possible. Once having been decided upon, it was announced to the world in the official government publication the *London Gazette*, and received without enthusiasm. Many newspapers editorially urged the Queen to change her mind; Labouchere in *Truth* put the general hope into undistinguished verse: 'One thing, at least, we cannot doubt, whatever be the plan / Your Majesty will make that route as lengthy as you can.'

When it was continually pointed out to the Queen how much disappointment the route had engendered, Victoria, as in so many jubilee matters, found herself forced to accept something more in line with public expectations. She therefore asked Lord Salisbury, himself not unencumbered with work, to draw up the

State or Semi-State? 157

route. As the Prime Minister juggled possibilities, the Lord Chamberlain's Department began to receive letters from residents and shopkeepers along the announced route, expressing in no uncertain terms how unpopular it would be to drop from the revamped route streets which it had already been announced would be included.

Lord Salisbury took the hint, and advised the Queen that streets already announced could not be dropped, though new ones might be added. In the end, he tacked on a great new sweep which made the final route run from Constitution Hill to Piccadilly, Regent Street, Waterloo Place, Pall Mall East, Cockspur Street and thence to Northumberland Avenue, the Embankment and Bridge Street. The return route, too, was rearranged, the Queen's route finally running from Parliament Street to Whitehall, Cockspur Street, Pall Mall, St. James's Street, Piccadilly and Constitution Hill. Some were still dissatisfied, but as officials in the Lord Chamberlain's Department, glad to shift responsibility elsewhere, quickly responded, now that the Prime Minister himself had approved the route, no further changes could be considered.

Given the Queen's decided notions about the jubilee and her nervous fear that she would be overtaxed during the hot weather she dreaded, whenever Lord Salisbury had a suggestion he wanted her to adopt, he had to put on the ways of the obsequious courtiers which he usually disdained. As Foreign Minister, however, he knew how important it was that the princes attending the jubilee be treated with the utmost consideration, lest they take umbrage and carry back resentments to their own lands. Entertainments with the Queen were necessary to achieve the proper effect, and so early in the jubilee year Salisbury took it upon himself to request that Victoria consent to a 'breakfast' for honoured guests who attended the thanksgiving service on June 21. His letter of thanks for her agreement is cast in such unexpectedly submissive terms that it is worth including. It also indicates to what lengths even that most unslavish man, the Marquess of Salisbury, felt he had to go in playing up to Victoria in such matters: 'Lord Salisbury with his humble duty desires to express respectfully his deep sense of Your Majesty's self-sacrificing kindness in consenting to have a breakfast at

Buckingham Palace after the Jubilee. He is very conscious of the labour, which such an entertainment will impose upon Your Majesty but every precaution will be taken to lighten it. He is sure that it will be very gratifying & that the effect will be highly beneficial.'

As the Queen gave way to ever greater anxiety about the jubilee, made worse by continuing criticism of arrangements she was determined not to change, she sprinkled her journal with entries like that of March 25, 'Worried by the constant questions about the arrangements for the Jubilee,' and complained that she would simply abandon it. In such circumstances, Salisbury must have felt glad he had previously adopted what was for him an exaggerated deference, for as spring approached he had another, significant favour to ask, which would entail for Victoria more work of the sort she was keen to avoid. He wanted her to pay a jubilee visit to Birmingham.

Salisbury had not determined upon this city at all idly. Indeed, his choice is an excellent example of how political considerations, while never publicized, sometimes influenced the arrangement of the jubilee. Birmingham was the home town of Joseph Chamberlain, who had first come to prominence as its dynamic, reforming Liberal mayor, going on to even greater notoriety as the leader of the Radical wing of the Gladstonians in the House of Commons. Over the Home Rule issue, he had withdrawn from Mr. Gladstone and taken a band of Radical Unionists to the support of the government. His newborn alliance was, however, threatened by the resignation of Lord Randolph Churchill from the Exchequer, when for a time Chamberlain thought he might be better off returning to his origins than remaining within a party suddenly much more orthodox. Although by March the spectre of Chamberlain's reunion with the regular Liberals (which would have galvanized the politics of Birmingham) had largely passed, Lord Salisbury was nonetheless eager to reinforce the Unionist sentiments of a city which had in the last election given all its seven seats to supporters of the government, both Conservative and Liberal Unionist, and so prove conclusively to Chamberlain that he was better off retaining his current alliance. It thus made good sense to get the chief symbol of Unionism, the sovereign, to go to Birmingham and spark a loyalist demonstration.

It is impossible to suggest just how much opposition Victoria put up to what was perhaps Salisbury's most important jubilee request to her; given the Queen's general disposition early in the year, she cannot have embraced the idea warmly. Nonetheless, because Salisbury was prepared to maintain his point in this instance, she acquiesced and set a date in late March for her visit.

Delighted that their city should be so honoured, the Birmingham City Council voted a good deal of money to decorate the Queen's route, while Chamberlain's lieutenants worked hard to ensure that there would be substantial crowds on hand. Additionally, the police spent extra time running in political dissidents, of whom it was thought Birmingham had more than its share; the Queen herself corresponded with Lord Salisbury about Irish and Socialist malcontents.

H.M. Hyndman and other Socialists were thus locked up for a time, although the report sent to the Home Office by Hyndman's arresting officer suggests that the department was being over-zealous. 'Had not the Detectives been present at a rally given by Socialists they would have evidently received very rough usage and treatment' from keyed-up loyalists. As Hyndman's memoirs, *The Record of an Adventurous Life*, later stated, 1887 was a very bad year for men of his opinions, but official Birmingham was taking no chances.

Given Chamberlain's assistance, the Queen's visit passed off just as Salisbury had hoped. As he told her on March 23, 'The visit will be of the greatest value, politically and publicly.' Chamberlain, however, was not quite so pleased. After the initial enthusiasm had dissipated, he wrote telling a 'Court official' (probably Ponsonby) that while the city had gone to great lengths on her behalf, the Queen's own lack of pomp and circumstance had been considered by some as an offence. Perhaps because she was aware of Chamberlain's importance to the government, Victoria saw the force of his complaint, although typically she was not prepared to see its relevance in relation to the forthcoming jubilee celebration in London. Nevertheless, the Queen promised that in future she would bring along a detachment of Household Cavalry when she ventured into the provinces. At the same time, however, she determined that she would not do so again in 1887, although prominent citizens of another great city were anxious that the Queen should come to them.

Perhaps no city in the realm was more essentially Victorian than Manchester where the first captains of industry had risen to sooty eminence and where the Anti-Corn Law League had worked successfully to fix the opinions and prejudices of the age. In Mancunian opinion, therefore, there was something peculiarly appropriate about the Queen who had given her name to the epoch visiting in her jubilee year the city which had so shaped it, especially when there was a great exhibition of the arts and manufactures of that reign to be opened. That there were also important political considerations for her doing so only increased local enthusiasm for a visit.

Although the Unionist party had done very well in the Home Rule elections in 1886, Manchester had proven a significant disappointment. There, before these elections, Conservatives had held five of the six seats; afterwards, they held only three, one of the returning members being the Prime Minister's nephew, A. J. Balfour. In the spring of 1887, with Balfour now Irish Secretary, one of his political associates, E. B. Muller of the *Manchester Courier*, wrote and asked him to do what he could about getting the Queen to visit Manchester. 'I would not be so exigent,' he wrote, 'unless I were convinced of the paramount necessity of getting HM here in the interests of the throne itself, not to speak of party considerations . . . I can say honestly that the Queen's refusal to take any notice of Manchester and its district would be a fatal error the consequences of which may well be serious.' Although perhaps smiling at Müller's apocalyptic assessment of the situation, Balfour accepted his main point and pressed his uncle to see what could be done. Once again Salisbury went to the well; this time, however, as he perhaps anticipated, the Queen refused. Given her age, the state of her nerves and the other demands upon her time, it was, she said, *'absolutely impossible'* to consider it. Because the Manchester Exhibition, with its notable retrospective of the artists of the reign, was a significant affair, being the largest of the several municipal exhibitions mounted in jubilee year, Balfour secured the Prince of Wales for its opening. Later still, in October, the Duke of Cambridge paid a visit, too; upon his return to London, he felt obliged to tell Cousin Victoria what she had missed. 'I have met with so loyal & cordial a reception . . . that I think it my duty to inform you of this, as in these days all marks of respect to the Crown, & good feeling toward members of your family must be looked upon as acceptable—& highly encouraging.'[4]

If the Queen's disinclination to adopt certain suggestions for celebrating the jubilee rightly aroused widespread disapproval, her failure to acquiesce in others was more justifiable. There was, for instance, an undercurrent throughout the year that the Queen should reciprocate to her subjects for their half century of loyal devotion by making some kind of gift. The Duke of Cambridge suggested that following the precedent of King George III's jubilee the Queen should give an extra ration to the army. In advising against the idea, Ponsonby pointed out that as the army was now much larger than it had been, such generosity would cost the Queen about £2,000 and could not be done without including the navy as well. He therefore recommended that if the idea was to be considered at all, it had better be done by the government. Always chary where her money was concerned, the Queen concurred.

Other schemes started who-knows-where. One rumour that the Queen would give six guineas and a silver cradle to any baby born on her jubilee day took flight with amazing speed. Given that average daily births in the United Kingdom ran at about 3,200, royal officials acted promptly to squash the story before it got out of hand. Even so, more than 400 applications for this non-existent bounty were received.

It was not in the Queen's character to consider such an outlay. Instead she continued her usual subscriptions, only supplementing them with gifts of £2,000 to the Imperial Institute and of lesser sums to the Church House and to the Countess of Dufferin's Fund, a proposal advanced by the Vicereine to assist the development of female medical departments in Indian colleges and universities. Inevitably there were those who disliked the Queen's caution on money matters, none more so than the radical newspaper *Reynolds's*, which week after week minutely scrutinized the monarchy.

> From a million to a stew-pan; I verily believe
> She'll take, take, take to the last day she lives;
> But then, you know, you seldom hear
> Of anything she gives.

Such sentiments, however disagreeable, were not very serious, although there was more than an element of truth in them. The Queen was most careful with her money, and having to put up nearly £50,000 from her privy purse to meet the expenses of the golden jubilee (as Sir Edward Hamilton learned from her private secretary during financial negotiations in advance of the diamond jubilee) made her exercise the closest watch on anything likely to need funds. Moreover, the fact that she was herself meeting the bulk of the jubilee expenses not only deprived the government of any leverage it would otherwise have had but entirely justified in the Queen's mind her insistence upon getting what she wanted.

While anti-royalist diatribes in *Reynolds's* were of little consequence, attacks launched on the Queen because of her preferred arrangement of the thanksgiving service in Westminster Abbey were of more significance.

The Queen was a good Broad churchwoman who so disliked the ritualistic fallals of the 'mass in masquerade' that she had had Disraeli take legislative action against them. Not only did she like her religion simple, she also liked it short and sweet. When it was otherwise the Defender of the Faith was given to fidgetting.

Because she had complained to Gladstone in 1872 that the thanksgiving service at St. Paul's was turning into a 'mere show,' the Queen took pains to ensure that the one arranged for her jubilee should be without fripperies. She had undoubtedly briefed Lord Salisbury on what she wanted before he wrote to the Archbishop of Canterbury in December, 1886; citing the likelihood of hot summer weather which always troubled the Queen, Salisbury told Benson that the prime requisite of the service was that it be kept short; there must be no instructive discourse or admonitory sermon such as had been included in 1872, which had made the service interminable. Indeed, there must be no flourishes whatsoever.

Archbishop Benson, distracted by the demands of the church

house proposal, did not seriously consider the matter for several weeks. When he did so, however, he was most conscientious about meeting the Queen's wishes. No item was added to the service without the question, 'Can this be shorter?' having been satisfactorily answered. After a good deal of tinkering, Benson drew up a service which would last exactly 27 minutes. It provided for no prayers, lessons or psalms, all of which the Archbishop initially seems to have felt could be dispensed with.

Catching wind of this stark arrangement, Canon Flood Jones of Westminster wrote to the Archbishop's chaplain, the Reverend Montague Fowler, to implore Benson at least to add an introductory versicle before the Prince Consort's *Te Deum*. Otherwise the service would begin too abruptly. Since the versicle took just one minute to perform, Benson included it; having done so, he decided there ought also to be prayers, so added exactly seven minutes of them. With that he submitted the result to the Queen, uncertain whether she would find 35 minutes too long. To his intense relief, she did not, even authorizing the inclusion of a short piece of scripture and a psalm.

As originally drafted by the Archbishop, the service had solely referred to the wondrous circumstance of the Queen's reign of fifty years and the benefits that had thereby accrued to the nation. Victoria's decision to extend the service slightly now gave Benson the opportunity to add a recognition of the important fact that it was a wondrous people over whom the Queen reigned. Thus after including Psalm 20 ('Exaudiat Te Dominus'), he took a lesson from 1 Peter ii, which included the key phrase, 'But ye are a chosen generation, a royal priesthood, an holy nation, a peculiar people. . . .' Here, at least, was some tardy recognition of the wider significance of the jubilee, and Randall Davidson, Dean of Windsor, congratulated Benson for having added it: 'I think your addition of both,' he wrote, 'takes away all objection to "Over Mastering" '.

Satisfactory though the completed service may have been to the Queen, it found no favour with her High Church subjects. Since the early years of the reign they had been campaigning against the very idea of special state services which, smacking of the erastian, were suspect. In 1858, they had succeeded in getting three such annual services abolished, those commemorating the execution of Charles I, the restoration of the monarchy in 1660, and the failure of the Gunpowder Plot. Only the one celebrating the accession of the reigning sovereign was retained, despite vehement criticism against it by High Churchmen, who disliked the fact that it had not been approved by church convocation and that its language glorified the crown in almost Elizabethan terms which belied the actuality of constitutional monarchy.

Moreover, many ritualistically-inclined clerics took exception to the loyal sentiments of the service praising Victoria's relations with the Church of England. This went down very badly with those who knew well enough that the Queen bore a heavy responsibility for the means of prosecuting ritual offences, and the High Church newspaper *Church Times* was not averse to pointing it out. 'So far from being a nursing-mother to the Church,' it wrote in one of its many articles on the issue, 'her attitude has never been other than markedly cold and unsympathetic. . . .' The newspaper also chastised her for 'having proceeded to direct acts of nonconformity' by which it meant, of course, her communion with the Church of Scotland, during her residence in the northern kingdom.

The final provocation for ritualists, however, was the Queen's decision to permit the Archbishops of Canterbury and York and the Dean and Chapter of Westminster to appear at the Abbey service in copes. Because this decision was not actually known until jubilee day itself, the criticism did not come until afterwards. Nonetheless, when it did appear, it was astringent. One correspondent to the *Church Times* wrote later in the summer that 'If ever there is another prosecution for vestment-wearing, I hope these antics will not be forgotten,' while the newspaper itself pointedly editorialized, 'We have thus the very highest authority possible for asserting that according to the true construction of the Ornaments Rubric the usual mediaeval vestments are still lawful in the Church of England.'

The matter continued beyond its natural life when a group photograph of the offending clergy in their unwonted copes made its way into a number of shopwindows in the capital. There it was prominently displayed to the malicious glee of the

Church Times, which wondered whether it might outsell those of the professional beauties of the day. Not likely, it sniffed, as the featured copes were 'sorry makeshift affairs,' an evaluation which must have pained Archbishop Benson, who had gone to great lengths to replace the velvet on his own cope, finding something suitable only at Lyons, where it cost £40.

As far as the Queen was concerned, the antagonism of the High Church party, while bothersome, was never too important; she had, after all, become used to it over the years. Nonetheless, coming at a time when there was so much other criticism about the jubilee, it may have contributed its mite to her already-considerable anxiety. In any event, after returning from Birmingham (and after spending most of the first three months of the year out of the public eye), the Queen retired first to Windsor for a rest and thence to the South of France for a lengthy holiday, leaving matters in London to take their course. When she was gone, the *Daily News*, which had so far held its tongue, at last could stand it no longer and on April 13 released its pent-up frustrations in a strong attack on the contemplated jubilee arrangements. 'It is high time that there should be some plain speaking on the subject of the Jubilee celebration; and it may be hoped that the Prince of Wales and Lord Salisbury will take an early opportunity, after the Queen returns to England, to point out to her Majesty that the Court arrangements are in every respect infelicitous, and will assuredly excite great and general disgust.'

Unfortunately, neither the Prince of Wales nor the Prime Minister was disposed to accept this commission. The Prince, of course, with his delight in the minutiae of pomp (for which he had a real flair) might well have seemed the obvious candidate, but Bertie's role in the jubilee was a limited one. Not only was he distracted by his ill-fated Imperial Institute, but he knew that the Queen placed no weight on the opinions of her middle-aged son; she thought him well meaning, of course, and genial but lacking in judgment, an evaluation which, he was aware, the Imperial Institute affair had done nothing to change. As for Lord Salisbury, except when some domestic or foreign advantage was to be gained (or more usually where matters taking their course threatened to bring problems), he was simply uninterested.

Who else was there?

No other member of her family had sufficient influence with the Queen to succeed in having her change her mind. Princess Alexandra's decided snub proved that. And no member of her Court did either. Her long-time ladies Jane, Marchioness of Ely and Jane, Lady Churchill stood in too much awe of their sovereign ever to dare mention the subject, while even Sir Henry Ponsonby, whose obligation it was to be aware of the critical comments being made and to submit suitable advice to the Queen, seems not to have felt he could broach the touchy subject with Victoria. There was thus no one who could save the Queen from herself and spare the jubilee its unnecessary problems.

Only Prince Albert could have done so, but it was not the Prince's counsel that she missed on the eve of her jubilee. It was rather that of her now deceased, very controversial highland servant, John Brown, whose presence at Court had not many years before led to much snide gossip. Why, rumour asked, did Victoria permit unquestioned liberties to this coarse, blunt-spoken man? Could it be that she had become infatuated, or that she had so far forgotten herself as to contract a secret marriage, thereby becoming, in the words of scandal-mongers, 'The Empress Brown'? Just before going from Windsor to the metropolitan celebration of her jubilee she showed how much she missed Brown, sending Ponsonby a note in which she lamented Brown's absence and remarked how helpful he would have been. Ponsonby's response was restrained: 'It is most true,' he wrote on June 20, 'that Brown's assistance at this moment would have been invaluable and that he would have saved Your Majesty much trouble & anxiety in many points.'[5] In fact, however, had Brown been alive he would probably only have stiffened the Queen's determination to do what she wanted, for despite his rough ways, John Brown was a canny courtier, who succeeded by giving his sovereign what she wanted.

In truth, Victoria had not a friend in the world, if by friend one means someone free to give unsolicited, candid and, if necessary, distasteful advice. After a half century of rule, she had outlived any member of the royal family who could do so, except the Dowager Duchess of Cambridge, who as the doyenne of the family might use the Queen's Christian name but took no other liberties. Equally, no politician dared to be blunt. Only Gladstone was her equal in terms of public service (Salisbury had been a mere lad of seven at the time of her accession), and, of course, Gladstone was the Queen's great *bête noire*.

Her lack of friends can be accounted for by what Tennyson termed the Queen's 'terrible height' above her subjects, which made her such an unapproachable figure and caused grown men with deeds of derring-do to their credit to quail before this shy, even timid, diminutive figure with soft, plump hands.

This development in the status of the monarch had come about gradually during the Queen's long reign; it had certainly not been present when her dissolute uncle King George IV sat on the throne or when his brother King William IV, succeeded him. The efflorescence of monarchy came much later in the century and was by no means inevitable. Britain's shifting position in the world helped it along, for when the hegemony of free trade began to be threatened in the 1870s, a defensive consciousness began to grow which sparked not only nationalism but the sleeping genius of imperialism. To a far flung, heterogeneous, haphazardly-assembled empire casually linked, the monarchy offered the best symbol of unity, as well as the security of continuity and tradition in a world of uncharted change.

Then, too, the rise of the Conservative party helped. It was not that in reality Conservatives were any more loyal to the idea of monarchy than orthodox Liberals, but that Disraeli had ingeniously (if tentatively) recognized the benefits to be gained by transforming his party into the vehicle of patriotism both national and imperial. The exercise was new and its outcome uncertain at his death in 1881, but it flourished in the years after, in part because Gladstone's 'Little Englander' disposition ill-suited the national mood. After Majuba the Grand Old Man did not return the drubbing the Boers had there inflicted, and dithered while 'Chinese' Gordon, staving off a horde of dervishes at Khartoum, at last became an unnecessary martyr.

Public failure to understand the intricacies of such complex situations did not prevent the Conservatives, benefitting from the irresponsibility of opposition, from capitalizing on them. A few years later, when Gladstone allied himself with the Irish Nationalists to bring Home Rule to Ireland, the crucial development of the Conservatives into the patriotic party was complete, for anti-Irish feelings were rampant and virulent among all classes of Englishmen. Along with all the other chattels of nationalism and empire, the Conservatives also captured the Queen, who under Disraeli's tutelage had no trouble discovering that she, too, was a Tory.

Ironically, the one person who had good reason to protest at this result and could have upset it was himself an earnest and devoted monarchist of scrupulous loyalty. As the perceptive Mary, Lady Ponsonby, once said, if Gladstone ever wavered in his allegiance to the throne, the game would be up, for he was the man who kept the Liberal party and the democracy in line. Indeed, it was because he was so great a monarchist that he was prepared to overlook the Queen's blatantly partisan behaviour during his second ministry and after, though her personal hostility deeply pained him.

Victoria, often petty and small-minded, seemed not to appreciate how dependent the throne was, how contingent her own well-being, on the Grand Old Man she so much disparaged and so openly loathed. Lesser men would have paid her back in kind, exposing with relish the sham of royal impartiality, but Gladstone did not do so; sadly, latter-day monarchists have all too often been insufficiently aware of what the throne owes to him.

As a result of his high minded rectitude and constant fidelity under great duress, the notion that the crown was in fact above politics took root, thereby assisting, despite the actual facts of the case, in strengthening the throne. High above the increasing storms and divisive battles of politics, so the accepted reasoning went, was an impartial, olympian arbiter, calm, judicious, fair, who always had the best interest of the people at heart. To such a figure were loyalty, constancy and deference due.

Of course in reality Queen Victoria, a partisan, obstinate, opinionated woman, often fell short of the standard. Child of the Hanoverians, she had come to the throne before the new theories of monarchy propounded by the likes of Walter Bagehot had gained a foothold, and her behaviour was often reminiscent of earlier, more rambunctious modes of kingship. Nonetheless, the olympian throne needed an olympian sovereign, and the jubilee presented a splendid opportunity to wink at the facts and transform a highly individual, flawed and imperfect woman into a towering figure of legend and myth suitable for the new demands of monarchy. In the avalanche of biographies of the Queen called up for the occasion, this is just what happened.

The purpose of these books was only secondarily to present the facts of the Queen's life. These, it was thought, were already well outlined. Rather, it was to show what a moral, useful, conscientious life the Queen had led and to exhort others, particularly young people, to follow her example. No one in 1887 stated the matter quite so baldly as the anonymous author of a diamond jubilee booklet entitled *Queen Victoria: Her Character Brought out by Incidents in Her Life,* but his reason for writing was the common one. 'This booklet is meant not to present Queen Victoria's history, but her character in the hope that many who admire her may be induced also to imitate her.' Had it been otherwise, the recently-completed series of the memoirs of Charles Greville, a superb source for the early years of the reign, must have been frequently cited. As they present an all-too-human and intimate account of Queen Victoria and her Court, however, not one of the jubilee biographers found it appropriate to utilize his findings; although true, they were very much at variance with the image such people wished to present.

Instead, they turned to those incidents which might easily be made into instructive moral tales. The famous line, 'I will be good,' supposedly uttered by the young Victoria upon learning her closeness to the throne was always prominently placed; whether it was true or not was unimportant. It was just the sort of thing an olympian sovereign would say and just the sort of dutiful example which ought to be put before children. There was even a jubilee song entitled 'I Will Be Good' with this instructive line: 'Let ev'ry English maiden make this her frequent prayer; that she the same high purpose may with her sovereign share.'

Such tales, which of course never dealt with the effect her lack of playmates may have had or the pernicious influence of the doubtful relationship her mother had enjoyed with Sir John Conroy, portrayed the young Victoria as stiff, saccharine, unlifelike. The Reverend Charles Bullock, one of the most characteristic jubilee authors, captured this angel child in banal verse in his book *The Queen's Resolve.*

> Fair thy childhood ever grew,
> Brightening with graces ever new;
> When growth of person was combined
> With growing graces of the mind,
> Till all the good and wise approved thee.
> And all, who ever knew thee, loved thee.

In the same way, each aspect of the Queen's life was purged of its individual character and made into a standard to be followed, nowhere more pointedly than in her domestic relations. As Mr. Bullock wrote, 'The Queen's household has been—what every palace should be—a model home.' Some writers carried this point even further, introducing for the first time in any significant way the maternal imagery which was to be so noticeable at both the Queen's diamond jubilee and at her funeral. It was particularly popular among Sunday versifiers like Isaac Jones, who wrote in his 'Jubilee National Anthem,' about 'Victoria, our gracious Queen/and mother of our land,' and Thomas Adams, whose poem 'The Queen's Jubilee,' proclaimed that 'Her Majesty is truly / The Queen Mother of her Empire.'

Once the process of apotheosis was under way, ever more extravagant claims slipped into the effusions of the jubilee writers. Mr. Bullock wrote without flinching that 'The Queen and her subjects are of one heart and one mind,' despite her notorious conduct throughout the Home Rule debate. The Reverend A. E. Humphreys, a Cambridgeshire clergyman, went even farther. In his 'Jubilee Hymn,' he placed her in a unique relationship with the Almighty. 'God, her Father, Husband, Friend / loving, loves her to the end.' Victoria herself had the good sense to call this kind of thing 'twaddle.' Nonetheless, although ridiculously extravagant, such sentiments are a good indication of the crucial transformation which had already taken place in public perception of the monarchy and its place in the nation. At no other time in the century, for no other monarch, could such ideas have been put forward without the writer being denounced as a toady and a sycophant. From the time of the golden jubilee, they became commonplace.

Despite the development of circumstances favouring the monarchic principle and the creation of a suitably mythic *persona* to occupy the throne, the real Queen Victoria with all her very human traits, was still very much on the scene and likely to upset all the careful contrivance. Which is just what she did when she returned from France in late April to undertake a series of functions, the most important of which was the opening of the People's Palace. There it was clear she had no intention of heeding any advice, no matter how sensible, about how she should undertake her public duties.

The idea for the People's Palace had originated in 1884, when the trustees of the Barber Beaumont endowment approached the Drapers Company about setting up an educational institution in London's East End. The same year in an unrelated development novelist Walter Besant published his book *All Sorts and Conditions of Men* in which he proposed that a 'Palace of Delight' be established in the East End, a place of intellectual and artistic culture, organized recreation and orderly amusement. A best seller, Besant's book excited much interest in the scheme already begun by the Drapers.

Unfortunately, the wide divergence between the Drapers insistence that the Palace be solely an educational institution and Besant's wish that it have a significant recreational dimension caused continuing problems. So did debates about whether it should be open on Sundays and if liquor should be allowed. Indeed, debate on these issues was so fierce that at one point in late 1886 the *Daily News* had written, 'There is no disguising the fact that the question of the People's Palace for East London has now become one of the disputed questions of the day.' In addition, ever since gangs of East End roughs had in February, 1886, invaded the West End, wreaking havoc in clubland and causing subscriptions to dry up, there had been financial problems, too. Nonetheless, the building was finished in time for the Queen's jubilee, and Victoria was prevailed upon to open it in person.

Almost as rare as a jubilee itself, the Queen's visit to the East End of her capital was a most unusual event. In large part her absence from the district stemmed from lack of interest in its pervasive problems, for domestic social issues and the condition of the working classes were of little concern to the Queen. Since she was coming to an area rife with unemployment, disease and overcrowding, however, one correspondent to the *East London Observer* in February thought that the opportunity should be seized to change her outlook. 'I think she ought to avail herself of the chance and really find out what is at the bottom of the existing poverty and destitution so that she may communicate to her advisers the things she actually saw.'

Then, too, the Queen shared with most of the privileged a profound suspicion of the creatures who lived in the East End, who were generally regarded as domestic hottentots, unwashed, uncivilized and best kept at arm's length. In dealing with such people, one had always to fear for the worst, as Archbishop Benson significantly reflected in his diary after returning from the opening of the People's Palace. 'The sight of those vibrating mighty ribbons of human faces and forms haunts the eye still, and I shall never forget it. . . . It made one shudder at the thought of what would be, if ever those were against us.'

The Queen's advisers, of course, were as prone as the Archbishop of Canterbury to shudder at that thought; they may also have been influenced by the (unfounded) suspicion in the air that the jubilee year was provoking anti-royalism and the growth of socialism, as Frances, Lady Dilke, told Sir Edward Hamilton in May. Both were likely to flourish in the noisome conditions of the East End. It was widely agreed, therefore, that the Queen should adopt as much gorgeous pomp as possible, for surely no one was more susceptible to it than the dispossessed? Predictably, however, Victoria dismissed any argument for the greater use of regal appurtenances, even though Lord Salisbury himself had approached her to do more. Apparently fearing that to give way in May would mean giving way in June, the Queen was adamant. On April 7, she informed the Prime Minister that, 'Sir Wm. Jenner [royal physician] cd easily if Ld Salisbury wishes & wd tell him write a letter to Ld Salisbury arguing that the Queen's strength must not be overtaxed . . . it is *not* loyalty to try & force the Queen, and the woman of nearly 68, to overtax and overwork her & possibly make her ill for sometime afterwards.'

Salisbury certainly knew that such a letter, no matter how persuasively written, would not (when published, as the Queen evidently intended) quiet the demand for suitable state, but as Victoria was at her most inflexible, the Prime Minister dropped the matter. The result was a meagre procession made up of five town carriages, a few hussars and some life guards, no more. As Salisbury had feared, it compared very badly with the lavish decorations put up along the way by Victoria's subjects, who, as the Queen whirled by at her usual over-brisk pace, could have seen very little. Inevitably, there was much criticism.

To compound the problem, despite advice to the contrary, the Queen insisted on opening the People's Palace on Saturday, May 14, the chief business day in the district. Even though local shopkeepers sent a petition to Buckingham Palace urging a change of date, Victoria would consider no alteration. She had made up her mind that May 14 was the most suitable date and would hear no argument to the contrary.

What she did hear, however, as she drove along the route to the East End was something which utterly confounded her. It was, she wrote to Lord Salisbury afterwards, 'a horrid noise *quite* new to the Queen's ears—"booing" she believes it is called.' Naturally, she blamed it on the Irish and Socialists, refusing to see that her own perverse conduct may have had its effect. Diplomatically, Salisbury concurred with the Queen, telling her that, 'It is of course impossible for any organization to prevent such ill-manners, and London contains a much larger number of the worst kind of roughs than any other great town in the island; for all that is worthless, worn out or penniless, naturally drifts to London. . . .'

Despite the booing, the irritation of the shopkeepers and the disappointment of those who had hoped for a brilliant display of monarchic splendour, the Queen's reception was a success. 'I was most thankful,' Victoria wrote in her journal, 'all had gone off so well. It was indeed a most satisfactory event, and showed the loyalty of the people.'

What explains this result in the face of the Queen's failure to meet popular expectations, indeed her positive refusal to do so?

In the end, the transformation in the crown's position in the later nineteenth century, a development which occurred to a considerable extent in spite of the sovereign, far outweighed the negative influence of the Queen's own stubbornness, which, while galling, dwindled to near insignificance beside the luxuriant growth of monarchy. The jubilee succeeded to a considerable extent despite the woman in whose honour it was taking place. There is, however, less paradox in this statement than there may appear, for wise observers had always recognized that the golden jubilee was not just an event personal to Queen Victoria. It had an aspect equally important, and indeed for towns and hamlets far removed from London more important than that. To the people at large, the jubilee was as much a commemoration of fifty heady years of unrivalled progress and of their own unexampled worth and superiority as it was an occasion to sing Queen Victoria's praises. As one of the characters in George Gissing's later novel *In the Year of Jubilee* rightly put it, 'Now, I look at it this way. It's to celebrate the fiftieth year of the reign of Queen Victoria—yes; but, at the same time and far more, it's to celebrate the completion of fifty years of Progress. National Progress, without precedent in the history of mankind! One may say, indeed, Progress of the Human Race.' It was Victoria's failure to grasp this crucial point which spawned so many unnecessary difficulties.

Out of the West End of London, away from the district where the obstinacy of the Queen, the perverse doggedness of high placed promoters, and confused, inadequate preparations exercised such a baleful influence, the point was recognized, was indeed the foundation on which the entire event was raised; outside London, therefore, the success of the golden jubilee was never so questionable, though West End opinion makers entirely overlooked developments in the provinces.

Jubilee celebrations outside London were very much alike. Most established a fund for some civic improvement or another generally adding another fund at the request of the Prince of Wales in aid of his Imperial Institute; later still most of them took yet another collection for an entertainment meant for children or the elderly. On jubilee day itself, most towns began with their own services of thanksgiving, based on the form of worship authorized by the Privy Council. In a typical jubilee sermon, as the Reverend Dr. Luard, chaplain to the mayor of Cambridge, said: 'There are many yet among us old enough to remember the beginning of the present Queen's reign, and who can call to mind the state of things existing then, and the changes which in so many ways have marked its progress.... We cannot but believe that the country has made in most directions a steady advance—in the power of making its members happier, in the subjection of disease, in the repression of crime, in enabling the poorest to live more like civilized beings, in helping all on their way to a higher life. And it is to thank God for these blessings, to commemorate the lapse of these years, thus on the whole spent happily, that we come together as a body....' Only after this progress had been duly recognized did the Queen receive her due.

Later in the day, all the trappings of civic pomp and circumstance were called up for a turnout on the common, with local clubs, friendly societies and the volunteers.

In the evening the great event was the jubilee bonfire. Much attention was expended on concocting impressive jubilee illuminations. When it became known that the government was doing nothing about illuminations in London, the first Duke of Westminster suggested that candles be set up in every window, an idea which sparked a host of hostile commentary. One correspondent to the *Daily News* asked in outraged terms if the Duke, probably the richest peer in the realm, had any idea what candles cost, while another wrote sarcastically, 'It [the spectacle] will doubtless be splendid, only surpassed by the subsequent and consequent conflagration.' The idea never caught on but in the countryside attention focussed on bonfires. On May 13, Victor Milward, High Sheriff of Worcestershire, wrote to the national press suggesting that the lighting of such fires be coordinated to begin at 10 p.m. on June 21, the opening signal to be given from Great Malvern. 'The Malvern Hills,' he wrote, 'are geographically nearly the centre of England, and are isolated in position; a very slight amount of county organization would ensure simultaneous illumination throughout the whole kingdom.'

On jubilee night more than 350 signal stations blazed throughout the land in a fiery display reminiscent of the one organized after the defeat of the Spanish Armada. 'It was a sight to be remembered and demonstrates most forcibly the value of such signalling, should an occasion ever arise when all our people need to be apprised of coming foes,' wrote a correspondent to *The Times* on June 25.

A. E. Housman got the tone of the event right, when he wrote in the opening stanza of *The Shropshire Lad* years later,

> Look left, look right, the hills are bright,
> The dales are light between,
> Because 'tis fifty years tonight
> That God has saved the Queen.

The bonfires successfully capped an entirely successful day.

CHAPTER SEVEN

IN QUEST OF HONOURS

THE OCCASION of the golden jubilee seemed to some a good time to amend the Queen's royal title explicitly to take into account the vast increase during her reign of the British dominions overseas. In the spring of 1887 two Tory backbenchers, Howard Vincent and George Baden-Powell, launched a campaign to this effect with, on May 7, editorial backing from *The Times*. Just as the first Colonial Conference ever was being convened in London the idea of such a change was supported by many of the colonial representatives in attendance.

But, as Colonial Office officials soon realized when they canvassed the self-governing colonies, whatever enthusiasm might exist in the imperial capital for amending the royal title, there was virtually none in the colonies. As the Governor of Victoria put it, 'My Govt. do not think proposition as to Queen's title an improvement but if HM in favour this colony will carry her wishes out.'

The Colonial Office might have gone ahead on this basis because the Queen wished for the change, but Canada's response made this impossible. If the Queen's title were changed, the Canadian government wired the Colonial Office, Canada would have to be explicitly mentioned. Since Canada could scarcely be included without all the other self-governing colonies being added as well, the matter took on a new complexion. Not only would the title become ludicrously unwieldy but some acceptable formula would have to be devised whereby the colonies were enumerated. Alphabetically? In order of size? By the date they had been annexed? And, of course, there was the frightful prospect of having to alter the title each time the circumstances of the empire shifted.

Under these conditions, the Colonial Secretary, a nondescript figure named Henry Holland, decided to leave matters alone. How he broke this unsatisfactory news to the Queen is not known; perhaps he fell back on Disraeli's argument to Gladstone in 1876, when the Grand Old Man had urged in the House of Commons that some mention of the colonies be added to the royal title. They were implicitly included, Disraeli reasoned, so there was absolutely no need to mention them.

This unsatisfactory result, for which the Queen unfairly held Holland responsible, angered Victoria—not because she much cared about adding the colonies to her title, but because the demise of the colonial scheme affected the question of when she could call herself Empress of India. By mid-July, it was clear that no progress would be made in either matter. She wrote pungently to Lord Salisbury: 'The Queen thinks it is better to make no alteration in her title now, but wishes *some day* the unnecessary and stupid restrictions as to when she is in public RI [Regina et Imperatrix] & when not and when the Title is to be used or not will be repealed.'

The problem that the Queen wished to rectify had arisen in 1876 when the Royal Titles Bill, which made her Empress of India, was passed. Contrary to legend, the Prime Minister, Disraeli, was not anxious to introduce this legislation, much as he liked the idea of empresses; Victoria urged him to do so, both because she wanted the imperial title and because Prince Albert, as long before as 1843, had suggested she should have it. Nonetheless, the proposal generated criticism not only from the Liberal press but also from London Society, which thought the title Victoria already had was quite sufficient. To get the bill through Parliament, it was decided that the title could only be used in India or concerning matters pertaining to India and that as regarded England and all her other possessions, Victoria would have to rest content as just Queen.

For a dozen years, she fretted under this provoking arrangement, an Empress in India, a Queen everywhere else, stubbornly initialling letters to royal officials 'VRI', waiting for the chance to change things, so that she could use her imperial title in Britain. Misled by what seemed to be growing public support for some recognition of her colonial possessions in the royal title, the Queen early let Lord Salisbury know what she was really after. On May 13, she told him that, 'If anything further is added the [imperial] title shd be *acknowledged once for all* &

not as was done in 76 to assuage the opposition *only* for certain occasions.' Overplaying a hand which she thought stronger than it actually was, Victoria indicated she would have difficulty signing any warrant adding the colonies to her title if it did not also satisfy her imperial aspirations.

As the Queen might have anticipated, such a threat had no influence at all on Salisbury. He had seen much less reason than Disraeli for having an imperial title in the first place and was still not convinced it ought to be used outside India. Though the Queen was most put out by this course of events, Salisbury was not distressed in the slightest. A good Conservative, he recognized that the best thing to do was often nothing. But the Queen was determined that even in small matters her imperial title should be used in England. She intended that her style on the English coinage should be one of these matters, and the unsatisfactory nature of the jubilee coins gave her an opening to press the matter home.

Beginning as far back as 1879, J. E. Boehm, R.A., Victoria's favourite sculptor, had been hired by the Mint to renew the Queen's effigy on the coinage, for it had remained constant throughout the reign. After he had done so, a number of pattern coins were presented to the Queen for her approval in August, 1885, and by the beginning of 1886 matters were so far advanced that the Hon. C. W. Fremantle, deputy master of the mint, thought Boehm might at last be paid for his several years of work. Fremantle thought the sum of £200 which the artist was to be paid a 'moderate' one. The new coins were now ready to be struck, but as it was apparently considered more appropriate to release them to coincide with the jubilee, nothing more was done officially in 1886.

Perhaps some hint that a change in the coinage was in the offing leaked out; in any case, in July the *Daily News* suddenly began to offer ideas on what kind of coinage was needed, having written on July 8 that 'Our coins are very well in their way, but they are commonplace and prosy.' 'Our English currency,' it continued, 'seems in the last hundred or hundred and fifty years to have had little history and no romance.' What was needed, the newspaper wrote, was a jubilee commemorative coinage worthy to mark the occasion.

Plans for the new coinage were left as they were until

Fremantle in May, 1887, officially informed the Secretary of the Treasury that at the Queen's pleasure certain changes were going to be made in the designs of the gold and silver coins and that a new double florin or four-shilling piece was to be added. Five days later a proclamation to this effect was published in the *London Gazette*.

Because it merely described the new coins in words only, it was impossible to evaluage the changes but when the illustrated Annual Report of the Deputy Master of the Mint was published, the coins were found most unsatisfactory. On May 30, the *Daily News* wrote, 'The crown has shrunk into a mere top-knot, and a certain stiffness in the figure suggests that her Majesty is balancing it on her head, from which it shows a decided tendency to slip off.'

A few days later an unusual attempt to explain how Mint officials had approached the task of designing the new coinage was published by C. W. Fremantle in the June number of *Murray's Magazine*. Entitled 'Our New Coins and Their Pedigree,' Fremantle's article critized the lack of artistic merit of the run of Victorian coins and suggested that the intention this time had been to create an artistically distinguished selection, retaining from the past only a reverse of 'considerable merit' by Merlin on the half crown and the 'beautiful design of St. George' by Pistrucci on the reverse sides of the five pound, two pound, sovereign and crown pieces. The *Church Times* retorted on June 10, 'We cannot join in the applause which has been bestowed upon the George of Pistrucci. . . . It is not likely that anybody going out to fight dragons would forget to put on any clothes except a helmet, a cloak and a pair of shoes.'

Major newspapers, too, disliked the designs. The *Daily News* returned to the attack on June 18, writing: 'The new coins compare unfavourably with the old. The natural grace and majesty of the Royal countenance might have been more distinctively brought out, and the little crown perched on the disproportionate head like the apple which William Tell's son was said to have been called upon to stand upon his head provokes, as we anticipated, the oddest comments.' Criticizing the brassiness of the £2 coin, its similarity in size and weight to the silver florin, and the absence of denominations, the *Daily*

News concluded that, 'It is quite possible that a cry will arise for the withdrawal of the new coins.'

In the midst of a growing storm of criticism, G. J. Goschen, Chancellor of the Exchequer, who was answerable in the House of Commons for the activities of the Mint, found himself called upon to account for the new coins. Mr. W. L. Bright, a Liberal M.P., asked whether the general dissatisfaction would not cause the dies to be altered; Hugh Childers, a former Liberal Home Secretary, suggested that denominations ought to be added; and Sir John Lubbock, M.P. for London University, indicated that some attempt would have to be made to distinguish between the sixpence and the half sovereign, which were identical in size and liable to be confused. What had Mr. Goschen to say?

The Chancellor of the Exchequer claimed that there had been less criticism than members thought about any practical difficulties with the coins, which had been designed with 'artistic' considerations in mind. 'There had been a great controversy,' he said, 'between the numismatists, or lovers of coins, and the more practical persons who passed the coins from hand to hand. . . . It was a matter in which there was a conflict of authority; but the Mint would be extremely reluctant to abandon the design.'

A conflict of authority between numismatists and practical individuals was rubbish, said Barclay Head, Keeper of the Department of Coins and Medals of the British Museum and Hon. Secretary of the Numismatic Society, who in the *Daily News* promptly rejected Goschen's argument. 'As Secretary of the Numismatic Society, I may perhaps be allowed to correct the Chancellor of the Exchequer in this particular, for I can assure him that the new coinage has given very general dissatisfaction to the members of the Council of the Numismatic Society. Some of the new designs were severely criticized by the President of the Society in his Annual Address, delivered before the General Meeting last week, in the course of which he expressed his regret that the Council of the Society had not been communicated with by the authorities before the choice of the new types.'

Asked again about the matter in the House of Commons, Goschen said that as the Mint was unable to meet public demand for the new coins, there was obviously some misunderstanding in the House about how popular they were. The *Standard* on June 29 dismissed this argument. 'The idea has been very prevalent that its quantity will be extremely limited. Hence the rush to get specimens while they might be had. With regard to the five-pound pieces, for which silly people have been paying large premiums, the statement has been deliberately put about that no more would be struck, and it was this rumour that raised the price.'

Whatever the reason (and the likeliest is that the public valued the coins as jubilee keepsakes), there was quite a run on the new coinage. Mint employees were paid overtime for work brought on by the continuing demand. But popularity with souvenir hunters in no way appeased those who thought the coins presented severe practical problems. Criticism focused on the sixpence, which, being the same size as the half sovereign and bearing no marked denomination, offered tempting opportunities for fraud. As 'Branch Manager' wrote in *The Times* on June 22, 'I think it is a great blunder that the new sixpence should be precisely the same in size and pattern as the new half-sovereign and that it bears no indication of value. It will be very easy to gild these coins and pass them through banks for half-sovereigns.' In the autumn, Goschen at last withdrew the jubilee sixpence and ordered a new coin to be circulated with its value clearly marked.

As soon as this change became known, Goschen and his deputies were subjected to all manner of advice about how all the other coins should be redesigned, too. A certain Mr. MacGeorge in December wrote to Fremantle pointing out errors in the arms of Scotland as portrayed on the new florin. 'The lion rampant, as you are aware, is not peculiar to Scotland,' he wrote. 'What constitutes the distinctive peculiarity of the arms of that kingdom is that the lion is represented within a *double tressure* floré and counter floré. But on the new Florin the lion appears within a *single tressure* only. What appears on the coins, therefore, *is not the arms of Scotland*. . . . This is a very serious error.'

'If you will look closely at the Scottish shield on the new Florin,' Fremantle two months later rejoined, 'you will observe that the tressure is really double, but it will no doubt be

9 (a) Lord Skelmersdale, 1877

(b) Colonel Henry Ponsonby, 1861

10 (a) Arthur, Duke of Connaught, 1887

10 (b) Lord Esher, 1907

11 (a) The Queen's Diamond Jubilee procession enters
     Pall Mall from St. James's Street

11 (b) Arrival at St Paul's

12 (a) The Queen drives out during the celebrations

12 (b) Illumination of the Fleet, Spithead

The death of the Queen:

Embarkation at Cowes

) The cortège at Windsor

14 The procession leaves Buckingham Palace

15 Royal mourners at Paddington Station

The funeral service in St. George's Chapel, Windsor

desirable to put the lines farther apart, and this will be done in future dies.' By return of post, Mr. MacGeorge tartly replied, 'I was quite aware that there were two *lines* surrounding the lion. But unfortunately it takes two lines to make a single tressure. . . . You say the correction will be made "in future dies" but I trust no more coins will be struck from the present die. It is wrong. The arms of Scotland are not represented at all. And the matter is important. There is nothing, I think, more essentially a question of State, nothing *more* clearly affecting the dignity of a great nation than the heraldic accuracy of its flag and its coinage.'

Critics of the Queen's effigy had more success than Mr. MacGeorge, for it was generally recognized that it was a poor piece of work. As Edward Poynter, R.A., said in July, opening an exhibition of student art work in South Kensington, 'Making all allowance for the necessity of pleasing an illustrious patron, that may have led Mr. Boehm to accept such structural absurdities as the toy crown and the straight veil, it was difficult to believe that a sculptor of his eminence should have turned out such a thoroughly bad work.'

Poynter was mistaken in supposing that Boehm had pleased his 'illustrious patron', for although he was the Queen's favourite sculptor, she was as dissatisfied as everybody else with this example of his work. As she told Goschen in June, 1888, after inspecting the proposed design for another effigy. 'She thinks this new design greatly preferable to the one struck last year, especially as to the size, for the other head was much too small.' She was not, however, ready to approve this design. 'She regrets the Crown not being on the head. As regards the likeness the underlip projects too much and the chin though correct in shape is slightly too short and the eye is not good. It lacks the beauty of workmanship of the original coin.'

But what Victoria really objected to was the fact that her imperial title had not been included on the proposed coin. She disingenuously chose to assume that this oversight could be rectified by juggling her other titles around to make space. 'Then she *must* insist on the Imp. being added before D.F. [Defender of the Faith]' she told her Chancellor of the Exchequer. 'Really there is room for one of her proudest titles while the D.F. is really a most unnecessary one having been given to Henry VIII by the Pope. There is plenty of room for Imp. as well as Reg. and D.F. and the Queen *must insist* on it.'

As both the Queen and Goschen knew, of course, the matter had nothing to do with space. Adding the imperial title to the British coinage might be attacked as an evasion of the statute which prohibited its use in the United Kingdom; Goschen wisely refused to come to any decision at this time. Instead, in March 1891, he appointed a committee to reconsider the design of the jubilee coinage, to include Sir Frederick Leighton, President of the Royal Academy; David Powell, Deputy Governor of the Bank of England; John Evans, President of the Numismatic Society of London; Richard Wade, Chairman of the National Provincial Bank; and Fremantle himself. It was, in short, just the sort of representative group that should have been called initially but in jubilee matters so seldom was.

Determined to ensure that the new coinage would be popular, the committee, instead of engaging a designer on their own responsibility, held a competition in which several eminent artists including Hamo Thorneycroft and Edward Poynter were invited to submit designs. Thomas Brock, R.A., was the winner.

The double florin was dropped from the new coinage, and the florin had its dimensions changed to become more distinctive. Although denominations were not included on the gold coins, it being thought that those who handled such amounts would be acute enough to tell the difference between them, all the silver coins were carefully stamped with their values. None of the new jubilee coinage designs was retained, although the celebrated reverse by Pistrucci remained on the gold coinage.

As for Victoria, her insistence upon the inclusion of her imperial title resulted at last in the gratifaction of her wish. As the committee's report stated, in an abbreviated form 'Indiae Imperatrix' was added to the coinage; this had been done, it said without comment, at the 'request of the Chancellor of the Exchequer.' If it was not the full recognition of her title that Victoria always desired, it was a mark of distinction she wished to have, and she valued it accordingly.

* * *

The Queen, of course, was not the only one who wanted to be honoured in 1887. As George Taubman Goldie, founder of the Royal Niger Company, wrote to Lord Lathom, 'Every one all over British territory expects to secure some honour on the occasion of the Jubilee. . . .' Goldie himself was no exception. Although Lathom had nothing to do with the selection of those who were to receive honours, Goldie contacted him in the hope that the Lord Chamberlain, who seems to have been an acquaintance, could be induced to lobby the Prime Minister on his behalf. It is hard to imagine Lathom broaching the subject with Salisbury; however, he did send Goldie's letter along. Given the fact that the then deputy governor of the Royal Niger Company did in fact receive a jubilee K.C.M.G., Salisbury may have been influenced by Lathom; if so, Goldie was luckier than most.

In fact, the Prime Minister found the entire business of honours, which took up a good deal of his time, both bothersome and distasteful. Indeed, Lord Salisbury was appalled at the persistence of individuals who wanted to be recommended to the Queen. Though Salisbury wished to maintain so far as was possible the select and meritorious arrangement inaugurated by Sir Robert Peel early in the reign, he found, gallingly enough, that political vicissitudes generally made it impossible to dismiss such wheedlers out of hand, as he would have liked to do.

The problem began with the spread of empire, for it was thought an imperial power needed imperial honours. The Most Exalted Order of the Star of India, although created in 1861 and enlarged in 1866, did not become full-blown with all the various classes of knights and companions until the Indian empire was proclaimed in 1876. A mere two years later, the Most Eminent Order of the Indian Empire was created, because it was felt one knightly order would not be sufficient to meet the demands of subcontinental worthies.

Once orders pertaining to India had been established, of course, it would have been thought invidious if nothing equal were available for individuals connected with the colonies. It was debated whether an entirely new order should be established for this purpose, but in the end it was decided to make use of the Most Distinguished Order of Saint Michael and Saint George—

at one time restricted to the reward of citizens of the Ionian islands. In 1877, it was enlarged to permit the Foreign Secretary to make nominations from throughout the colonies.

Once the process of augmenting the honours had begun, it became more difficult to hold the line, for the more people who had them, the more wanted them. Henceforward there was continuing pressure both to increase the number of places in the existing orders and to create new awards altogether. During the year 1886 both eventualities occurred.

In September, the Distinguished Service Order was created, a new award which to those who discerned a cheapening of the honours system had disquieting features about it. Designed to recognize military valour, it differed from other such awards, because its holder was accorded precedence among the knightly orders, coming just after members of the Royal Victorian Order. Begun without knights, which it may have been thought could later be added, its membership at the beginning was restricted to companions only. Significantly, however, and unlike any of the other orders, there was no limit to the number of individuals who could be granted this distinction. On November 11, the *Daily News* grumbled, 'It is difficult to see why we need a new order; but perhaps those who are nearer the fountain of honour know best.' In a rare display of concurrence the *Daily Telegraph* agreed, writing, 'To the civilian such an enamelled cross as that which is to deck the breasts of the Companions of the new Order is a useless gewgaw.'

Not only was this new honour added during the year, but as a result of the Colonial and Indian Exhibition a sizeable increase was made to the colonial order of St. Michael and St. George. This was done to gratify the Prince of Wales, who himself assiduously lobbied Mr. Gladstone, then Prime Minister, for favours for his friends. As the Prince's biographer, Sir Sidney Lee, genteely put it, 'During the summer he importuned the Prime Minister with more than usual pertinacity for titular honours on behalf of his numerous co-workers. . . .' While Gladstone was willing to go so far as to leave the order of St. Michael and St. George bloated, he did not yield to the Prince's desire to do the same with the Most Honourable Order of the Bath. He also refused Bertie's desire to have Sir John Rose, one of the commissioners of the exhibition, made a peer.

In ordinary circumstances the 'extra' members of the Order of St. Michael and St. George, although taking their titles immediately, would have had a long time to wait for attrition among the regular members before they could occupy one of the enumerated places. The convening of the first colonial conference in 1887 and the golden jubilee made this impossible, and in March, 1887, Lord Salisbury reluctantly had to recommend an increase in the number of knights and companions in the colonial order. This followed hard on the heels of an enlargement of the Order of the Indian Empire which was extended to permit the designation of knights grand cross and knights commander in time for the celebration of the Queen's jubilee in India. Between these two orders just under three hundred new titles of knighthood had been created. While in practice some gentlemen might hold places in two orders, or rarely in three, and while some might hold hereditary honours, it was nonetheless a substantial increase.

More distressing to the Prime Minister, what was occurring with the knightly orders was also taking place with regard to the hereditary honours. Here the unstable political situation was leaving its mark. By the 1880s, it was established practice that upon a dissolution of parliament or upon a change of ministry, the Prime Minister was permitted to draw up an honours list composed mainly of hereditary honours and knighthoods. Throughout the halcyon period of mid-Victorian stability, when governments were assured of their parliamentary majorities and held long tenure, this practice was unexceptionable. Thus, with only three ministries between 1868 and 1885, there were only three gazettes of honours. Between 1885 and 1886, however, there were again three ministries, each producing its honours list; in addition, there was that special list gazetted in 1886 at the conclusion of the Colinderies exhibition. Realizing that the impending golden jubilee would inevitably bring demands for still further honours, advocates of the small and select system were rightly alarmed. The *Standard* reported in February, 'There will be a Jubilee Gazette of honours, and, indeed, rumours are abroad that it is likely to be a tolerably exhaustive one. . . .' Lord Salisbury, of course, was working to keep it more tolerable than exhaustive, but his problems were manifold, for the old certainties about what kind of people ought to receive honours were no longer clear cut. Ironically enough, it was Salisbury himself who had unwittingly helped to blur them.

When Lord Salisbury's 'Caretaker' administration went out in January, 1886, the Prime Minister recommended that Sir Henry Allsopp and Sir Charles Mills be elevated to the peerage, and in due course they were, taking the titles Baron Hindlip and Baron Hillingdon respectively. The *Daily News*, as was only to be expected, complained. On February 6 it wrote, 'There are not two less distinguished men in the country.... But they are rich. They have spent money in the Conservative cause, and so they and their descendants are for an indefinite time to legislate for this unhappy country.' In a general way the *Standard* concurred bemoaning 'the frequency with which these distinctions have recently been bestowed.... That honours of every kind have been a good deal cheapened of late years is beyond dispute and denial.'

Superficially the two newest peers had the conventional claims for consideration. Both had succeeded their fathers as baronets; both had served as Tory M.P.s. The *Daily News* might have dubbed them Tweedledum and Tweedledee peers. More significantly, however, both were active businessmen in the City of London, Hindlip as a partner in the brewing firm of Allsopp & Sons and deputy chairman of the Great Northern Railway, while Hillingdon was on the board of the London banking firm of Glyn, Mills & Company. Between 1876 and 1886, only four commercial or industrial peerages had been created; in the next decade, there were no fewer than eighteen starting with Lords Hindlip and Hillingdon.

What was happening?

One reason why such men had now to be considered was that they had money, which in the changing circumstances of the 1880s political parties needed. To begin with, a Corrupt Practices Act had been passed in 1883 which limited local expenditure on elections and made it necessary for the central party organizations to increase their spending on national promotion. Additionally, the increase in the number of constituencies under the Reform Act of 1885 increased the parties' need for money. Finally, there were simply more elections and more contested elections during this period than there had been previously.

Devotedly partisan as these heavy contributors may have been, few of them parted with their money without the expectation that they would be rewarded in some fashion; for many, an honour was reckoned to be suitable recompense. Between 1870 and 1885, 58 new peerages were created; in 1885–86 alone 25 were added. In 1887, another nine followed, with baronetcies following the same inflated course.

Rich men from commerce and industry were not the only ones applying pressure to change the traditional honours system; leading members of the professions joined in attempting to overthrow the virtual monopoly of honours enjoyed by royalty, the landed classes, government, civil service and the forces. By the 1880s the medical profession was clamouring for its share and was supported by many leading organs of opinion. *Punch* was one of them, with Mr. Punch early in 1886 saying, 'I wish Her Most Gracious Majesty would . . . be pleased to award some special recognition to meritorious medical men. Distinguishing titles would not be bad things, such as the Marquis of Magnesia. . . .' By the time of the jubilee, medical opinion was supremely confident that it was at last about to be recognized in a major fashion.

At the same time others were working for enhanced recognition of individuals distinguished in art and literature. Every now and then during the reign a leading writer such as Lord Tennyson or painters like Sir John Millais or Sir Frederick Leighton were honoured, but as the scientific periodical *Nature* wrote in June, 1887, 'Literature and science, and we might add art, have no access to the Throne.'

To improve matters and systematize them, Sir James Linton, President of the Royal Institution of Artists in Water Colours, conceived the idea of a new order to be called The Rose, a full-blown affair of knights and companions, which Linton thought might be opened to ladies, too. The *Daily News* got wind of the idea in December, 1886, and the *Court Journal* endorsed it on New Year's Day, but it was not until January 20 that Linton wrote to Princess Beatrice to see whether the Queen's youngest daughter would intercede with her mother.

Victoria seems to have smiled on the notion; predictably, Lord Salisbury did not. Not only was he opposed to any increase in the number of decorations, even though these were to be personal, but he doubted the wisdom of establishing a special order for artists. Wouldn't other groups then feel that they had cause for consideration, too? Nonetheless the Prime Minister's first response was diplomatically understated. 'Ld Salisbury does not think idea quite practicable as suggested but is open to conviction.'

By March matters had not advanced; indeed a letter Salisbury had just sent to the Queen was interpreted at Windsor as indicating that the Cabinet disapproved the idea of the order. In response Ponsonby wrote that the Queen wanted Sir Frederick Leighton and other leading artists to be consulted on the matter. He also gently added, 'The Queen hopes you do not mean that the Cabinet are opposed to the idea, but rather that there are other more important questions that must postpone the consideration of this one.' This, however, does not seem to be what Salisbury meant, for the matter progressed no farther and by Jubilee day was a dead letter.

Although Salisbury dispensed with the matter of The Rose without difficulty, he could not so easily deal with the other jubilee honours, which were proving very provoking indeed. In May while forwarding some suggestions from Benjamin Jowitt, Master of Balliol College, Oxford ('Would it not be well and inexpensive [and] greatly conduce to the popularity of the govt . . . to shower freely knighthoods and baronetcies on literary & scientific men?'), Goschen had commiserated with Lord Salisbury: 'When is the "honour" correspondence to end? It is frightful. . . . How fearfully foolish men are about honours.'

Salisbury tried to have as little as possible to do with knighthoods and knightly orders, leaving them, as far as he could, to be taken care of by responsible ministers or service heads, who followed their own rough rules of thumb in considering inclusion and promotion and, knowing the Prime Minister's disposition in the matter, tried to keep the number of recommendations as small as possible. But with the best will in the world those involved in drawing up the English jubilee list found that they could not squeeze all they wished to be accommodated into the existing vacancies. As a result, the Order of St. Michael and St. George was permanently enlarged, and even the Order of the Bath was to be increased. The question, of course, was by how much?

In March, Edward Stanhope at the War Office sent Lord Salisbury what seems to be the only existing detailed memorandum on appointments to the knightly orders; it deals exclusively with the Order of the Bath. Stanhope probably rightly assumed that Salisbury knew nothing about it. There were then vacant, he wrote, in the order's military division 4 grand crosses; 10 knighthoods; and 42 companionships, mostly in the navy. On the civil side, there was only one G.C.B. available, 2 K.C.B.s and 9 C.B.s. Stanhope proposed that 5 military and 2 civil grand crosses be added; 11 military and 6 civil knighthoods, and 28 military and 10 civil companionships. Because Salisbury was perfectly prepared to follow reasonable advice when he found it in the matter of honours, Stanhope's memorandum was adopted almost without change. When he wrote to the Queen on the matter on May 11, the Prime Minister only added 4 companionships to the civil side.

Why Salisbury found it necessary to add the extra companions is not clear; perhaps to keep the proportion at roughly two to one between the military and civil divisions. It was certainly not because he was interested in who got them. On June 2, he sent his secretary Manners a note: 'Can you explain to me who are the persons of whom I [have] given a list over-leaf & who are down in my book for C.B. I have not a notion who they are.'

The only intended C.B. brought especially to the Prime Minister's attention was the one earmarked for the second Earl of Iddesleigh, deputy chairman of Inland Revenue. Iddesleigh's father, who had been well known in Conservative circles as Sir Stafford Northcote, had been pushed from his place as Foreign Secretary at the beginning of the year in the reshuffle of the Cabinet following the resignation of Lord Randolph Churchill. Despite his long service to the party and high position, Iddesleigh had learned of his 'resignation' in the press; almost immediately afterwards, he had died in the anteroom of Salisbury's office while waiting to see the Prime Minister, who had himself assumed the earl's place. There had been unpleasant mutterings in some quarters that the old man had been ill-used. Perhaps to lay some of the bad feeling to rest, Goschen, who as Chancellor of the Exchequer was Iddesleigh's official superior, pressed for his decoration, telling Salisbury on April 7 he felt 'very anxious' on this matter. More than a month later, Alfred Milner, Goschen's secretary, wrote to the Prime Minister's secretary that 'Iddesleigh stands on special grounds.' In no other case did Goschen press so hard, and in the event Iddesleigh got the C.B.

It was not G. J. Goschen, though, who had the greatest influence with Lord Salisbury in the matter of honours, but William Neville, first Marquess of Abergavenny.

Born in 1826, son of the fourth Earl of Abergavenny, Neville had had a long career as a backstage political operator, working up to the important position of Disraeli's principal party manager. Abergavenny's was a shadowy, elusive power, which he necessarily kept as ill-defined as possible. As Eric, Lord Chilston has written in his biography of Aretas Akers-Douglas, *Chief Whip*, 'Abergavenny's influence was potent but unseen....'

In the spring of 1887, Abergavenny sent Salisbury a long, undated memorandum suggesting suitable Conservative candidates for jubilee honours. In it, he put forward the names of four gentlemen who should be considered for peerages; two peers who might be promoted; ten names for baronetcies; and two for knighthoods. On April 14, he followed up his original memorandum with a further short note in the interests of his protégé, Aretas Akers-Douglas, who had been chief conservative whip since 1885: 'Then *last* but *not least*, all our friends in & out of Parliament would like to see Akers-Douglas a P.C. [Privy Councillor]. He is one of the best, if not quite the best & most popular Whips either side ever had.'

In urging these names, Abergavenny generally concentrated on two considerations: their party services and ability to maintain the honour. Thus, as he pointed out to Salisbury in recommending Samuel Cunliffe-Lister, High Sheriff for Yorkshire, for a baronetcy, this man was not only the 'largest employer of labour in the county' and had laid out over £800,000 in the purchase of land but also had fought several losing election contests in the West Riding. Abergavenny also put forward the name of Sir Algernon Borthwick for a baronetcy.

Borthwick, proprietor of the Conservative newspaper the *Morning Post*, had been grumbling for some time that his strong support for the party, both in the House of Commons, where he served as member for South Kensington, but more importantly in his publication, had gone unrecognized. On

June 11, he sent a letter to his colleague Andrew Montagu, writing, 'I may say, I have been a very loyal and powerful supporter. But there [is] a limit to what a man will stand. . . . I care little for honours in themselves, but I certainly feel being the only man whose services have been absolutely unacknowledged.'

Montagu duly sent this overstated letter along to Lord Salisbury, as he was no doubt intended to do, but Abergavenny had already acquainted the Prime Minister with Borthwick's complaint. 'I can't help thinking it would be *good policy* to offer him a Baronetcy,' he concluded.

In the event, both Borthwick and Cunliffe-Lister received their awards. Having got what he wanted, Borthwick's tone changed considerably. On jubilee day, he wrote to Salisbury 'that the recommendation to Her Majesty should have come from a Statesman so illustrious as yourself is most flattering' and promised 'that in the Future, as in the Past, my earnest service will be given to the great constitutional cause.'

Cunliffe-Lister, however, was less pleased with his baronetcy. Indeed, he had refused it when it was offered and was appalled when he found it published on jubilee day. Four years later he finally received the peerage he really wanted, becoming the first Baron Masham.

Of the other recommendations made by Lord Abergavenny, eight received honours, though H. W. Eaton, M.P. for Coventry, whom the marquess had suggested for a baronetcy, received a peerage instead. Why? Sir Edward Hamilton, that astute observer, recorded that the talk in clubland was that Eaton had helped the impecunious Tecks out of financial difficulties and so established a claim on the Royal Family. Like Abergavenny, however, Hamilton thought a baronetcy would have been 'ample.' It would also have been more convenient for the ministry, since the by-election which followed his elevation to the peerage as Baron Cheylesmore resulted in a Liberal victory.

More of Abergavenny's recommendations might have been accepted had not Lord Salisbury been rightly reluctant to risk losing other seats to the Liberals. Both the Prime Minister and Lord Hartington, who suggested the names of Liberal Unionists for consideration, had good reason to be careful of which

M.P.s were advanced. Between the end of January and mid-May, there were 6 by-elections. Before these elections, each party had held three seats; afterwards the Liberals held four and showed a substantially improved margin in a fifth.

In the end, five M.P.s were given peerages: four Tories and one Liberal Unionist. Both Lord Salisbury and Victoria were worried about how the ensuing by-elections would turn out, and on July 16 Victoria expressed her anxieties to the Prime Minister. 'The Queen appd the last Peers with regret as she fears that there may be more trouble with the elections but hopes Ld Salisbury hears favourable accounts.' He did not. Before another six weeks had elapsed, the Liberals had won two more Tory seats and were cock-a-hoop about their further chances for gain. Gladstone, sensing Micawber-like that something was turning up, wrote a jubilant article on 'The Electoral Facts on 1887' in the September issue of *Nineteenth Century*. 'The rational Tory, and still more any Dissentient who may be inclined to the practice of forecast, will probably regard the results as of very marked significance. They may even begin to ask themselves in a reflective temper, *where is all this to end?*' The correct answer to Gladstone's significant query was that it ended in a love nest in Eltham. For there Charles Stewart Parnell, the Irish leader, and the winsome Kitty O'Shea were carrying on the notorious liaison which would shatter so many Home Rule hopes. That convulsive fact would twist Gladstone's insistent question into irony, but it was left to be discovered later.

Although the jubilee honours published in the finest print took up three and a half columns in *The Times*, most of the rest of them were routine: mayoral knighthoods and dozens of naval and military awards and promotions. Only one other group commanded Lord Salisbury's attention. On May 11, the Queen after one of several meetings with her Prime Minister on the subject, recorded, 'Saw Ld Salisbury, & talked a good deal about the Jubilee & the honours for my Relations & other people, about which he was most kind. But there are great difficulties about many.' So, indeed, there were.

Royalties, living in an atmosphere much regulated by gradations in rank and precedence, are as prone as lesser men to look favourably upon stars and ribands. No one knew this better than Queen Victoria, who with her 'royal mob' of relations and princely connections continually found herself subject to wheedling advances. Upon the occasion of her jubilee, everyone had a request for Victoria. The Princess of Wales wrote a characteristic letter in June on behalf of her physician, Sir Oscar Clayton, who had treated her for diphtheria the year before. 'I have *one* petition at heart,' she wrote, 'which I really beg you to grant for my sake. It is for poor little Clayton I plead who really did save my life last year, when he was totally ignored & badly treated because he was forbidden to say what was really the matter with me. . . . So please dearest mama do kindly grant my request & make this poor little man happy. . . . Even the smallest thing like C.M.G. wd delight him.' He got 'the smallest thing.'[1]

On June 5, Victoria's nephew, Ernest, Prince of Leiningen, who had been captain of the royal yacht, wrote with a request so close to his heart 'I have never mentioned it to any body, *not even* Marie' (his wife). He wanted his civil G.C.B. turned into a military one. He had, as he pointed out, seen 'plenty of active work in my younger days,' unlike certain other admirals like Sir G. Phipps Hornby, 'our so-called "only admiral",' who had 'never seen a shot fired.'[2] As Ponsonby told the Queen, the Prince of Wales was championing his cousin Ernest's request.

The Prince's adoption of Leiningen's cause may well have prejudiced whatever chance it had; in any event, like the rest of Bertie's suggestions, it was turned down. As Ponsonby told the Queen on June 6, 'Lord Salisbury was not prepared to recommend that any of the names suggested by the Prince of Wales should be submitted for honours.'[3] Unlike Gladstone, whom the Prince could influence and who in 1886 had been persuaded to recommend many royal associates for honours, Salisbury found no reason to gratify the wishes of a man he held in scant regard.

Yet another relation was particularly exigent, the Queen's cousin by marriage, Francis, Duke of Teck. The great tragedy of the Duke's life was that his father, heir to the King of Wurttemberg, had thrown away his rights to the succession to contract a morganatic marriage with a beguiling Hungarian charmer. As a result, Francis was a mere serene highness. This fact mattered not a whit to Queen Victoria, who felt he had been unjustly deprived of his rights, nor to Princess Mary of Cambridge, who, both ageing and rotund, thought herself lucky to marry the penniless but handsome Teck. However, the stain of his birth distressed the duke, who spent his life lamenting his blighted fortune and preening himself on looks which were never so good as they had been. On the occasion of the jubilee, he set out to do what he could about rectifying the first of these matters.

The Tecks were never shy about asking Queen Victoria for favours, but in this case they were most pressing. In May Ponsonby learnt of the matter, telling the Queen that Teck would like to be gazetted an English 'highness,' but if this were impossible, could she make him a general instead? The Duchess of Teck, he added, had asked that her children should be similarly advanced.

On May 13, the Queen brought the matter to Lord Salisbury's attention recommending that the duke's request be granted. 'It cd hurt no one,' she told him. However, it was to be made personal to Francis himself and could not therefore be passed on to his children. The Queen was insistent on this point, for to make the distinction hereditary, as she could have done, would allow the younger Tecks equal rank with the children of the Queen's own daughters Princess Christian and Princess Henry of Battenberg, both of whom had married princes of lesser standing than themselves. Whether the Queen's good deed made the tiresome Duke of Teck happy is doubtful, because such patents of higher rank generally went unrecognized by punctilious continental courts, as Henry Battenberg had already learned. Later, to gratify his wife Queen Mary, who was the Duke of Teck's only daughter, King George V raised her brother, the second duke, to the same exalted degree.

In addition to these matters, the Queen had also to decide what other honours she herself would distribute to mark her jubilee. In May she determined she would give no decoration higher than the Grand Cross of the Bath and would give this award solely to princes who were related. One grandson was to have it, three grandsons-in-law and two cousins, one of whom was the Crown Prince of Austria, with whom Victoria claimed a tenuous relationship, because he had married her cousin, Stefanie of Belgium.

Unfortunately, Lord Salisbury did not approve the Queen's decision. At the moment, he was working hard drawing up the Mediterranean Agreements in which Austrian participation was important. He therefore persuaded a reluctant Queen that it was in Britain's best interests to treat the heir to the Austrian throne with distinction; Prince Rudolph, he said, must have the Garter.

In acquiescing to Salisbury's request, Queen Victoria let it be known her agreement would be based on one condition: the bestowal would not be considered a precedent for the award of other imperial heirs. She meant, of course, the Tsarevitch. Anxious to express her displeasure with the treatment accorded by the Tsar to Prince Alexander of Bulgaria ('dear Sandro'), Victoria wished to withhold the Garter from the future Nicholas II. Although Lord Salisbury was at work to defuse Britain's tense relationship with Russia, he wisely said nothing. After all, the Tsar's representative to the jubilee, the Grand Duke Serge, as a grandson-in-law, would be getting the G.C.B., the highest British decoration he could ever expect. Moreover, the Prime Minister was certain that when he needed the Garter for 'Nicki,' he could persuade the Queen to be reasonable. Which is just what happened.

One other honorary Grand Cross of the Bath went to the Khedive of Egypt, an important figure who it was felt ought to be conciliated. In this case, the Queen made no attempt to prove the dusky ruler a relation.

As far as her own staff went, the aged Colonel Maude and the up-and-coming Fleetwood Edwards were both granted knighthoods, and Sir John Cowell was made a privy councillor. The Queen wished Ponsonby to have the only civil G.C.B. she proposed to give. Ponsonby, however, wanted to decline it. On the last day of May he told Salisbury, 'To speak plainly, I don't want the G.C.B. But of course I can't say so to H.M.' Not only was he averse to accepting honours, but he felt his acceptance would place him in an awkward position with other members of the Household whose claims for consideration he had consistently declined to advance to the Queen. Since Victoria was not to be denied, Ponsonby, however unwillingly, found himself promoted to the dignity of a Knight Grand Cross of the Bath.

When at last the honours list had laboriously been pieced together, the Prime Minister wrote to W. H. Smith, 'I feel so convinced of the universal execration with which the list of honours . . . will be received, that I think it will be best not to publish it till the very day of the Jubilee. Otherwise, the wrath of the undecorated might imperil the Crime Bill.' Salisbury's instinct proved correct.

Truth had a field day with the new honours. 'The list of Peerages is an admirable one,' it wrote. 'With the exception of Sir George Armstrong [a Liberal Unionist armaments manufacturer] there is no man of any note in it.' It also noted that 'Mr. Eaton's Peerage has created the most surprise, because, although long an M.P., he has only been remarkable as a legislator on account of the glossiness of his hat and the excellent cut of his coat.' The *Daily News* joined in, 'Lord Salisbury has not often displayed more openly his contempt for everything and everybody, especially the Queen and the House of Lords. . . . None [of the new peers] except Lord Armstrong enjoy any personal distinction. . . .'

Less partisan opinion was also disgruntled. The *British Medical Journal* was crestfallen at discovering that the profession's high expectations had in no way been met. 'The list of Jubilee honours,' it wrote, 'has altogether fallen rather flat . . . it is not calculated to produce much sensation in the medical profession.'

To do him justice, Lord Salisbury had tried to forestall such criticism by proposing to the Queen that Sir William Jenner, her physician, be advanced to a G.C.B., but Victoria would not hear of it. On June 9, she tartly informed him, 'Since 72 or rather 71 he has done nothing remarkable for the Queen & our family & indeed *positively refused* to attend her in Scotland or abroad since 79.' Not only that, which really ought to have been sufficient, but also, 'No physician has ever been made a G.C.B. & the Queen owns she thinks it too much.'

All in all, there was so much criticism of the honours list that the rumour arose that it would be reopened—a rumour which gained greater currency when in August a new gazette of honours was published for Ireland. Why Ireland was neglected in the original list is by no means clear, but as a certain Mr. de Vesci in July told Alfred Milner, who passed the information to

Arthur Balfour who passed it to Lord Salisbury, 'I think it would be inconceivably stupid to neglect Ireland.' When the Lord Lieutenant, the sixth Marquess of Londonderry, complained to Balfour in the same sense, a strong Loyalist list was drawn up, a list endorsed without enthusiasm by Victoria. As Ponsonby wrote to Lord Salisbury on July 30, 'The Queen thinks this a large number of knights for Ireland but if you consider them necessary Her Majesty will agree.'

Predictably, Lord Salisbury had no intention of reopening the honours list. The fact that many who had been disappointed of a more substantial honour received a jubilee medal may have helped him resist doing so. This medal, designed by Empmeyer as a commemoration of the occasion, was struck in gold for the Queen's family and her royal guests, in silver for members of the Queen's Household, officers commanding the guards of honour along the parade route and the naval officers commanding ships reviewed at Spithead, and in bronze for just about anyone. Sir Fleetwood Edwards wrote to Ponsonby-Fane that the housekeepers at St. James's Palace should have it. 'Will you kindly hold an investiture?' he asked.

The Queen had characteristically opinionated views about the importance of the medal and ordered that it should rank above all war decorations. This brought criticism from those who had won their honours in more audacious ways than by attending the jubilee, but to those without much field service, it allowed the pleasurable experience of appearing bemedalled at Court.

Once conferred, of course, the Queen wanted the medal to be worn—a command which gave the Archbishop of Canterbury pause. 'I rather suspect,' he wrote in his diary, 'it is the first time that an Abp. has worn a decoration and I am not sure that he ought.' Yet like its more than a thousand other recipients, his grace did so, though no doubt more sheepishly than the rest.

Throughout jubilee summer there were continual sallies about honours. Sir Charles Warren pressed the claim for consideration of the London police who had worked extra hours throughout the affair. On June 24 the *Daily Telegraph* endorsed the idea. In the end his men received the jubilee medal and the grant was again extended when the City of London police managed to get themselves included. Ultimately, some 14,000 bronze medals were distributed. Later, certain members of the Home Office were chagrined to discover that clerks in the Metropolitan Police had also been included, although on jubilee day they had been on holiday.

So long as there were honours, of course, there had been intrigues and strategems to get them, but the kind of pestering which went on at the time of the jubilee was new in its brash insistence. The late Victorians had become star-struck; there was a real craze for honours.

Refused, an honour caused dissatisfaction; granted, it was seldom thought sufficient. In both cases, it was the catalyst for a volatile reaction producing umbrage, resentment and indignation. In the circumstances, it is no wonder Salisbury chose to keep the number of individuals touched by this poisonous process as small as possible.

CHAPTER EIGHT

THE ARMED FORCES SALUTE

THE PASSING of jubilee day in no way concluded the celebration, for there were still three great military reviews to take place—and to give more vexation.

The first to be considered was that of the regular forces, and in October, 1886, the first Viscount Wolseley, adjutant general to the forces, contacted Sir Henry Ponsonby and suggested a plan that would 'impress foreign powers with an idea of the vast size and great resources of Her Majesty's Empire.'[1] Twenty to thirty thousand regular troops should be ordered up, ten or twelve thousand militia, fifty thousand volunteers, some battalions of Canadian militia and assorted representatives from the colonies. It was a grand idea, and it immediately caught the Queen's attention. It would do very well, she said, in May and at Aldershot.

In the event, things did not at all work out along these lines. When the Cabinet was asked to consider this scheme it did so with vast reluctance: there was, it reckoned, far, far too much expense involved in implementing Wolseley's 'splendid idea' (as Ponsonby had called it). And so, it was considerably scaled down—and broken up. There would be two smaller reviews, one of volunteers, the other principally of regular troops.

Although no doubt irritating to Wolseley, who had a taste for grandiose designs, this decision was generally felt to be unexceptional. The regulars would still have their review at Aldershot, the volunteers, they thought, would march past the Queen in Hyde Park, the site of so many past scenes of triumph. 'The right place for the Review,' wrote the *Volunteer Service Gazette* on March 26, 'is the old place—Hyde Park.'

But, alas, this old place was to be denied the volunteers, who were informed that they would have to parade instead on the treacherous and obstacle-studded ground before Buckingham Palace.

Just who made this decision is not clear from the record, but it probably came from officials in either the Home Office or the Office of Works, for they had acted similarly in 1880. Then the volunteers had been forbidden to use Hyde Park because of policing difficulties and the trouble of making convenient arrangements. In any event, this unexpected result left the volunteers both angry and apprehensive, for they had good reason to believe that the complexities of the chosen ground would give the ill-prepared amateur troopers the severest test.

To guard against the worst, the general commanding the Home District was called in to give advice. He did so, but only after two bodies of regular troops had practised on the site to determine which formations, some quite rare, could be used. The *Daily News*, usually a booster of the force, took this occasion to sneer at the volunteers for needing such assistance, saying, 'German soldiers would probably not be greatly vexed or seriously upset by the obstacles nor would they be likely to require any preliminary preparation for a march-past, no matter what obstacles the chosen ground might present.'

Such an opinion could only have added to the gloom of the volunteers who after many slights and much anxiety had generally come to feel that the jubilee had been an unsatisfactory time for them. After all, Edward Stanhope, the Secretary of War, had muddled their preparation for jubilee day by an uncertainty about whether volunteers should be allowed to participate in local celebrations. It was, said the *Volunteer Record*, an example of 'unpardonable bungling and mill-stone thick-headed stupidity' on the part of the War Office and made for a bad start.

Then the favoured volunteer site for the review had not been selected. Then the force that was to be assembled was reduced, both because some troops had been siphoned off to increase the brilliance of the Aldershot review and because others had chosen, curiously enough, to spend time on military manoeuvres instead of on an ornamental march-past. The cumulative effect of these pinpricks had left the volunteer force decidedly testy and towards the end of June the *Volunteer Record* complained that, 'There is one class of Her Majesty's subjects, and that one not the least loyal of all, which has not much to be thankful for . . . in connection with the festal proceedings. It is needless to say that this is the class which embraces the long suffering members of the citizen army.'

Only one thing was left to increase their dismay, and it, too, occurred. Days before the event was to take place, the review's time was pushed ahead to 2.30, an hour on a Saturday afternoon when many volunteers would still be working. And so, the *Volunteer Record* moaned, another 6,000 men were lost to the march-past, leaving the newspaper stoical, at best, about what was to take place.

What actually happened on July 2, however, defied any expectation of ineptitude and embarrassment to the consternation of every doomsayer and the delight of every fretful volunteer.

The 24,000 volunteers gathered without incident and did successfully what had not been expected of them. The early units wheeled without a hitch at the saluting base after entering from the Mall into Green Park and got away in good order despite the trees and lamp-posts, so that the movement of the troops in the rear was not checked. They broke into double time when required and kept at it for a considerable distance without flagging; formed fours correctly when ordered and wheeled left and right when expected. Their performance wrote the previously dubious *Daily News* was a 'distinct and unqualified triumph.' The volunteers, of course, were cock-a-hoop.

Unfortunately the enthusiasm of the *Daily News* was rarely echoed elsewhere, for the general impression was that while the march-past had been all very well it in no way lessened or disguised the dangerous ill-preparedness of the force. 'Gasping self-admiration,' wrote the *Standard*, which was set on volunteer improvement, was utterly out of place. 'The legitimate satisfaction which is felt in some quarters because twenty-four thousand men can be paraded and marched past the Queen, should be moderated by the notorious fact that their training, especially in the work of war, is slight.'

The volunteers, in short, stood on notice that their continued existence would have to be based on something more than a spurious success with what the *Standard* called 'the mere pomp and panoply of glorious war.' The fact that most volunteers had not yet recognized this essential fact of that defensive, troubled time lay at the root of their frustrations and difficulties throughout the jubilee.

It was different with the regular forces, although they were far from immune from criticism, because reviews had never held for them the same importance as they did with the volunteers.

The truth is that the Aldershot review of July 9 was not a very important event, despite the fact that the 60,000 men who took part in it constituted probably the largest body to be reviewed during the reign. So ordinary was it, indeed, that a pruning commission of the Public Records Office had no hesitation some years ago in destroying its organizational file.

It was an occasion distinguished as usual by discomfort, for the Long Valley where the review was held was, in the words of a souvenir booklet, a 'notorious purgatory.' And despite the inspiration of Richard Harrison, commander of engineers, who apparently was the first to have the idea of watering the review field, clouds of dust and small stones were blown alternately into the faces of spectators and troops. Getting away from this scene was not easy either, since the transportation arrangements were notably inadequate.

Still, for most, it was a satisfactory event, although the *Standard*, having marked the scarcity of cavalry and the complete absence of artillery, threw out a cautionary review. 'Until the country insists upon a properly proportioned army, it will be impossible to regard such parades . . . with unmixed satisfaction.' However, the concern of even the *Standard* was fairly perfunctory, for like the general run of Englishmen it cared less about the army than the navy and was much more interested in the impending review of the senior service.

Unlike the other jubilee events, the Spithead naval review was generally organized efficiently and methodically by Admiral Sir George Willes, the commander-in-chief at Portsmouth, who was in charge of its day to day operations. He was assisted by Captain Lord Charles Beresford, the irrepressible Fourth Sea Lord, who may have been Willes' liaison with the Admiralty in London but who in any event never missed an opportunity to ensure the review's usefulness as a naval promotional event. Once it had been decided that the review was to be limited to the reserve, training and channel squadrons of the Home Fleet, no vessels being taken from their foreign duty stations, both Beresford and Willes went to their various work. Beresford pushed to ensure adequate representation of press and influential visitors and took yet another party of M.P.s to the Portsmouth navy yard so that he could persuade fellow lawmakers not to take too seriously all the favourable publicity he expected to generate about the fleet. At the same time, Willes on June 4 began publishing an information bulletin which was despatched to all participants. Over the next weeks it dealt with matters pertaining to naval stores, charts, leave, and visitors in a simple, straightforward way which must have benefited other aspects of the jubilee, too, had anyone thought to implement it.

Unfortunately Willes did not have the same control over the reviewing vessels headed by the royal yacht *Victoria and Albert* as he did over those which were to be reviewed. As a result the careless ways of the Court and the problems resulting from considerations of place and precedence soon made an inevitable appearance. At the request of the Foreign Office, the Admiralty was asked to accommodate two sons of the Duke of Aosta, brother of the King of Italy. For unstated reasons, however, the Duke wished them to maintain the strictest incognito, which meant they could not be placed among the other royal guests. Admiralty officials worried, though, that if the princes did not find their alternative accommodation sufficient, they would complain that they had not been treated with the regard due their rank.

More vexing was the difficulty of knowing what should be done with the Hessan es Sultaneh of Persia. With some difficulty, Lord Salisbury had persuaded him to stay on for the remainder of the jubilee events after the Hessan had threatened to leave because of the snubs to which he had been subjected. Nonetheless, for the review it was decided that he should not be allowed to travel with the other royalties but should be given a place on the vessel carrying the diplomatic corps. Despite his having thus been lowered a notch, it was also decided that the Persian prince should not be given a royal salute, for fear of causing umbrage among his prickly fellow travellers. Just how prickly they were may be surmized from the anxiety which arose at the Admiralty when it was found that the diplomats would have a four minute walk from their special London train to the Portsmouth dockyard. Serious consideration was given to the idea of running them direct to the harbour, but in the end this presented such insuperable traffic problems that the organizers decided to run the risk of diplomatic umbrage.

Less privileged people could be far more easily dealt with. If the Mayor of Portsmouth was causing concern by distributing too many invitations for his Admiralty-provided ship, he could be leaned upon; do so at once, Beresford warned in a minute, 'or he might ask all Hampshire.' More simply, most applicants for places on the reviewing vessels could be advised to look for accommodation on the commercial vessels advertising day trips. Thus when the irrepressible George Potter wrote to the Admiralty to ask for places for members of his London Working Men's Association under the guise of securing representation for labouring men, this was what he was advised to do.

Fortunately for Potter dozens of commercial selections were available. The British Cruising Association chartered the *Bonnie Doon* and offered *de luxe* treatment and champagne at five pounds five, while the vessels of the Southampton and Isle of Wight Steam Packet Company offered the bargain rate of 10*s*.6*d*. for the day. Despite their large numbers, in almost every case these vessels were dealt with on a routine basis: once the review 'field' had been determined, the larger commercial vessels were given their places directly by the Admiralty, and Captain Wharton, the naval hydrographer, issued a set of general regulations for captains of all ships, large or small. In only one instance was there a problem.

The *Great Eastern* was the largest steamship built in the nineteenth century. She was 680 feet long, weighed 23,000 tons and was designed to carry 4,000 passengers. At her launching she was five times the size of any vessel afloat and her construction was heralded as another wonder in a wonderful age. 'Here is a work,' wrote *The Times* on November 4, 1857, 'by the side of which all the achievements of former times would be diminished to nothing.' Difficult to handle, however, the *Great Eastern* proved to be a financial disappointment. By the time of the jubilee review, she was nothing more than a floating exhibition hall on the Mersey, whence Liverpool city officials were working to have her removed. To her owners the review seemed to present a perfect opportunity to weigh anchor and make money elsewhere. They therefore applied to the admiralty for mooring space in the Solent.

Admiral Hood, one of the Lords of the Admiralty, greeted this request with dismay. While other Admiralty officials were no better pleased, they did not see their way to refusing the owners without arousing unnecessary antagonism. However, the permission they reluctantly gave was accompanied by a condition: the *Great Eastern* could come to the review, but she was to be moored far out to sea nowhere near the other large commercial vessels. While she could not, therefore, run afoul of them, her passengers would not see much, either.

In these circumstances, her owners changed their minds. The *Great Eastern* did not go to Spithead, and the decision was taken shortly afterwards to break her up. 'There is an end at last,' *Truth* wrote on December 28, 'of the Great Eastern, whose career has been a long and unbroken series of failures and disasters.' The skeletons of two welders were found in the salvage of the ship, a sort of *memento mori* she had carried since the star-crossed day of her launching.

Basically well organized, the review nonetheless had aspects which reminded contemporaries of the confused preparations for the main part of the jubilee. Its actual date, for instance, gave problems. The first day chosen was picked without consulting the Queen. Thus when she was told about it on March 2 by Lord Salisbury, she noted in her journal that it was a time 'when I could not go down to Portsmouth to see it.' The date to which it was promptly changed, July 23, was to give trouble of another kind.

Incredibly, the Admiralty had selected the day without carefully gauging what the tides would be like. Towards the end of May someone found that they would be running in such a way that no large ships could come into Portsmouth harbour before 9 p.m. Thus if tired guests wished to disembark earlier, participating vessels would have to lay on additional small transport to convey them ashore, at considerable expense and inconvenience. After an internal Admiralty discussion about whether to change the day of the review yet again, it was finally decided it was better to leave it as it was and to hope for the best. Unfortunately, *Truth* caught wind of the situation and on both June 23 and June 30 drew public attention to what it called a 'characteristic Admiralty blunder' and 'Whitehall all over.'

Potentially more embarrassing was the discussion going on within the Admiralty about how the review vessels should be arranged. Willes had himself suggested two plans which were, he thought, likely to prove popular. Either, he wrote, the masted ships should be placed outside the main lines or they should be divided into two columns to the eastward, the unmasted being positioned to the west. Willes indicated that he preferred the first plan because as far as manning the yards and illuminating the vessels were concerned, it was a more picturesque arrangement.

The Admiralty felt, however, that Willes' preferred plan would be too difficult to implement. So ill-prepared were many officers and ratings that Admiralty officials were certain that such a complicated arrangement would cause confusion and perhaps even collisions when it was time for the ships to take up their assigned positions in the cruising squadrons and flotillas of the post-review manoeuvres. By the same token, it was decided not to have any general evolution of the fleet for fear of untoward incident.

The wisdom of these decisions quickly became apparent. On July 13, after the vessels had begun to arrive off the Spithead Roads, came the first 'incident'. The royal yacht *Victoria and Albert* and the troopship *Orontes* collided, providing a diverting display for the Crown Prince and Princess of Germany, who were on hand. There were irritated comments in the press that the German royalties should have seen such a demonstration of naval carelessness.

A few days later, the *Black Prince* struck the *Agincourt*. Like the previous collision, there was neither damage nor injury but further press grumbles about bruises to British pride. On July 19, however, a more serious accident occurred. This time two first-class ironclads, *Ajax* and *Devastation*, were involved. In broad daylight and fair weather, these two powerful members of the Steam Reserve Squadron ran into each other, so damaging the *Devastation* that there was doubt whether she could remain in the review lines. Following hard on the two previous collisions, this one caused widespread consternation. The *Standard* demanded to know if the crews were at fault or if the ships themselves were unmanageable, while the *Daily News* pointed out how humiliating such repeated demonstrations of incompetence were for the country, especially as this one had again taken place before the eyes of the Crown Prince of Germany. 'Foreign visitors,' it wrote on July 21, 'ought to be kept out of the way until our bumping races of ironclads have come to an end.'

Fortunately there were no further accidents before the day of the review, though on the 23rd itself yet another unfortunate incident took place when a gun on the gunboat *Kite* exploded, injuring several ratings and killing one of them. Immediately the spectre of ordnance problems arose again, just as they had the year before when a similar accident on the barbette *Collingwood* caused the *Daily News* to predict dramatically, 'We are on the eve of a new panic in regard to the navy.' This time, however, investigation of the accident showed that the explosion was the fault not of weapon deficiency but of an ill-trained and inexperienced crew.

All these accidents before the review made concerned observers feel it more than ever essential to take a long, hard look at the condition of the fleet. Knowledgeable opinion was, of course, under no illusions about its condition. Sir Edward Reed, the eminent naval architect whom the *Manchester Guardian* called in July 'a very candid friend of the Admiralty,' told the House of Commons after the review that he hoped no one would suppose that more than half a dozen ships, or at the most eight, of all those reviewed were fit to go to war. Echoing this opinion, Admiral Hewett, who commanded one of the cruising squadrons during the manoeuvres, told a friend on the day of the review, 'Most of what you see is mere ullage.'

The most explicit confirmation of this opinion came in a long article on the review fleet published in *The Times* on July 22. It went into a full analysis of the eight major groups of review vessels into which most of the 128 pennants present were divided: broadside armour ships (9); turret ships (15); barbettes (2); partially protected vessels (3); unprotected (5); gunboats (31); torpedo-boats (40); and one protected vessel.

While the analysis offered by *The Times* did not quite confirm Sir Edward Reed's gloomy appraisal, it was not a comforting one. Each class present at Spithead had, it wrote, major flaws in design, armour and weaponry. The broadside ships, for example, were obsolescent not only because of age, but also because of deficient armour protection and poor weaponry. The barbettes suffered from inadequate armour and had guns of doubtful utility. Indeed, as a result of the explosion in *Collingwood* in 1886, the Admiralty had advised barbette captains to refrain from firing their weapons unless absolutely necessary. Finally, even the turret ships, which included not only *Ajax* and *Devastation* but Admiral Willes's flagship *Inflexible*, the pride of the fleet, were hardly free from drawbacks. Many were sheathed in armour likely to be penetrated by guns of equal or sometimes even less power than their own. Fortunately, they had only a small draught of water which enabled them to get away from trouble by hugging the coast. This may have enabled the turret vessels to stay afloat, but it hardly instilled confidence in the general public as to their ability to defend the realm. Indeed, although *The Times* left readers to make their own deductions, very few of the ships were actually equipped to do so.

Two factors mitigated anxiety about this situation. One was the torpedo-boat craze. At the time of the review, they were widely regarded as a sort of naval panacea, reckoned to be both cheap and deadly. The idea owed much to the French who under the influence of the *Jeune Ecole* had introduced them in great numbers with the expectation that in swarms they might effectively interfere with British commerce at will and even take on capital ships without the need of committing their own thrifty nation to an expensive building programme. This comfortable notion, to which by 1887 the Admiralty had responded in kind, did not even last out the year, however. In the manoeuvres which followed the review, 24 of the 40 participating torpedo-boats broke down and 19 of the vessels reported up to 23 casualties. Faith in the efficacy of the torpedo-boat was never the same again.

When Edgar Sheppard, Sub-Dean of the Chapels Royal, wrote upon his return from Spithead that 'Such a gathering was never seen before or ever will be seen again,' he may not have known how accurate an appraisal he had penned, but in fact the fleet which was to be reviewed by the Queen was an outmoded thing already marked for extinction.

The Armed Forces' Salute

How aware the Queen was herself of this crucial development is difficult to say; she was not a close observer of naval affairs and probably had no idea that she was participating in the last great naval review of a fleet which had for most of her reign a reputation for strength and seaworthiness which it could not in fact sustain.

It is most unlikely that as the Queen and her exalted guests made their way out to sea at a little past three o'clock on the brilliant afternoon of July 23, any such suspicion was uppermost in any of their minds. Leading the *Victoria and Albert* away from the Queen's marine residence at Osborne was the Trinity House steamer *Galatea*. Following in the wake of the royal yacht came a train of Admiralty vessels containing assorted domestic and foreign dignitaries. As soon as the *Victoria and Albert* left the dock, the flagship *Inflexible* began booming out a royal salute of 21 guns, each volley answered by one from the shore batteries. Then as the Queen entered the lines, ratings manned the yards, while officers pushed visitors below so that Victoria would not see them. Lord Charles Beresford had urged that the civilian guests whose needs he had been assiduous in attending to be allowed to remain topside to see the Queen pass by, but in this instance he made no headway against Admiralty tradition. The guests thus missed the picturesque sight of Queen Victoria sailing by, waving her handkerchief and acknowledging the cheers of the fleet by inclining her head, now left, now right.

Once the entire line had been passed on the forward course, the Queen's yacht did not, as expected, immediately turn around but sailed out to sea for about an hour. When, at last, she returned, the *Victoria and Albert* anchored in the midst of the fleet and, following the precedent of the naval review held in connection with King George III's golden jubilee, the Queen ordered the presence of the officers commanding the various vessels through which she had just passed.

As these officers, dressed in what the *Daily Telegraph* termed the 'full glory of gold lace and epaulettes,' began arriving, there was a small, embarrassing incident. Upon the instructions of an officer attached to Admiral Willes's staff, all the officers from the visiting French courtesy vessels appeared and waited to be presented to the Queen. Because the Captain of the *Iphigénie*, the commander of the French flotilla, considered himself well versed in protocol matters, he doubted the correctness of this invitation and had the Englishman repeat it again. Yes, it was *all* the officers, not just the captain himself. Nonetheless, as the captain had suspected from the start, he was the only one expected on board the royal yacht. The Prince of Wales, however, smoothed the matter over and made sure all the Frenchmen were in fact presented to his mother, but the fact that he did so did not prevent an indignant comment on the matter being included in the captain's official report to Paris.

By the time these formalities had been completed, it was past seven in the evening and the royal yacht weighed anchor to return the Queen to Osborne House. As she departed, the guns of the fleet again boomed out a royal salute. It was considered noteworthy that once Victoria had gone, the weather changed as banks of dark, rolling clouds gathered, obscuring the illumination of the ships which ended the day's events.

Despite this dimmed finale, the day had been the kind of rousing success that the most frenzied naval promoter could have desired. As the *Daily Telegraph* characteristically enthused: 'On Saturday the superb series of festivities connected with the national celebration of the Jubilee Year of her Majesty's reign came to a most brilliant and impressive conclusion. . . . It was the fleet guarding their hearths and homes which was shown to Englishmen the day before yesterday, and in a strength and aspect eminently calculated to fill them with proud, confident and patriotic exultation.' Only certain French observers, already irritated at the *contretemps* on board the *Victoria and Albert*, took exception to such high-blown sentiments.

Following the usual practice on such occasions, a number of foreign governments had despatched ships to participate in the Spithead review. Ostensibly meant as a mark of honour to the Queen, such demonstrations were in fact a way for other seafaring nations to keep *au courant* with the latest British naval developments.

Though the Netherlands and Germany also sent ships to Spithead, it was the French who took most interest in the occasion and who sent not one but two vessels. It was evidently intended in Paris that both the naval attaché in London and officers of the small flotilla should make good use of their time by securing intelligence data. Unfortunately the attaché, a certain Captain Roustan, as he apologized to the Minister of the Marine and Colonies, had been too busy with other matters to devote much attention to the assignment. Moreover, the man he had sent to inspect the construction site of the ironclad *Trafalgar* had been denied admission by the police so that the technical information he could send back was relatively paltry. If this aspect of his mission had been less productive than he would have liked, Roustan went on, he felt certain the Minister would find the rest of what he had to say satisfactory. Perhaps to excuse his own delinquency, the attaché dismissed the review as an event without professional interest, nothing more than 'a spectacle for the public,' a spectacle, furthermore, which had been badly arranged. It lacked both precision and efficiency; even the Queen's procession had been carelessly arranged, the distances between the ships being too great. Compared to such bungling, the naval attaché noted, the French had made a very fine showing. He went on to speculate that word of the splendid French presence had influenced the Italian government to pull out of the review; in any event, the expected Italian vessel had never shown up.

Despite French complaints, Lord Charles Beresford had good reason to be pleased with the review. It entirely fulfilled its purpose as a promotional device for the navy. Yet Beresford's self-satisfaction was very nearly blighted by what the *Daily News* called 'a refreshingly comic interlude in the too-serious drama of politics.' It seems that Beresford, while aboard the royal yacht, had hoisted a private signal to his wife, thereby committing a breach of naval regulations. When the incident was reported in the press, Beresford offered to resign, but although the Prime Minister did not much like his rambunctious and free-wheeling Fourth Sea Lord, this was not the issue on which to eject him from office. Beresford was not, however, to hold his place much longer; in January, 1888, he submitted yet another letter of resignation, because he did not approve of the government's attempt to minimize naval expenditures. This time, Lord Salisbury accepted the resignation, informing the Queen that Beresford 'is too greedy of popular applause to get on in a public department. He is constantly playing his own game at the expense of his colleagues in the Department, which causes much irritation.'

It was Salisbury, however, and not Beresford who had misread the situation, for the country was by now ready to approve just the sort of enhanced naval preparedness that Beresford had always had in mind. Much as Salisbury disliked doing so, therefore, in November, 1888, he was forced to enter Britain in the end-of-century naval armaments race. As a result, in 1889 the Naval Defence Act was passed through parliament which substantially increased the size of the fleet and appropriated over £21 millions to meet the new naval costs. Moreover, unlike previous bouts of enthusiasm about and interest in the navy, this one, ominously, was not followed by a period of lull and disinterest. Instead, because the nation continued to be obsessed with the need for strong defences the reverse was true.

As a result, ten years later when the diamond jubilee naval review took place at Spithead the 'ullage' so much in evidence at the golden jubilee had been swept away. This was, of course, a circumstance which delighted Beresford, who in a pamphlet published for the occasion by the Navy League wrote contemptuously of the earlier review fleet: 'No more absolute criterion of its heterogeneous character need be instanced than the fact that the entire category of vessels has, with about half-a-dozen exceptions, been relegated to training squadrons or port-ships while scarcely a single example of its battleships and not one solitary specimen of its cruisers is found in the fighting lines of the lists of vessels which are to compose the magnificent British fleet on June 26.' Rear Admiral Sir Sydney Eardley-Wilmot was more pungent when in his memoirs, *Sixty-Five Years Afloat and Ashore*, he compared the two reviews, calling 'the first a motley collection of ancient constructions, the second a really fine fleet [which] afforded striking evidence of the progress in ten years.'

In truth, it was progress which was generally apparent throughout all the aspects of the diamond jubilee.

CHAPTER NINE

SIXTY YEARS A QUEEN

ON SEPTEMBER 23, 1896, Queen Victoria passed a notable historical milestone, becoming, by a day, the longest reigning sovereign in England's history. Until then her grandfather, King George III, had held the record. Characteristically, Victoria, with her precise turn of mind, had no desire to mark this date but let it be known that any commemoration should be put off until she had sat on the throne sixty years to the day —June 22, 1897.

As soon as this decision was publicized, suggestions began to be made about what any commemoration should include and what its official name should be. Among the earliest suggestions was one made in *The Times* by the twelfth Earl of Meath, who wrote that some endeavour should be made in 1897 to include the teaching of patriotism and loyalty in the schools. 'No effort is made,' he said, 'to show the rising generation that the love of Queen and of country is no mere idle sentiment, but is capable of being sustained by reasonable argument. . . .' He even suggested what text might be used: Mr. Arnold-Foster's *Citizen Reader*.

Competing with such disinterested suggestions were those made by promoters, who, as in 1887, saw the opportunity to further their own projects. Among the first into the field was the first Baron Hobhouse who had something to present called the 'Queen's Commemoration and Victorian Open Spaces,' a scheme designed for the acquisition and preservation of park land. He was followed by the first Baron Playfair, who urged that the South Kensington Museum, still unfinished, should be completed to mark the event, and by Frederick Temple, Archbishop of Canterbury, who, learning from what had happened to him when he was Bishop of London at the time of the golden jubilee, urged as the church's commemoration project that a special collection be taken for the 'Clergy Sustentation Fund' which was used to augment clerical stipends.

But in the name of what event were these collections to be taken?

By the end of January, 1897, a number of suggestions had already been made, among them 'The Queen's Commemoration' and even 'Jubilissimee.' More and more, however, 'Diamond Jubilee' was the name which generally appealed. 'It is short, apt and descriptive,' Miss Clara Boulnois wrote to *The Times*. Some did not like it. Sir Matthew Ridley, Home Secretary, let Sir Arthur Bigge, since 1895 the Queen's private secretary, know he thought it inappropriate. ' "Jubilee" has got its meaning from the old Jewish law & is certainly inseparably connected with a notion of 50 years. "Diamond" is understood because it is used to mark the completion of 60 years of married life. . . .' The phrase was not, therefore, 'strictly correct.' Lord Hobhouse went even farther. In *The Times* for January 28 he inveighed against such corrupt usage. 'To make the compound expression tolerable we must use the word in some new and, as yet, unexplained sense, and why should we destroy its time-sanctioned meaning, and at the same time make unavoidable confusion with the true Jubilee celebrated ten years ago?' Bigge evidently felt the same way and in asking Victoria what name she wanted expressed himself confidently that the 'Diamond Jubilee' was a title 'Your Majesty would not approve of.'

In fact, the Queen was much taken with it and, despite the misgivings of the purists, authorized its use. Unless, however, certain matters of finance could satisfactorily be arranged, there would be no state celebration to which this title might be applied.

The golden jubilee had been, for the Queen, most expensive. As Bigge told Sir Edward Hamilton, assistant secretary at the Treasury, it had cost her about £50,000 from her privy purse, and she was resolved to pay nothing this time. An intricate series of negotiations was begun to see what could be worked out.

Complicating matters, Victoria was also adamant that she would not permit the use of state ceremonial, would not get out of her carriage on jubilee day (though as Bigge told Hamilton the Queen 'was prepared to drive about as much as she was wanted to do') and would not allow any crowned heads to attend. This prohibition, which was made on the grounds of Victoria's advanced age (she was now 77) and the amount of attention she would have to give her regal colleagues, was meant to block the attendance of her continually-irritating eldest grandson. The Emperor William of Germany had, in fact, begun to make inquiries about the date of his grandmother's jubilee in the autumn of 1896; opinion in England was hostile to him, because of his incendiary telegram of congratulation earlier in the year to President Paul Krueger of the Transvaal on the success with which this inveterate foe of the British had dealt with the imperialistic incursion of Dr. Leander Starr Jameson and his raiders.

Sensible though it may have been to keep the Kaiser out of England, the Queen's decision was well received neither in Berlin nor in much of official London. The Queen's eldest daughter, the dowager Empress Frederick, pressed both her brother, the Prince of Wales, and the Queen, to allow the Emperor to come. As soon as she did so, the Prince of Wales directed his private secretary, Sir Francis Knollys, to write to Bigge in order to reinforce his mother's resistance. On January 29, Knollys warned that the Emperor 'would arrive with an enormous suite & would try & arrange things himself and endless trouble would arise. HRH is certain the Queen will regret it if she gives way. . . .'[1]

Mindful of how obnoxious William had often made himself during past visits, Victoria needed no persuasion. On January 30 she told her private secretary to inform the Prince of Wales that 'there is *not* the slightest fear of the Queen's giving way abt the Emperor William's coming. It wd *not* do for many reasons & the Queen is surprised that the Empress wd urge it.'[2]

When this decision was made known to the Cabinet it produced much irritation from those who wished to take advantage of the diamond jubilee to demonstrate that Britain's so-called 'splendid isolation' was simply a phrase and who were willing to swallow the Germain Kaiser in order to bring all other available monarchs to London. As Lord Salisbury, again both Prime Minister and Foreign Secretary, informed Bigge on January 31, both the current Conservative Chancellor of the Exchequer, Sir Michael Hicks Beach, and his Liberal predecessor, Sir William Harcourt, 'had agreed that they would pay without stint for big Royalties and the reception of them. They were therefore much grieved at the announcement of 'no crowned heads' . . . and weep over [them].' Since his pet idea had been vetoed, Hicks Beach gave way to near intransigence, angry that instead of sovereigns the usual mob of impecunious 'princelets' (as he called them) would be descending upon the country. Thus when Hamilton approached him at the beginning of February, the chancellor brusquely declined to provide funds for an entertainment for children in London and refused to commit himself on whether he would undertake the cost of entertaining naval officers. 'At present,' Sir Edward informed Bigge, 'he is not very "open handedly minded," though money would flow even from him like water, if the Crowned Heads were to come.'

Throughout February, Hicks Beach continued to remain in a funk, until at last even the Prime Minister, as uninterested in such things as ever, was forced to see that something would have to be done. He therefore asked Sir Edward Hamilton again to raise the matter with his chief. 'I yesterday broached the subject of Jubilee expenses again with the Chan. of the Exchequer by direction of Lord Salisbury, who seemed to be rather in awe of his colleague,' Hamilton wrote in his journal for February 21. 'Beach was stiff. So I dropped the matter, which must be allowed to soak.' An impasse threatened for as Hamilton noted, 'The Queen is most loath to show Herself at all, & declines to be put to extra expense. It is in short a question of "No money, no Jubilee".' When Hamilton mentioned these difficulties to the Prince of Wales on the evening of February 20, the heir to the throne predictably chose to berate the minister involved. He was, Hamilton recorded, 'very much down' on Hicks Beach. Hamilton, always diplomatic, 'begged him not to jump to conclusions prematurely,' and sensibly counselled patience: 'It will probably come all right in due time.'

Like most bouts of petulance, Hicks Beach's did in time pass; only three days later when Hamilton yet again brought up the subject of the expenses he found the chancellor 'in a much more amenable humour.' He was willing to agree to provide money for all the extraordinary expenses of the year both from the Queen's privy purse and the various Household departments, expenses which it was then being estimated would run at about the 1887 level. Hamilton promptly passed the good news to Bigge, who also heard the next day from Sir Francis Knollys that the Prince of Wales meant to take advantage of this change of heart to get Hicks Beach to agree, too, to pay £1,600 towards the cost of repairing the state harness. This was not, Knollys told Bigge, justifiable. 'I confess myself that I do not see why the govt. shd pay the £1600, but the P of W is going to try & make them swallow the whole £50,000.'³

This was not merely unjust but foolish, given the chancellor's temper for the past month, and it is fortunate that he did not take the Prince's importunity amiss (though Hamilton later noted that Hicks Beach had been 'alarmed' by the request). In the end the repair of the state harness was not considered an extraordinary expense, and the chancellor refused to meet it. On the other hand, 'nothing could have been more amicable than he was' about all the essential points, as Knollys reported to Bigge. Moreover as Hamilton recorded later, Hicks Beach also 'made no difficulty' about coming up with the money for bringing over colonial and Indian troops and for covering the expenses of eleven colonial premiers invited to London for the occasion.

It is doubtful whether these colonial premiers, whose inclusion constituted one of the most notable innovations of the diamond jubilee, would have even been thought of had not the more desirable crowned heads been banned. When they were, however, the fertile imagination of Joseph Chamberlain, Colonial Secretary, conceived the notion of replacing them with the leaders of Britain's self-governing dominions. Chamberlain presented this splendid inspiration to the Prime Minister on January 19 in a memorandum, pointing out that 'there has never been in English territory any representation of the Empire as a whole, and the Colonies especially have, hitherto, taken little part in any ceremony of the kind.' To impress both Englishmen and foreigners with the extent of the Empire and the loyalty of the Queen's subjects, the opportunity should be seized to correct such negligence.

Chamberlain therefore suggested that the premiers of the self-governing colonies be invited to the jubilee as guests of the government. Furthermore that each colony should send a representative sample of its military forces, especially cavalry, and that these troops should provide an escort for their respective premiers on jubilee day. He also asked that the Queen receive the premiers and allow for a march past of colonial troops. Naturally, he told the Prime Minister, the occasion might also be utilized for informal talks on 'many subjects of the greatest interest to the Empire, such as Commercial Union, legislation with regard to immigrants from Asia and elsewhere, and other similar subjects.' In conclusion, Chamberlain was glad to tell Lord Salisbury that these proposals had been submitted to the Prince of Wales, who had authorized him to say that 'he entirely approves of them and thinks that a unique demonstration of this kind would be both useful and popular.'

The fact that Chamberlain, the second most powerful member of the government, bothered to seek out the Prince of Wales's opinion and to note his approval, is a recognition of the heir to the throne's significant role in arranging the diamond jubilee. Ten years before he had not occupied such a position; at that time there had been a general feeling, entirely shared by the Queen, that the Prince would confuse matters by making irresponsible, costly suggestions and that it was better for him to be excluded. The short-sightedness of such a policy became glaringly apparent as the old Queen grew even older, and at last the politicians who might well have to deal with the Prince as King began taking pains to make certain he was consulted. Finally even the Queen, always the chief stumbling block to any scheme to make better use of her eldest son and heir, recognized the inevitable.

Thus when the opinion began to be heard towards the end of 1896 that there should be an organizing committee to oversee the coming diamond jubilee and to ensure that the same kind of muddle and lack of coordination which had marked its predecessor did not occur again, the Queen acquiesced in the appointment of the Prince of Wales as its head. That her confidence in him was still not complete may be gathered from the fact that she also appointed his brother, the Duke of Connaught, to assist in the matter. But as Connaught had neither aptitude for pageantry nor imagination, Bertie's control was never in danger.

As originally constituted on January 23, 1897, the non-royal members of the Diamond Jubilee Committee were: the fourteenth Earl of Pembroke, Lord Steward; Lord Lathom, Lord Chamberlain; the Duke of Portland, Master of the Horse; Lord Edward Pelham-Clinton, Master of the Household; Sir Spencer Ponsonby-Fane; Sir Fleetwood Edwards, Keeper of the Privy Purse; Sir Arthur Bigge; and Sir Edward Hamilton. The day before the first meeting was held on February 2, the Prince of Wales recommended that the Honourable Reginald Baliol Brett, Permanent Secretary of the Office of Works, be added. 'I suppose it is all right,' Knollys told Bigge somewhat uncertainly upon learning of the appointment. 'The Office of Works will have much to do with whatever is done in the way of celebrating the Diamond Jubilee & under these circumstances H.R.H. thought the Depart should be represented.'[4]

The committee first met on February 2 at Marlborough House with the Prince of Wales in the chair. The efficiency with which it handled its business, especially given the early date, was unprecedented. In part such dispatch resulted from the fact that royal officials had been informally discussing the diamond jubilee ever since the previous October when Sir Arthur Bigge drew up the first rough outline of proposed events. In part, of course, the organizers relied heavily for guidance on the precedent of the golden jubilee with which most of them had had experience, taking pains not to duplicate its mistakes. As a result the minutes of even the first committee meeting indicate a professionalism never before apparent in the arrangement of royal events.

On Saturday June 19 the royal guests were to arrive in London. The Master of the Household stated that he expected between 40 and 50 of them who should, so far as possible, be lodged in one hotel with no royal residences other than Buckingham Palace itself being employed. He suggested to the committee that royal and colonial representatives should be housed together, but, opposed by the Prince of Wales, this idea was declined as altogether too innovative.

Most of the discussion at that first meeting dealt with how the Queen should show herself to her people on June 22, which was to be jubilee day. Sir Edward Hamilton stated that this was an event to which the government attached great importance and was prepared 'to contribute largely towards the expenses attendant upon it' but only if something suitable could be arranged. The main problem was the Queen's adamant refusal to leave her carriage.

The first proposal advanced (the minutes are conspicuously silent about who presented it) was that the Queen should drive in procession to St. Paul's Cathedral, which it was understood was to be used if a religious ceremony was decided upon. Upon her arrival a service of thanksgiving already taking place inside the cathedral should be transferred to the outer steps (which were to be covered for the occasion) and there be brought to a conclusion with 'some sort of Te Deum & Benediction.' Allowing countless opportunities for confusion, the congregation and participants being moved from within the cathedral to the steps outside, it is not surprising that this suggestion 'was almost unanimously decided to be unsuitable and impossible.'

What then was to be done?

The committee rejected the Tower of London as a possible site because of the difficulty of access. A reception of all the mayors of the United Kingdom to be held outside Mansion House was also dismissed as was the possibility of using St. Paul's as a place to present an address but ignoring the ecclesiastical function of the edifice. Hyde Park, too, was talked of as a location where the Queen on her ride around London might be addressed, 'but there were also many objections to this.'

Eventually it was decided that no such commemoration would be complete without some sort of religious ceremony (which 'certainly was expected') and that perhaps the Queen could be persuaded to enter St. Paul's from a private pavilion to be erected at the side of the cathedral. Sir Fleetwood Edwards was designated to present this idea to Queen Victoria along with two other possibilities: a visit to Mansion House, there to receive an address, and a drive through the City without stopping, an address to be presented in Hyde Park.

None of these suggestions in the form in which they were put forward by Edwards favourably impressed the Queen, who especially disliked the notion of entering St. Paul's in a lift. Nor did she approve the idea made earlier by Schomberg McDonnell, the Prime Minister's secretary, who thought that the Queen's horses might be taken out of their traces at the cathedral and her carriage drawn up the main aisle by men. 'It would be a magnificent spectacle,' he told Bigge; horses would be better, of course, but bringing them into the building would undoubtedly 'shock people.'[5] Instead, while the main committee took up the matter of arranging for congratulatory addresses from the Houses of Parliament, the Queen let it be known she preferred a suggestion which seems first to have been made by Sir Arthur Bigge in a November, 1896 letter to McDonnell: there should be a religious service at St. Paul's, held in open air in front of the cathedral, with the Queen remaining in her carriage. Asked for his opinion on this unprecedented operation, Randall Davidson, Bishop of Winchester, told Edwards on February 14, 'It is clear the thing can be managed, and, given fine weather, it may be very effective in all respects.'[6]

To make suitable arrangements for this service, the first of the main organizing committee's subcommittees was established. Called after its chairman, the Dean of St. Paul's (the Very Reverend Robert Gregory), it included the Archbishop of Canterbury; Mandell Creighton, Bishop of London; Bishop Davidson; Brett; Colonel Sir Edward Bradford, Commissioner of Metropolitan Police; and the third Baron Methuen, who on jubilee day was to be chief of staff to the Duke of Connaught, who had been given ceremonial command of the troops.

Although nothing much was settled at the first meeting of the committee (which seems to have been held on February 22), the second gathering on February 27 was more productive. The steps of the cathedral were to be occupied by bishops, clergy and choirs 'in proper ecclesiastical dress,' the latter to be supported by two military bands, which Lord Methuen was to find. The service, which was to take only about twenty minutes, was to consist of a Te Deum '& probably some prayer & hymns' and would close with a benediction. 'Such a ceremony in the very heart of the City,' as Archbishop Temple told the Bishop of Winchester, 'would be an expression of thanks to God not soon to be forgotten.'[7] As Bishop Davidson told Sir Arthur Bigge, however, this would be true only if the service were seen in the proper perspective, as only an aspect of jubilee day, not as its focal point, unlike the thanksgiving at Westminster Abbey in 1887. 'If the S. Paul's Service were regarded as the objective,' he wrote on March 1, 'it would be in my opinion unsatisfactory in all ways as the service itself wd seem miserably inadequate to such an occasion.' Its incidental character had to be established. 'This ought to be made clear beforehand,' Davidson continued, 'so as to show that it is not "The Queen going to S. Paul's" but "The Queen's triumphal procession through the capital of the Empire," the drive, or procession, including a stoppage at S. Paul's where a Te Deum will be sung.'[8] If it was properly understood, there was no reason why this service should not be the success the Archbishop of Canterbury anticipated.

The Prince of Wales was not so sure, and when he read the Archbishop's plan to the next meeting of the general committee, he 'was plainly undecided as to its being the best arrangement.' His objections, however, were those of detail; those of the Queen's cousin, Princess Augusta, Grand Duchess of Mecklenburg-Strelitz, were more basic. Upon hearing the appalling news about what kind of service was going to take place she exploded to her niece, Princess Mary, Duchess of York. 'No! That out-of-doors service before St. Paul's! has one ever heard of such a thing! After a 60 years reign to thank God in the street!!'[9]

Despite the Grand Duchess's outraged incredulity and some occasional misgivings on the part of the Prince of Wales, the Queen herself was well satisfied with the unusual arrangement, for it not only assured that the service would be short but also that she would not suffer from the sense of confinement which so often made her churchgoing unpleasant. The Queen's insistence on this arrangement meant more work both for the Office of Works which had to arrange for seating at the west entrance of St. Paul's and for those arranging the parade route and the procession through London, which as the chief item of jubilee day was now considerably more important than its undistinguished predecessor ten years before.

In charge of arrangements for the Office of Works was Reginald Baliol Brett, at the time the forty-five-year-old permanent secretary of the department, son and heir to the first Baron Esher. Over the years a legend has arisen that, in the words of his biographer, Peter Fraser, Brett 'stage managed' the diamond jubilee. In fact, there is no discernible substance for this claim. Brett was only added to the general committee as something of an afterthought, having spent a productive week-end at Sandringham with the Prince of Wales, where he managed to persuade the chairman that it would be wrong for the Office of Works to go unrepresented on his committee. Thus despite the reservations of Sir Francis Knollys (who in expressing them to Sir Arthur Bigge evidently thought the Queen's private secretary agreed), Brett was asked to become part of the committee's deliberations. Once included, of course, he managed in his customary, often obsequious fashion, to make himself useful; there is no evidence in the record, however, that Brett had more influence or did more than might have been expected because of his official position. Instead he seems to have busied himself with its duties, superintending the necessary arrangements outside St. Paul's (both seating and the placement of carriages during the service) and authorizing the construction of grandstands along the parade route. Had he attempted to assert himself unduly, either in the committee or more characteristically behind the scenes (for Brett had a devious turn of mind), he would surely have been put down by the likes of Bigge and Knollys, neither of whom was ever known to shrink when it came to asserting their own positions.

Thus Brett found himself confined to the task of constructing about 20,000 seats, some built for domestic and foreign dignitaries, the rest rented for 12s. 6d. in aid, as it turned out, of the Royal Military Benevolent and Royal Naval Fund and the Civil Service Benevolent Fund. Later, the Office of Works was also given responsibility for watering the large force of cavalry and artillery which marched on jubilee day and for camping some 10,000 participating infantry in Hyde Park.

Quite properly, Brett's official responsibilities gave him membership on the second of the diamond jubilee sub-committees, the one headed by the Master of the Horse and charged with ordering the route and handling the processional arrangements. Its other members included Sir Henry Ewart, Crown Equerry; Sir Edward Bradford; Lord Methuen; Colonels Byng and Carrington; and Lt.-Col. Henry Smith.

The most important meeting of this committee was held on February 25 when a tentative route through London's West

End was drawn up. It was a route, however, which the committee hoped Queen Victoria would allow to be considerably extended so as to include a wide sweep south of the Thames, an idea put forward by the Bishop of Southwark. Two days later the Duke of Portland took this recommendation before the main committee, where it was made known that it was 'strongly supported' by Arthur Balfour, Conservative Leader in the House of Commons, 'as taking in a dense population who had never had an opportunity of seeing H.M.' For unknown reasons, the representatives of the Lord Chamberlain's Department opposed this extension; perhaps they had learned all too well that the Queen generally preferred the shortest route possible. Knollys told Bigge, 'I imagine they have nothing to do with it.'[10] He was right; they didn't, and, besides, Victoria had already let it be known she would ride howsoever long she was desired to, so long as the diamond jubilee expenses were entirely met by the government.

Once this matter had been settled, there remained the more troublesome problem of determining who should be in the procession and where they should be placed. Although the Queen had characteristically declined to consider using the accoutrements of full state, members of the organizing committee were full of suggestions how to make the final result more imposing than it had been at the time of the golden jubilee. The orchestral conductor Henry J. Wood, for instance, had written to the Lord Chamberlain at the beginning of February suggesting that bands should be used; even if they were not allowed to march in the procession, he said, they ought to be placed at intervals along the parade route. Committee members agreed with him that it had been a great defect ten years before that there had been no rousing martial music in the parade, and this time they saw to it that there was. Other matters gave more trouble. Would the Lord Mayor of London waive the corporation's privilege of presenting an address at the boundaries of the City? He would not, not only because the corporation was thereby allowed to exercise jurisdiction in the City but also because the troops would otherwise be marched through without permission.

Would the colonial premiers go in the Queen's procession and be escorted by troops from their respective dominions? No, they were to have a small procession by themselves, accompanied, but not escorted, by their troops, for, as the Prince of Wales had strongly pointed out, no subject could properly have an escort.

And what of the navy? In February the general committee had decided that a suggestion made by George Goschen, First Lord of the Admiralty, to include a contingent of bluejackets in the procession was impractical, because it would delay the progress too much. Goschen, however, refused to let the matter die and secured the backing of the Prince of Wales. Just as the matter was going before the Queen for her final approval, Lord Wolseley, now Commander-in-Chief of the army, caught wind of it and protested. 'Whilst most anxious to meet the navy as our sister service in this & in all other matters,' he wrote, 'I feel that their request is very much what a request would be from us to have the Life Guards on board the Fleet during the coming Naval Review.'[11] The controversy over the bluejackets plunged the royal chairman into a depression. As Knollys told Sir Fleetwood Edwards, 'The Prince of Wales is beginning to be much worried about the arrangements and gets rather in despair about them sometimes as when something or another is ready for the Queen's approval, it is upset.'[12] In the end, reluctantly, the Queen approved the presence of the bluejackets, although she thought Wolseley was right; even so a detachment of naval guns was added to the procession.

As members of both the Duke of Portland's committee and the main committee hammered out further particulars about the procession, they became unpleasantly aware of how their efficiency in settling the route early was leading to abuse. On March 23, Sir John Brunner, a Liberal M.P., asked the Home Secretary whether he was aware that certain landlords on the line of route were ejecting tenants in order to rent the premises for a higher return? Mr. Darling, a Liberal colleague, suggested that Sir Matthew Ridley keep in reserve the possibility of diverting the route so as to contravene any scheme of this kind, a suggestion which was met with cheers.

In a session where there were few momentous public issues, this matter was taken up with alacrity. Two days later Mr. Harry Marks, a Radical who sat for a division of the Tower Hamlets, announced that he was going to introduce a bill to enable magistrates to restrain evictions until the day after the procession. Eleven other M.P.s, including the ever ready Labouchere, joined with him in introducing the measure.

Was such a bill necessary? When the Home Office looked into the matter, it found that 'few if any' eviction cases had been brought before the courts and that there was therefore no reason to amend the law. The fact that their bill had no chance of being passed did not seem to bother its proponents a whit; they blithely continued to bring up the matter in the House until the end of May, a convenient stick to beat grasping landlords, unsympathetic magistrates and an uncaring government.

Such irresponsible behaviour did not worry the government as similar activities had done in 1887. Since then there had been a sea change in the political situation to the complete advantage of the Unionist coalition which at the time of the diamond jubilee had an enviable majority.

Thus there was no need to be concerned either about what the much depleted Radical ranks might do or their Nationalist allies, who after Parnell's death in 1891 and the defeat of Gladstone's second Home Rule bill in 1892, had fallen upon similarly hard times. The Irish, to be sure, felt obliged to point out on the floor of the House of Commons that the occasion had nothing to do with their unhappy land and that in consequence they would not attend any ceremony honouring the Queen. *The Times*, however, discovered that such blustery sentiments were a sham; no more than the most loyal Englishman could the Nationalist M.P.s absent themselves from such a notable historical event. On June 8, the newspaper exulted that 'We know . . . that many of [the Nationalist M.P.s] have taken non-transferable tickets for the stand on Speaker's green to view the Jubilee procession with the other members of the legislature. . . . Convictions which cannot withstand the temptation of a reserved seat can scarcely be regarded as intrinsically formidable.' So, in the changed circumstances of the late 1890s, did *The Thunderer*, once ridden with anxiety about the future of the United Kingdom, regard the fractious Irish and their unceasing demand for self government.

These circumstances, of course, played comfortably into the hands of Lord Salisbury. No more interested in the diamond jubilee than he had been in the golden, the political situation in 1897 gave him even less reason to concern himself with it. His only desire was that it should pass quickly away while causing the least disruption to the normal processes of government and his own well established routine. Happily for the Prime Minister's habits, it was a wish he had very largely fulfilled. No legislation had to be brought in except for the brief Metropolitan Police Courts (Holidays) Act, which enabled the Home Secretary to close such courts on jubilee day. Opposition to it came not from Radicals and Irish Nationalists bent on wreaking havoc in the House of Commons, but from bureaucrats who wondered at the necessity for such legislation. 'The matter seems a very small one to pass an act about,' grumbled H. E. Simpson, one of the principal clerks, but without it magistrates who had been forced to go without a jubilee holiday in 1887 would have missed another in 1897.

Only in the business of allocating the honours could the Prime Minister have found the diamond jubilee as disagreeable as its predecessor, yet even here things proved less tiresome. In 1887, a complicated and uncertain political situation had forced the Marquess of Salisbury at least to listen to the unceasing importunities of persons desiring honours. In 1897, in full command of the political scene, he was under no such compulsion. He could, therefore, with near impunity, do with honours what he liked best: deny them. Nonetheless, it was impossible even for Salisbury to turn the clock back to Sir Robert Peel's small and select system and his ready adoption by the time of the diamond jubilee of such novel and inflating tendencies as birthday and new year's gazettes of honours showed that the Prime Minister for all his wistfulness about the past was very much a creature of his time.

As such he was willing to propose the adoption of special statutes for the jubilee year which would enable the Queen to make appointments in both the Order of St. Michael and St. George and the Order of the Bath on an *ad lib.* basis without having regard to how many vacancies there actually were. The only concession to the old regime was that the ranks held by these extra members were not to be filled upon becoming vacant. Once this point had been settled, his staff and the usual department heads set about drawing up the least objectionable list. 'We are knee deep in Honours here,' Schomberg McDonnell wrote to Sir Fleetwood Edwards from the Foreign Office on June 2 'and shall be thankful when the lists are finally settled and submitted.'

When Lord Salisbury at last sent them to Windsor three days later he felt bound to do a little explaining to the Queen. 'He is conscious that [the honours] are voluminous. It would hardly be otherwise. The occasion is so unique and the pressure from all sides is so great.' Nonetheless, he told the Queen he had tried, 'successfully,' to keep the number of hereditary honours to a minimum. 'The baronetcies are not more numerous than they were at the Jubilee ten years ago, and the peerages are less numerous.' Might he therefore propose that the painter George Watts be made a privy councillor? Although the Prime Minister had done his best, even going so far as to combine the new year and birthday honours so that there would not be three lists in the jubilee year, the Queen saw fit to deny him this request; it was altogether too unusual to consider having an artist, however respectable, made a privy councillor. This distinction was being left for the colonial premiers, who at Chamberlain's urging were all awarded it.

Watts was only one of the many disappointed in the honours scramble, as Sir Edward Hamilton noted approvingly as he scanned the newly honoured on jubilee day. 'The list of honours is almost as uninteresting as it is long,' he wrote. 'Fortunately there is next to no new Peers and a very few promotions in the Peerage. Here Lord Salisbury has shewn excellent judgment at the expense presumably of causing disappointment right and left, including (I am afraid) Horace Farquhar who was led to expect that the promised coronet would be at his disposal now.'

Hamilton was referring to his friend Sir Horace Farquhar, Bart., a Liberal Unionist M.P. and member of the London County Council. A month earlier at a party at the Farquhars, Sir Horace had taken Hamilton aside and confidently confided his expectation of a jubilee peerage. He had, he said, worked hard for the Unionist cause in London and 'has provided more of the "sinews of war" than is required under the now accepted tariff for the bestowal of peerages.' Sinews of war or no, Salisbury felt secure enough to shatter such confident expectations; it was not until the new reign that Farquhar, who was close to the Prince of Wales, received his peerage, ending up both an earl and Lord Chamberlain, too.

As far as the Prince of Wales was concerned, the Prime Minister's lack of interest in the diamond jubilee was no drawback. It was enough for his ministry to pay, leaving the Prince's committee free to attend to the organization. This body continued formally to meet at least through the middle of May by which time most matters had been settled, though such items as the national thanksgiving service for Sunday, June 20 and the presentation of addresses from the Houses of Parliament on June 23 remained to be dealt with. Once the general plan had been determined, it was left to the responsible departments to carry it out.

As in 1887, the Chinese were the first to enquire whether the Queen would accept a special diamond jubilee mission. As Thomas Sanderson of the Foreign Office minuted after meeting with Sir Halliday Macartney, councillor and English secretary to the Chinese legation in London, 'I did not show any signs of rapture.' In fact, Mr. Sanderson had no idea what Foreign Office policy was in the matter when in December, 1896, Sir Halliday broached the subject, because no one had yet considered it.

Learning from what had happened ten years before, the decision was taken early to sound out the governments with British diplomatic personnel to see whether special envoys or princely guests might be expected.

This procedure generally worked well, for it not only forced foreign governments to think in plenty of time about whether they were going to send a representative but who that representative would be, a matter of importance where precedence had to be considered. It also alerted London to potential problems. When, for instance, Sir Ernest Satow, envoy in Tokyo, approached the Japanese Foreign Minister in April to see whether the emperor would be sending an imperial representative, he found that the snubs given to Prince Komatsu in 1887 left the Mikado in doubt about despatching another prince to England. Or, as Sir Ernest delicately phrased the difficulty on April 2: 'I believe hesitation arises from doubt as to whether same treatment would be accorded as to princes of European royal families.' In recognition, however, of the growing Anglo-Japanese entente which was functioning so well for both nations in Asia, the emperor was anxious to overlook what had happened before and to send an imperial prince, if only Lord Salisbury would give assurances about his cordial—and equal—reception. No less interested than the emperor in fostering continued good relations, Salisbury was happy to do so.

The representation of the Kingdom of Saxony also posed minor problems. On April 1, Lord Salisbury was informed by the British envoy, G. Strachey, that in Dresden there was a good deal of confusion about the diamond jubilee. King Albert, he said, had returned from, of all places, Berlin under the misapprehension that the Queen desired representatives only from those courts to which she was related, which did not include that of Saxony. In due course the King's erroneous impression was corrected, and he appointed one of his sons, Prince Frederick Augustus, to represent him. By that time the Lord Chamberlain had been advised that another of the King's sons, Prince Maximilian, had in the summer of 1896 moved to London, renounced his princely status and taken orders as a Roman Catholic priest. He was now at work as a missionary in the East End. 'Would it not be a graceful act to request Prince Max to accompany his brother in the Royal Procession on the 22nd?' a certain Joseph Moores asked Lord Lathom. Sensing trouble, the Lord Chamberlain pushed the suggestion over to the Foreign Office, where it was buried.

Most of the jubilee representatives, either princely or diplomatic, were known to the Foreign Office well in advance of the day, though the Prince of Wales was 'much surprised' on April 29 to learn that its information about who was coming was (typically) not being shared with the Lord Chamberlain's Office. In at least two cases there was again confusion about the guests, though in neither instance was the Foreign Office itself to blame.

On June 11, Sir Edmund Monson, British Ambassador in Paris, informed the Foreign Office about a jubilee mission sent by the Sultan of Morocco and now resting in the French capital before travelling on to London. The French, it seems, were not pleased that this client state had sent such a mission, apparently fearing that while in England its members would be adversely influenced by perfidious Albion. While assuring the British Ambassador that he wished to facilitate the mission's departure, therefore, M. Hanotaux, the French Foreign Minister, set about making difficulties so as to retard it.

With an insight that all foreign ministers should possess, Hanotaux saw that the Sultan's envoy was himself the weakest reed. Having never before travelled outside his country, he was unnerved by what Monson termed his sudden 'plunge into civilization.' Furthermore, as Sir Edmund wrote privately to Lord Salisbury on the same day, it was likely 'that the Ambassador has been frightened, and it may be that an attempt has been made to deter him from proceeding on his mission to England, and that fearing the consequences to himself should he disobey the Sovereign's order, his nerves have become somewhat shaken.'

Monson, however, was not at all distressed by M. Hanotaux's duplicity and manoeuvring. Rather the reverse. The Moor, he knew, had left Tangier with a suite of nearly 40. As the housing expenses of diplomatic personnel were on this occasion to be met by the Foreign Office, the prospect of such a large party was appalling. So, while Hanotaux played on the weak-minded envoy's unsteady nerves, a certain Consul Maclean was despatched to Paris to see what he could do about reducing the envoy's suite to manageable size. A compromise was reached, and on June 12 F. H. Villiers of the Foreign Office informed Ponsonby-Fane that 'In spite of strenuous procedural struggles, I am sorry to say the Moor has beaten us & is coming, but we have reduced his suite from nearly 40 to 3!' As it turned out, though, the Moroccan mission never reached London, as the envoy was so much shaken by his first encounter with western life and the intrigues of great power diplomacy that he could not bear to travel farther and so remained, at ease, in Paris.

When at last it seemed that all arrangements were complete, Villiers sent Ponsonby-Fane a despairing communication: 'Alas,' he wrote on June 16, 'a Greek has been announced.' Perhaps the Greek government may be excused for having deferred their decision so long; their nation had, after all, only the month before signed an armistice to conclude an unsuccessful war with Turkey. Though the Greeks had provoked the war, sympathy in London was very much on their side, because of continuing Turkish attacks on the Armenian population of the Ottoman Empire. Indeed the Women's Liberal Federation formally protested to Lord Salisbury against the visit of a Turkish jubilee envoy. 'It appears to condone conduct which the majority of the British nation hold in abhorrence and is an insult to Her Majesty as Queen and as woman.' Despite the lateness of their decision to attend, the defeated government in Athens felt it could not miss the opportunity to send an envoy and take any advantage of the situation it could. After all, Britain would no doubt be influential in arranging the peace which had yet to be negotiated between Turkey and Greece.

But what of the Chinese who had been the first to enquire about jubilee missions? After the Foreign Office had assured the Chinese legation in London that, contrary to Sanderson's earlier opinion, the Queen would indeed be delighted to receive an envoy from Peking, one was designated by the ruling yamen.

Unfortunately, when he reached Vancouver, an epidemic of smallpox had broken out, and His Excellency was held in quarantine on Victoria Island in circumstances which showed that to local authorities a Chinaman was a Chinaman, mandarin rank and diplomatic status notwithstanding. Alerted by the Chinese legation to their envoy's situation, the Foreign Office approached Joseph Chamberlain to see whether the Colonial Secretary could improve matters. 'He is at present lodged in a tent on an island,' Sanderson wrote of the envoy on May 1, 'and torrents of rain are falling.' Whether Chamberlain was able to do anything for the poor man is not clear, but upon reaching London the ambassador from the celestial empire, by now no doubt crestfallen and indignant, shut himself away in the legation, declining Foreign Office hospitality and playing only an inconspicuous part in the proceedings.

As had become clear ten years before, it is always easy to bruise the amour propre of foreign representatives, whether diplomatic or princely. Nothing is more certain to do so than to arrange them improperly in the order of precedence. Most of such difficulties are avoidable and would not have occurred had there been some general system in existence for sorting out important guests and arranging them properly. Nothing of this kind had ever been set up in London, and the Foreign

Office found itself rather enviously eyeing the order of diplomatic precedence which the Russians had used in May, 1896 for the Coronation of Tsar Nicholas II. This seemed especially desirable in London because it had not unduly offended anyone. Besides having already passed muster on the international scene, it also had the advantage of advancing nations to the forefront which it was wise for Britain to honour.

On May 31, Villiers, who had charge of the matter for the Foreign Office, wrote to Ponsonby-Fane suggesting that special envoys other than those of princely rank should be divided into three categories—first the envoys from states normally maintaining embassies in Britain. While this meant that Spain and Turkey would both be prominently placed, it was more significant that France and the United States would be. The second group would comprise envoys who had been given the rank of ambassador for this occasion but who came from states maintaining legations in London. The final group was to consist of envoys from nations with legations but who did not hold the rank of ambassador. In each case the order of precedence within each group would be according to the date of the envoy's arrival in London.

Though Lord Lathom gladly endorsed this sensible scheme, the place of the representative of the Vatican, as in 1887, was again a problem. Villiers left the matter outstanding when he sent the list of precedence to the Queen, and Victoria when she approved it told Sir Fleetwood Edward that Lord Salisbury himself would have to fix the prelate's place. Salisbury adopted the precedent of 1887 and informed the Vatican that its representative would be received as a special envoy and not as a nuncio. As there were no formal relations between London and the Vatican, however, it was still not clear into which category the Roman Catholic envoy should be fitted. Superfluously warned by the Committee of Protestant Alliance that trafficking with papists had its political dangers, Salisbury wisely buried the special envoy in the midst of the second group of diplomats placing him just before the hapless Chinese ambassador.

Arrangement of the princely guests was less troublesome than it had been ten years before. There were no crowned heads to worry about and the non-European princely contingent was smaller. It included no one such as Queen Kapiolani, whose dark skin and high standing had in 1887 affronted nearly everyone. Kapiolani, however, still figured in the diamond jubilee: by now an ex-queen, thanks to the American annexation of Hawaii and the ending of the monarchy, the widowed Kapiolani despatched a congratulatory address to her sister Queen Victoria on May 22. The British Consul General in Honolulu accompanied it with a letter in which he informed Salisbury that as her 'position, dignity and rights' were recognized by the Hawaiian government, she ought to get an appropriate response.

Kapiolani's regal status had assured her the enmity of most of the European princes, but none of the so-called oriental royalties had been immune from disdainful treatment. Perhaps as a result the Shah of Persia decided in 1897 to send a special envoy rather than a member of his imperial house. Like so many other matters in Teheran, this one was immediately caught up in a web of intrigue. When the first envoy appointed was replaced in May by another, Sir Mortimer Durand, the British minister, saw it as the diminution of the influence of the Fernan Firina.

The King of Siam told the British envoy in Bangkok that he would have come himself had Queen Victoria been prepared to allow it; since she was not, he would send his young son, the Crown Prince. As this youngster came on the understanding that he would not have to attend evening events and was to have only a limited part in the proceedings, he gave no cause for hostile feelings. Whether such feelings could have been avoided had a large contingent of Indian princes been on hand is dubious, but to the relief of the organizers, domestic calamity on the subcontinent kept most of them away.

1896 had been a year of acute famine and disease in India the ill effects of which in that poor country were persisting. When, therefore, the possibility of Indian princes coming to the jubilee began to be mooted, there was much opinion against it. As Sir Francis Knollys told Bigge on January 14 the Prince of Wales hoped that 'a visit from the Indian Princes will not be pressed as if it were known that they had been urged and encouraged to come he thinks the public would consider it a mistake in view of the famine.' Perhaps not so incidentally, a visit from such princes ought also to be discouraged because it would increase the expenses of the event as well as lead to further difficulties. 'The Prince of Wales says there would be another objection to the Indian Princes coming over, vizt that they would clash with the other Princes who will be over here.'[13]

Although Lord George Hamilton, Secretary of State for India, thought it wise to have the ninth Earl of Elgin, the Viceroy, inform princes that the Queen would receive them and enquire about which would accept her invitation, it was in these circumstances not surprising that only three Indians, none of the first rank, journeyed to London.

As far as the jubilee in India was concerned, the Viceregal government, as in 1887, left its arrangement entirely in the hands of the populace. Despite a brave despatch from Simla printed in *The Times* towards the end of April that spontaneous efforts being made throughout India, the pinched conditions of the country ensured that the final result would be meagre. As a final blow, Calcutta was struck by a devastating earthquake on the eve of the jubilee which forced the cancellation of not only the thanksgiving service in the cathedral but also the royal *feu de joie*. Thus the diamond jubilee was never an important occasion in the greatest of Britain's colonies.

Given the tribulations of her Indian subjects, the Queen might have been expected to propose that those few princes who travelled to her jubilee should at least have their housing expenses met by the government, as were those of all her other guests. No doubt reluctant to establish a costly precedent, the India Office refused to recommend this course, even though a year before they had done so for the visit of the son of the Amir of Afghanistan. Though this decision risked affronting the Indians, it minimally lessened the burden of the Master of the Household.

Lord Edward Penham-Clinton, son of the fifth Duke of Newcastle, had taken on this post in 1894 after the death of Sir John Cowell. A much more voluble man than his predecessor, Pelham-Clinton was not averse to telling other royal officials about how taxing his work of housing the Queen's guests was, particularly with the pace increasing as the jubilee approached. What further complicated his work was that, unlike Cowell, he had not only princes to worry about, but a number of diplomats, too. This innovation apparently stemmed from the Queen's wish to give particular attention to the special French envoy, the Duc d'Auerstadt, which she could not do unless she accepted his peers, all 25 of them.

'It is the entertaining of these blessed missions that places us in a mess,' Pelham-Clinton told Ponsonby-Fane on May 20. Not only was there insufficient room for them in the Buckingham Palace Hotel, which had again been rented for the occasion (at a cost of £4,000), but what was to be done with them once they arrived? 'They cannot feed with the Royalties or with the Household,' Pelham-Clinton continued. 'Is there no loyal subject who will give the Queen a house?' In response to this *cri de coeur*, the first Baron Burton and the first Baron Iveagh lent their London houses, so that two more residences would not have to be rented. So did Mr. G. Holford, the owner of Dorchester House. As, however, Mr. Holford was comparatively poor, Sir Edward Hamilton successfully pressed for him to get £400.

As the jubilee drew nearer, Pelham-Clinton grew quite frenzied. On June 10 he was upset when he found he had to provide for an unexpected representative of the Grand Duke of Mecklenburg-Schwerin. 'This is not quite fair of the Foreign Office,' he told Ponsonby-Fane. 'I have not got a room at my disposal & am too busy to run about to hotels to look for one.' Three days later, having solved the first problem, new tidings from Princess Christian caused him renewed anxiety. 'She has telegraphed something about the Turk!' he informed Ponsonby-Fane. 'All my plans are again upset. I find the Grand-Duke of Hesse's *suite* are not "roomed." I shall have to turn out Baden & Bolivia I think and find rooms for them in some other Hotel. Oh, what work it is!'

In the end Pelham-Clinton seems to have coped successfully with all his problems. In doing so, however, the Master of the Household spent a good deal of money. That he was on the defensive about this is clear from a letter he sent to Ponsonby-Fane on July 4 concerning his expenses. As he rather stiffly pointed out, there was a 'very large number' of guests to provide for, and because he had not known until 'rather late in the day' how many rooms he would need, some had had to be booked at very high rates. Moreover, despite the fact that both

Lords Burton and Iveagh had lent their houses, several others had had to be rented, along with furniture, plate and linen. Then there were floral decorations to consider and servants and who knows what. As a result 'The Lord Steward's account will be very large for everything has been done thoroughly well.' Which is just as it should be, Pelham-Clinton concluded, for 'all that is done in the name of the Queen *must* be done well.' Such thinking helped to swell the diamond jubilee accounts to some £80,000.

Despite some initial reservations on the part of the Chancellor of the Exchequer, the government did not mind paying this considerable sum, for by and large things had been done thoroughly well. Only in one department was there a conspicuous difference.

Unlike 1887 when he had been responsible for arranging for the national thanksgiving in Westminster Abbey, the Lord Chamberlain (Lord Lathom) and his Department did not have a comparable role in the diamond jubilee. They were not unemployed, of course; a number of Court functions fell to the Lord Chamberlain's Department to arrange, such as the presentation of an address by United Kingdom mayors and provosts on June 23 and the state ball on June 24, but none of them was out of the ordinary. Even so, the Lord Chamberlain's Department provided the diamond jubilee with its one glaring instance of traditional confusion.

On June 23 both Houses of Parliament were scheduled to present congratulatory addresses to the Queen. Due to the large numbers of peers and M.P.s who would have to be accommodated, it was decided that the two houses should do so successively in the Ball Room at Buckingham Palace. Matters got off to a bad start when the Speaker of the House and members arrived a quarter of an hour too soon and were engulfed in a tide of departing peers. When at last the Speaker managed to make his way up to the Queen, many M.P.s were still not in the room. Indeed some had not yet managed to get in by the time the Speaker had finished reading the address and was already retiring.

M.P.s who had come to the Palace and missed the ceremony were understandably put out. George Goschen, First Lord of the Admiralty, was particularly irritated and took Lathom to task for the confusion. In return Lathom wrote that, 'I think what you say about the reception of the House of Commons most unkind and really not warranted.' 'But we all of us did feel the contretemps acutely,' Goschen replied from aboard the Admiralty yacht *Enchantress*.

This second letter from Goschen prompted Lathom to a more rousing defence of his administration. To begin with, he told the First Lord, he could not 'find anybody ready to make any specific charge of incivility.' Even if such a charge were to be made, however, all concerned ought to take into consideration the fact that it was the Queen herself who had (characteristically) ordered both receptions to be conducted within an hour, 'in spite of three remonstrances from me.' Considering that between 1600 and 1700 persons had to be manoeuvred into and out of the royal presence in that time, Goschen ought to see what a hard task the Lord Chamberlain had had. Besides, as he reminded Arthur Balfour in excusing himself to the Leader of the House of Commons, it was not so much his fault as the Speaker's. Surely Balfour remembered that the Lord Chamberlain had asked him to pause until all members were present, but he was too impatient to do so.

All these explanations, which indeed seem to indicate that some of the blame belongs to the Speaker, did Lord Lathom no good, for he was widely regarded as a muddler. 'Fortunately,' Sir Edward Hamilton wrote of the incident, 'it was the only fiasco we have had, and the responsibility deservedly rests on the Lord Chamberlain's Dept. The fact is Lord Lathom is not an efficient Lord Chamberlain, and Spencer Ponsonby Fane is a little past his work.'

Because it was the House of Commons which had been affronted, Victoria decided to invite members, wives and daughters to Windsor for an unscheduled June garden party, to be held at her own expense. She did so not because she herself felt any responsibility for the affair (though had she listened to Lord Lathom in the first place it would not have occurred) but for purely pragmatic reasons. As Hamilton noted on June 29, 'This happy thought of the Queen's is, I know, entirely her own doing and is a wise act on her part in view of the Jubilee Vote which will have to be taken.'

Other difficulties which arose in 1897 concerned some of the collection funds set up to take advantage of the occasion. Again the Prince of Wales and this time his Princess, too, found their efforts being criticized.

In 1896, while raising money for Guy's Hospital in South London, the Prince had become acutely aware of the precarious financial circumstances of the metropolitan hospitals. He therefore decided that a diamond jubilee commemoration fund to augment hospital endowments should be launched. Unlike the Imperial Institute he had promoted for the golden jubilee, this scheme, he reckoned, was so obviously a public service project that he could not be faulted. Unfortunately the Prince was mistaken.

Under the influence of Henry Burdett, described by Sir Edward Hamilton as a 'clever & energetic fellow, who has irons in every fire,' the Prince aimed to do something more ambitious than promote a one-for-all donation. He decided, instead, that contributors should be asked to pledge an annual recurrent sum. 'Should the Prince of Wales's scheme be successful,' Knollys told Bigge on January 22, 'and people competent to give an opinion in a matter of this nature anticipate no difficulty about it, the London hospitals will for the future be placed on a sound financial basis. . . .'

As quickly became evident, however, there were no grounds for the confident anticipation suffusing Marlborough House. As *The Times* pointed out on February 3, not only were donors unwilling to bind themselves to make payments in perpetuity but there were so many other schemes before the public that there was no certainty about the success of this one. Finally, in an implicit warning all too reminiscent of 1887, the newspaper pointed out yet another disadvantage of the Prince's hospital plan. 'Making an appeal for a scheme the details of which are not before the public' was sure to lead the Prince into difficulties. He was therefore advised to think over the whole matter very carefully.

The Prince had already made up his mind, however, and had no intention of following this good advice. Neither did Burdett. On February 28, therefore, when the Prince's newest promotional colleague called on Sir Edward Hamilton to see whether the Inland Revenue Office would be allowed to sell special stamps to would-be subscribers (it would not), that astute civil servant took advantage of the occasion to pass on some home truths.

The Prince's friends, he said, were tired of his endless solicitations for public projects, which though ostensibly requests were in the nature of royal commands. The strong implication was that on this occasion the Prince should not expect enthusiastic support. 'I took the opportunity of telling him,' Hamilton recorded in his diary, 'that he could not proceed with too great caution in this matter. If he does not, he will get the Prince of Wales into trouble.'

The situation darkened as the Duke of Westminster let it be known that beyond contributing £100 to the Prince's proposal, he would do nothing. He meant to concentrate his efforts on increasing by £100,000 the endowment of the Jubilee Nursing Institute begun in 1887 and he was having a hard enough time doing so. The Duke's decision was a blow for two reasons: not only did it mean added competition in a field where the objects of solicitation were related but the Duke was also Lord Lieutenant of the County of London in which the hospitals to be benefited were located.

Fortunately in the end common sense triumphed over the Prince's unduly ambitious and ill-conceived notion. By the end of the year some £227,000 had been contributed to his hospital fund; only a tenth of this amount, however, was promised as an annual recurring subscription.

Just as it seemed the Prince was out of the woods, his wife, Princess Alexandra, suggested holding a series of jubilee feasts for the outcast poor. Characteristically, she wished no one, however indigent or afflicted, to be turned away. This was still the Victorian era, however, and the unheard of catholicity of the Princess's invitation was not generally approved. The appeal confidently launched on May 1 had by May 11 garnered only some £3,200, not nearly enough to accommodate the hordes of poor people expected.

No wonder the fund was faltering, Mr. Charles Montagu of the King Edward Mission, Ragged Schools, informed *The Times*. It was not, after all, meant for the deserving poor but for 'beggars, vagrants and disreputable people,' too. Surely, he said, the aged poor and struggling widows should have their share 'as I am sure the Princess intended they should.' Much more astringent was the writer of a letter signed A.R.P., which ran concurrently. 'If the advantages of the fund were to be confined to the really deserving poor there would be something to be said in its favour, although experience shows that even then the disadvantages far outbalance the advantages; but, as it is, the sum of money subscribed will be as completely wasted as if it had been thrown into the sea.'

Under the circumstances the Princess was forced to adopt regulations which excluded from her scheme those taking poor law relief, individuals not residing in the particular district on May 1, single persons in receipt of more than 10 shillings a week or families earning more than a pound. In addition neither tramps were to be allowed nor the habitually intemperate, lazy or disorderly. So outlined the fund might well have proved a success (though Sir Edward Hamilton doubted it) even had not the tea magnate Thomas Lipton anonymously contributed £25,000 to it, so earning not only the Princess's gratitude but a knighthood. In the end the fund raised enough to allow approximately 400,000 of the deserving poor to be feasted under its auspices on June 24.

By that time, of course, jubilee day had already come and gone, the brilliant success that organizers had hoped to bring about. 'Tout se passa en parfait ordre, favorisé par un temps splendide,' as the Hereditary Prince of Montenegro telegraphed to his father.

The Queen herself had been up early on the morning of June 21 after having passed a restless night, disturbed by the summer's heat and by the noise of the bustling crowds milling in the London streets. As she put on her jubilee finery—a dress of black silk embroidered with silver and featuring grey panels, a chiffon cape and a bonnet trimmed with ostrich feathers, the courtyard filled with those participating in the procession. So extended was it that while the first section featuring colonial troops and premiers was moving out, Victoria had time not only to breakfast but, shortly after 11 a.m., to send a telegraphic greeting to her subjects round the world. 'From my heart I thank my beloved people. May God bless them.' Shortly afterwards Captain Oswald Ames of the Life Guards, at six foot eight inches the tallest man in the British army, led off the main procession. Well might the Montenegrin prince call it 'unique et grandiose.'

Much more imposing than its predecessor ten years before, this parade was a splendid conception. Bands playing martial and patriotic airs alternated in its early stages with soldiers in full dress. Awash in gold braid, medals clanking, there rode the aides-de-camp to the Commander-in-Chief, the aides-de-camp to the Queen, the Headquarters staff and Field Marshals. They were followed by 100 equerries, gentlemen-in-waiting and military attachés who preceded deputations from the First Prussian Dragoons ('The Queen of Great Britain and Ireland's own') and the Indian Imperial Service troops. Later still were carriages containing princesses from Victoria's house and those from throughout Europe, and a phalanx of 36 princes on horseback.

Finally came Victoria herself, preceded by the Commander-in-Chief, Lord Wolseley, and flanked by the Duke of Cambridge, the Prince of Wales and the Duke of Connaught. Plainly-dressed, even dowdy, this red-faced little old lady was not only the cause for this gorgeous display but the constant subject of attention. As she passed along the route waves of unending cheering accompanied her. 'It was not the grandeur, the dignity, or the display which were impressive,' the Bishop of London said in a report which the Queen asked him to write of the day, 'it was the intimacy and the sincerity of the respect and affection felt towards the Queen which was in the air and brought home to every heart an overpowering emotion in the thought of what England had become under her rule and what she had done for England.'[14]

This loyal sentiment was perhaps nowhere more apparent than at St. Paul's Cathedral where the two archbishops of the realm waited for the sovereign on its steps along with members of the government, 500 choristers, and two bands. Perhaps 15,000 others crammed every available bit of space nearby. Once the Queen had arrived at this heady scene, the short service was quickly dispatched: it began with a Te Deum and was followed by the Lord's Prayer, a collect of thanksgiving and a benediction uttered by the Archbishop of Canterbury. Then the choir sang two verses of the Old Hundredth Psalm.

The plan had been that during the singing of this hymn, the carriages which had been waiting in the square would move on so that when it was finished the Queen's carriage would proceed. Despite rehearsals, there was a snag. The carriages did not move, and when the hymn was over there was, in the words of the Bishop of London, 'a pause of intolerable silence.' The aged Archbishop Temple acting with 'splendid audacity and disregard of decorum interpreted what was in everyone's mind & called out "Three cheers for the Queen".'

'Never were cheers given with such startling unanimity & precision. All the horses threw up their heads at the same moment, & gave a little quiver of surprise when the cheers were over. The band and chorus, by an irresistible impulse, burst into "God Save the Queen." ' Well might the Queen express herself satisfied to the Archbishop of Canterbury and Bishop Creighton before her carriage continued on its way.

As soon as it did so, moving on to the Mansion House and across London Bridge to the South Bank, the choir boys, able to restrain themselves no longer, broke ranks, most of them rushing to question the Bishop of London about what they had just witnessed, one stuffing his pockets with gravel on which the Queen's carriage had rested. 'Bishop of London,' Archbishop Temple said laughingly, 'you are spoiling those boys.' While they gambolled, the rest of the massive crowd walked away in silence, so Bishop Creighton told the Queen. 'There was too much for words to express.'

When at last the words did come, however, they were everything that could have been hoped for, a giddy stream of dazzling superlatives. Only Rudyard Kipling in his 'Recessional', published in *The Times* on jubilee day attempted to put things in perspective:

> The tumult and the shouting dies
> The Captains and the Kings depart:
> Still stands thine ancient sacrifice,
> An humble and a contrite heart.
> Lord God of Hosts, be with us yet,
> Lest we forget—Lest we forget

However profound Kipling's sentiments, the fate of vanished Nineveh and Tyre was not what the organizers wished to reflect upon just now. Because of their efforts, careful planning and conscientiousness, it seemed the bogey of organizational ineptitude and muddle, so typical of royal ceremonial, had at last been dispelled. The cosmic validity of Kipling's sobering truths, less often heard at this exuberant moment of imperial confidence than ten years before, would have to give way for a moment at least to jubilation about an unprecedented accomplishment which surely had closed a confused chapter in the history of the monarchy. 'The pageant was wonderfully well arranged,' Sir Edward Hamilton happily noted in his journal, 'so good as to be a complete refutation of the common slur on our inability to organise.'

As shortly became clear, however, Sir Edward Hamilton's blithe assessment was premature.

EPILOGUE

As the nineteenth century turned into the twentieth, Queen Victoria continued to live and work on. In her eighties, crippled with rheumatism, ever more blind, the Great White Queen showed no sign of laying down her burden. Indeed in the face of increasingly gloomy war news from the South African front where England's Boer antagonists were proving unexpectedly difficult to defeat, her activities actually increased. 'We are not interested in the possibilities of defeat,' she told Mr. Balfour, now Chancellor of the Exchequer. 'They do not exist.' Plucky and indomitable, Victoria in those days gave every indication of going on forever, and by a polite fiction no one questioned the possibility.

This attitude at last began to trouble Mr. Almeric Fitzroy, who in his capacity as Clerk of the Privy Council would be professionally concerned with the accession of a new monarch. Therefore in the waning days of 1900, he took up the subject of a prospective change in the sovereign with his chief the Duke of Devonshire, Lord President of the Council. Despite Lord Salisbury's protest against 'gruesome proceedings,' Devonshire authorized Fitzroy to consult government departments about what would have to be done in the unexpected event of the Queen's demise. Fitzroy had scarcely begun to do so, however, when on January 18, 1901, it was announced that the Queen's health had been much strained and that she must therefore abstain from transacting business. A mere four days later she was dead.

Nothing, absolutely nothing was ready. And no one knew quite what was to be done. But two matters had to be urgently considered: the funeral of the old sovereign and the accession of the new.

Fitzroy's work had not, of course, progressed so far that

there were no questions about the proclamation of the King. Moreover the available precedents conflicted. But at least he had been able to squash the attempt of the Home Office to summon the Accession Council and regulate its precedents. Having done so, he was confronted with the fact that the new monarch saw no pressing need to convene the council, apparently feeling that it might be postponed until the first wave of grief and shock had passed. Lord Salisbury, however, with a mind to reassuring the public and an eye on the piles of red boxes stacking up, insisted there could be no delay, and the King consented to go up to London from Osborne House the day after the Queen had expired.

At St. James's Palace where the Council was held, matters went better than might have been anticipated given the short notice and the large number of privy councillors who needed to be sworn. The pens didn't work very well to be sure and Fitzroy had to force out the Lord Mayor of London who insisted upon advancing a 'preposterous claim' that he, too, was a Privy Councillor and as such entitled to stay; notwithstanding, both the Lord Chamberlain and the Master of the Horse who were present told Fitzroy 'they never saw so large a function better arranged.'

Once the Lord Mayor and other City officials had been removed, the King entered the council chamber. There he delivered a brief address, during which he announced that he would reign under the name of Edward VII, despite his parents' firm expectation that he would be known as King Albert Edward I.

It was only later in the day that a remarkable thing about these remarks was noticed: there was not a copy of them to be had. The King had spoken without notes, and no arrangement had been made to take down what he said. When Edward discovered this fact, he was, Fitzroy laconically noted, 'rather surprised.' He set the Clerk of the Council on the unexpected task of reassembling just what had been said. In the end Fitzroy managed to do so by drawing on Lord Rosebery's capacious memory and on the sovereign himself, who provided an 'extremely illegible' revision. Once this tiresome task was completed, it was time to get on with the late Queen's funeral.

Already some arrangements had been undertaken at Osborne House. The first of these was to call in the 60th Rifles from

Parkhurst Barracks to provide a guard over the Queen's coffin. Upon their arrival, however, it was quickly discovered that the troops had no idea what to do and that there was no one on hand to assist them. They had never been taught to reverse arms and the drill book was of no help in showing them how to do so. Muddling through, the captain in charge with the assistance of Sir John M'Neill, Senior Equerry, and Captain Frederick Ponsonby, a junior member of the Household, created his own ceremonial under which the men were relieved from their duty every hour.

Matters scarcely improved after the Duke of Connaught discovered that the Queen's Company of Grenadier Guards was entitled to stand guard over a sovereign's coffin, for when two Guards officers turned up at Osborne, Ponsonby found them 'extremely sketchy' about what should be done. They ended up simply copying the invented ceremonial of the 60th Rifles. Only when Arthur Lloyd, Captain of the Queen's Company, arrived did things improve. Under his direction changing the guard of honour in the specially-prepared *chapelle ardente*, thick with the cloying scent of tuberoses and gardenias, became an impressive event.

Meanwhile back in London a heated discussion had taken place about just who would have control over the Queen's funeral. The fifth Earl of Clarendon, Lord Chamberlain, had advanced the claim that his department should be put in charge. He did so because of the availability of experienced staff and the fact that the Lord Chamberlain's Office had taken care of all the royal funerals during the reign, including that of the Prince Consort. Finally, Clarendon cited a directive issued by the Queen during the time when Lord Sydney was Lord Chamberlain which indicated that the funerals of kings, queens, or heirs apparent should be directed by his office. The Lord Chamberlain therefore let it be known that he expected to have the job.

When the fifteenth Duke of Norfolk was made aware of Clarendon's plan, he was most irritated. A mild-mannered, modest man on his own account, the Duke had no intention of allowing his hereditary prerogatives as Earl Marshal of England to be diminished, as they permanently would have been had he allowed the Lord Chamberlain's claim.

It was scarcely surprising, of course, that Queen Victoria had given Lord Sydney the directive Clarendon now brandished, for after the death of the Prince Consort she had determined absolutely to avoid state ceremonies even unto death. Nonetheless, Norfolk protested, from time immemorial the funerals of sovereigns had been state ceremonials arranged by the Earl Marshal and the College of Arms, and he could not allow such an ancient right to be abridged.

Asked to decide the issue, King Edward ruled in favour of the unwontedly assertive Earl Marshal, who thus carried the day. However, as the astute Fitzroy noted in his diary, 'in the next ten days Norfolk may have cause to repent having so strongly preferred his claim, as without any regular organization he will have to arrange all the details of a notable pageant —I am afraid, with no great help from the Lord Chamberlain's officials.' And so it proved.

Whatever their merits as antiquarians and genealogists, the grandly-named officials of the College of Arms had no experience in the business of arranging the great national ceremonies which had evolved during Queen Victoria's reign. Indeed since the Duke of Wellington's funeral a half century before the Earl Marshal and Heralds had had no part at all in the ordering of ceremonies. Thus they were totally at a loss as to how to approach the considerable task of arranging the Queen's funeral. Their inexperience and ineptitude quickly threatened to reduce the occasion to chaos.

Norfolk for his part approached matters deliberately enough. Having won the right to arrange the funeral, he adopted the precedent of the diamond jubilee organizing committee, and, as chairman, called together representatives of departments concerned. Among those asked to join were Lord Roberts, Commander-in-Chief; the Duke of Portland, Master of the Horse; Sir Henry Ewart, Crown Equerry; Sir Edward Bradford, Commissioner of Metropolitan Police; Reginald Baliol Brett, by now second Viscount Esher, Permanent Secretary of the Office of Works; Mr. William Forbes, general manager of the London, Brighton and South Coast Railway; Lord Pembroke, the Lord Steward; Lord Clarendon; Sir Spencer Ponsonby-Fane; and from the Earl Marshal's office, W. A. Lindsay, Windsor Herald; Farnham Burke, Somerset Herald; and

W. H. Weldon, Norroy King-of-Arms, who because of the illness of Garter Principal King-of-Arms acted in his stead throughout the proceedings. Later the Earl of Selborne, First Lord of the Admiralty, and Sir Francis Mowatt, Permanent Secretary of the Treasury, were added to the group. By January 28 it was fully constituted.

Just how the committee approached its work will probably never be known, since no minutes seem to have survived. Like its diamond jubilee predecessor, however, its members surely worked to create an overall plan and to assign areas of responsibility. Such a rationalizing tendency proved no match, however, for the dogged ill-preparedness of the College of Arms.

On January 31, two days before the funeral was to take place and only a day before the first part of the pageant was to begin at Osborne, Fritz Ponsonby hurried to London. Ponsonby, the engaging son of Queen Victoria's long-time Private Secretary Sir Henry Ponsonby, had been asked by Edward VII to superintend arrangements at Windsor, and he wanted to see if he was expected to handle the funeral procession there as well. What he discovered at the Earl Marshal's office, though, appalled him, for there reigned 'absolute chaos.'

The Heralds, without precedents to guide them and accustomed to doing their work at a leisurely pace, had been, Ponsonby found, 'swept off their feet with the urgent arrangements for the funeral.' They seemed to have no organizational system or general plan. 'Everyone was engaged in working out the little bits of detail most suited to their capacity.'

All this was bad enough, but when Ponsonby asked for the Windsor arrangements, he was staggered to hear that absolutely none had been drawn up. 'We haven't finished Osborne and London yet,' one of the heralds wailed. Ponsonby, entirely taken aback, momentarily gave way to despair. 'I suddenly realized that the Windsor part would be a fiasco, and I should be blamed.'

Recovering himself, the young equerry demanded to see the Earl Marshal, who, it turned out, had no idea that his subordinates were failing in their work, supposing that there was a well developed skeleton programme. Learning the worst, the Duke advised Ponsonby to see Lord Roberts and to work up the necessary ceremonial.

As Ponsonby swung into action, some hint of what was happening in the Earl Marshal's office reached the public, for Norfolk, admitting that things had 'proved far more complicated than was anticipated,' was forced to cancel a press conference he had scheduled in order to announce the funeral arrangements.

As this was happening, Ponsonby began to sort out the Windsor arrangements. He first secured Lord Roberts' permission to order up the necessary troops. Then he set about dictating a programme, an 'astonishingly difficult' task given the fact he had nothing to go on and that no one knew who was expected to attend. When at last he had finished, Ponsonby submitted what he had to the Duke of Norfolk who made a few alterations. The programme was then sent off to the printer, and Ponsonby left for Osborne where next day he was to participate in the first part of the funeral, moving the Queen's body to the mainland. He got barely three hours' sleep.

In the afternoon of February 1, bluejackets of the Royal Yacht carried the Queen's body from the *chapelle ardente* and placed it on a gun-carriage flanked by the equerries. Guards of the Queen's Company marched in single file on either side of the procession down to Trinity pier where the coffin was placed on the Royal Yacht *Alberta* which thereafter proceeded through a long line of warships firing minute guns as the departed sovereign left her marine palace for the last time.

Although these arrangements went without a hitch, there had been a number of changes in them as they developed. Local civic officials were dropped from the procession when it was found that including them would mean doing the same with London and Windsor officials when the funeral reached them. Then, too, there was a good deal of scrambling concerning the naval arrangements. At first the Royal Family was to accompany the Queen's body in the *Alberta*; then they were shifted to the *Victoria and Albert*. Foreign naval vessels specially despatched to the event were originally to be placed in the review lines; then they were removed. And there was a good deal of confusion about where the Queen's body was to be put ashore. All these matters were faithfully reported in the press.

Equally there had been difficulties about the London proceedings which were to take place on February 2, not least of course because the arrangements for them were not completed and finally announced by the Earl Marshal until the evening before the event was to occur. As so often in the past, the original processional route this time between Victoria Station and Paddington, did not give general satisfaction. On this occasion, however, its shortness seems entirely to have been due to pressure from the metropolitan police, who had recently experienced difficulty with London crowds and who thus wished to take no chances with a long route. Discreet criticism from the press, however, forced the route to be redrawn.

Then there was some confusion about just who was going to participate in the London procession; at one time it was understood that Members of Parliament were to march in it with clergymen and representatives of the law, universities and civic government. When nothing came of this plan, however, it bothered almost no one except the M.P.s, and as the *Daily Telegraph* noted, 'Few will regret their absence from the cortège.'

What was regretted, though, was the fact that the Queen's body was not to lie in state at St. Paul's. There was a good deal of comment about what was seen as a singularly unfortunate omission. Given the Queen's explicit desire to keep her obsequies as simple as possible (which she put forward in two memoranda to the Prince of Wales in October 1897, and January, 1898), she may very well have forbidden such an event herself. London's part in the funeral was thus limited to a two-hour procession through streets hung with purple and black mourning and lined with enormous crowds silent and respectful.

At Windsor where the last stage of the funeral was to take place, Fritz Ponsonby had at last succeeded in arranging things. Any chance of relief at its conclusion, however, had been destroyed when the King on Friday, February 1 asked him to make the arrangements for the Queen's final burial at Frogmore on Monday.

Just how he was going to cope with the Queen's actual interment was very much on Ponsonby's mind as he arrived in Windsor on Saturday to oversee the last part of the public funeral. In due course the Queen's body was taken from the train, and the King and all the dignitaries positioned for their walk to St. George's Chapel, where the service was to be held. When all was ready, Ponsonby signalled the band to begin the *Dead March* and the officer in charge to start.

Unfortunately the horses which were to pull the gun-carriage had been left in the bitter cold of that February day for a long while without exercise. They were thus restive upon taking up their load, and the two wheelers started to kick and plunge at the unexpected weight. In an instant the traces were gone, the horses were rearing in the direction of the King and the German Emperor, and the coffin seemed likely to topple into the street. It was pandemonium. 'Such a mishap had never occurred to me,' Ponsonby said later with impressive understatement.

At once he directed the head of the procession to stop and went to tell the King what had happened. After he had reported, he heard Prince Louis of Battenberg, a staunch navy man, inform the sovereign that if the horses could not be replaced the naval guard of honour might be used to drag the gun-carriage.

When this expedient was actually adopted, however, the military men present were outraged at the unexpected honour to the senior service. Sir Arthur Bigge, Queen Victoria's last Private Secretary, told Ponsonby that he was ruining the whole ceremony and rushed off to expostulate with the King. 'Right or wrong,' King Edward told him, 'let him manage everything; we shall never get on if there are two people giving contradictory orders.'

After the bluejackets were put in place, using bits of rope and some of the horse trappings, the proceedings began again. But all was not quite over. Another horse at the end of the procession reared up and got a front leg entangled in the bridle of the beast next to him. Before any damage was done, however, a quick-thinking trooper promptly dismounted and cut the bridle allowing the horses to continue. There were no further incidents en route to the chapel.

Within St. George's, however, there had been additional confusion and a good deal of crowding which came about because the Earl Marshal's staff had forgotten to assign the seats in the choir. This time it was Ponsonby-Fane who set matters right by moving some of the more important people from the nave and putting them in the choir.

As for the service itself, it turned out to be an impressive thing with its solemn music by Croft, Wesley and Purcell and the sonorous declaiming by Norroy King-of-Arms of the 'Styles of Her late Most Sacred Majesty of Blessed Memory.'

'Thus it hath pleased Almighty God to take out of this transitory life into His Divine Mercy, the late Most High, Most Mighty, and Most Excellent Monarch, Victoria by the Grace of God of the United Kingdom of Great Britain and Ireland, Queen, Defender of the Faith, Empress of India, and Sovereign of the Most Noble Order of the Garter.'

It still remained, however, to commit the Queen's mortal remains to the crypt at Frogmore, and here again Ponsonby was in charge of the arrangements.

He found he first had to convince the King that artillery horses rather than sailors ought to be used to pull the gun-carriage, otherwise the army would take it hardly. The King, who had liked the effect of the improvisation, was difficult to convince and only gave way with ill-grace. 'Very well, the gun-carriage will be drawn by the Artillery, but if anything goes wrong, I will never speak to you again.' Several rehearsals were carried out to make sure nothing did go wrong, one held at the mausoleum in the dead of night.

On this occasion, however, nothing untoward happened with the procession, although Ponsonby did receive a tongue-lashing from the King for forgetting to include the name of his son-in-law the Duke of Fife in the published programme. Ponsonby got his own back by reminding the King that he himself had approved the proof.

At last on February 4 the final stage of the great funeral pageant was begun, and it was largely a family party which walked behind the gun-carriage to Frogmore. Largely but not entirely for among the mourners Ponsonby spotted 'a dignified gentlemanly-looking man with several medals' who had previously applied to him for tickets to the mausoleum. Now Ponsonby saw him among the German suite.

Inside Frogmore, surrounded by the mortuarial splendour for which Victoria had once pined, Ponsonby's reverie was broken by a voice whispering in his ear, 'Who is the old bird with a beard?' and a finger pointing at his majesty of Belgium. When he turned around it was the bemedalled gentleman; Ponsonby himself quickly ejected him.

Later in the day in the Quadrangle of the castle near the Sovereign's Entrance, Ponsonby came upon a gaggle of crowned heads and princes and among them, very much at his ease, was the same English officer he had thrown out of Frogmore. Again Ponsonby intervened, 'much to the relief of the Royal Family,' took his man in tow, and went for a policeman.

Later it came to be known that the poor man was mentally defective, which made Ponsonby particularly relieved that his presence had not, apparently, been noted by the German suite —least of all by the All-Highest himself. It was just the kind of thing they would have found hilarious.

So often so close to disaster on the occasion of the Queen's funeral, it was now left for royal officials as they faced the new King's Coronation, the next great royal event, to see whether or not the imp of confusion could at last be expelled from the Court.

NOTES AND BIBLIOGRAPHY

A Note on Sources

It was from the first decided not to include footnotes and the usual scholarly apparatus with this book. Interested individuals are instead referred to the extensive notes and detailed bibliography contained in my doctoral dissertation, 'Queen Victoria's Golden Jubilee, 1887'. Its two volumes are to be found in the collections of Widener Library, Harvard University and the British Library, London. An exception has been made regarding materials held by the Royal Archives at Windsor. Citations from royal papers are as follow:

Introduction
1. F46/96

Chapter 1 Nil

Chapter 2
1. PPBoxG

Chapter 3
1. F46/89

Chapter 4
1. F45/116
2. F46/56
3. F46/112
4. Journal, March 17, 1887
5. F45/137
6. F46/107
7. F46/55
8. F46/55
9. F46/16
10. PP/BoxG
11. F46/76

12. N44/65
13. F47/70

Chapter 5
1. PPVic.BoxG
2. PPVic.BoxG
3. PPVic.22779
4. PP1/22/12
5. PP1/22/15
6. PP1/22/25
7. F45/5
8. F45/9
9. PP1/22/37
10. PP1/22/46
11. PP1/22/52
12. PP1/22/53
13. F45/279
14. PP1/22/70
15. PP1/22/71
16. F45/27a
17. PPVic.BoxG
18. PPVic.BoxG
19. PPVic.BoxG

20	PPVic.BoxG	5	F46/116
21	PPVic.BoxG		
22	PPVic.BoxG	*Chapter 7*	
23	PPVic.BoxG	1	F46/112,113
24	PPVic.BoxG	2	F46/59
25	PPc,BoxG	3	F46/61
26	PPVic. BoxG		
27	PPVic.BoxG		
28	PPVic.BoxG	*Chapter 8*	
29	N44/12	1	F45/7
30	ADD.MS.A/15/4782		
31	F45/81	*Chapter 9*	
32	F46/40	1	R45/39
33	F47/29	2	R45/40
24	PPVic.BoxG	3	R45/70
35	PPVic.BoxG	4	R45/44
36	PPVic.BoxG	5	R45/7
37	PPVic. BoxG	6	R45/56
38	PPVic.BoxG	7	R45/57
39	PPVic.BoxG	8	R45/77
		9	VicAddcM33A/8/2870
Chapter 6		10	R45/92
1	PPVic.BoxG	11	R45/146
2	F45/119	12	R45/149
3	F45/120	13	R45/18
4	F47/67	14	R46/75

For general readers it is hoped that the following select bibliography will prove useful.

Short Reading List

(all books published in London unless otherwise noted

Allingham, H. and Radford, D., eds. *William Allingham: A Diary*. Macmillan, 1907.
Anonymous. *From an Eastern Embassy*. Herbert Jenkins, 1920.
Aston, Sir George Grey. *His Royal Highness the Duke of Connaught and Strathearn*. George G. Harrap. 1929.
Benson, Arthur Christopher. *The Life of Edward White Benson*. Macmillan, 1899.
Beresford of Metemmeh and Curraghmore, Admiral Lord. *Memoirs*. Methuen, 1919.

Brett, Maurice B., ed. *Journals and Letters of Reginald Brett*. Ivor Nicholson and Watson, 1923.
Buckle, George Earle, ed. *The Letters of Queen Victoria*. John Murray, 1924–30.
Boyd Carpenter, William. *Some Pages of My Life*. William and Norgate, 1911.
Cecil, Lady Gwendolen. *Life of Robert, Marquis of Salisbury*. Hodder and Stoughton, 1932.
Chilston, Eric, third Viscount. *Chief Whip: The Political Life and Times of Aretas Akers-Douglas, First Viscount Chilston*. Routledge and Kegan Paul, 1961.
— *W. H. Smith*. Routledge and Kegan Paul, 1965
Collier, Hon. E. C. F., ed. *A Victorian Diarist, Extracts From the Journals Of Mary, Lady Monkswell, 1873–1895*. John Murray, 1944.
Colson, Percy, ed. *Lord Goschen and His Friends*. Hutchinson, n.d.
Dyson, Hope and Tennyson, Charles, eds. *Dear and Honoured Lady: The Correspondence of Queen Victoria and Alfred Tennyson*. Macmillan, 1969.
Fitzroy, Sir Almeric. *Memoirs*. Hutchinson, 1925.
Garvin, J. L. *The Life of Joseph Chamberlain*. Macmillan, 1933–4.
Grenfell, Lord Francis Wallace. *Memoirs of a Field-Marshal*. Hodder and Stoughton, 1925.
Jersey, Dowager Countess of (Margaret Elizabeth Villers). *Fifty One Years of Victorian Life*. London: John Murray, 1922.
Kuykendall, Ralph S. *The Hawaiian Kingdom: The Kalakaua Dynasty*. Honolulu: University of Hawaii Press, 1967.
Lant, Jeffrey L. 'The Archbishop, the Prince and the Troubles Which Cast a Shadow Over Victoria's Jubilee,' *The Times*, August 29, 1977.
— 'Dashing Lord Charles Made the Navy Sit Up,' *The Times*, June 25, 1977.
— 'The Jubilee Coinage of 1887,' *British Numismatic Journal*, vol. 43, 132–41.
— 'The Jubilee and the Nationalists,' *The Irish Times*, June 10, 1977.
— 'Lord Salisbury and the Honours Scramble,' *The Times*, December 5, 1977.
— 'Poor Queen Kapiolani, and the Snubs and Insults She Had To Put Up With At Victoria's Jubilee,' *The Times*, July 23, 1977.
— 'Queen Victoria's Golden Jubilee of 1887,' *Nineteenth Century*, vol. 3, no. 2 (Summer, 1977), 74–9.
— 'The Spithead Naval Review of 1887,' *The Mariner's Mirror*, vol. 62, no. 1 (February, 1976), 67–79.
— 'A Guest but Not Quite Welcome: Queen Kapiolani of Hawaii at the Golden Jubilee of Queen Victoria of England,' *Aloha* (the Magazine of Hawaii) summer issue, 1978.

Liluikalani, Queen. *Hawaii's Story by Hawaii's Queen.* Boston: Lee and Shepard, 1898.

Lindsay, W. A. *The Royal Household.* London: Kegan Paul, 1898.

Longford, Elizabeth Countess of. *Victoria, R.I.* Weidenfeld & Nicolson, 1964. (New York, 1964, published by Harper & Row as *Victoria: Born to Succeed*, 1965.) Reprint New York: Pyramid Books, 1966.

Lucas, Reginald. *Lord Glenesk and the Morning Post.* Alston Rivers, 1910.

Lyall, Sir Alfred. *The Life of the Marquis of Dufferin and Ava.* John Murray, 1905.

Lynd, Helen Merrill. *England in the Eighteen Eighties.* Oxford University Press, 1945.

Morley, John. *The Life of William Ewart Gladstone.* Macmillan, 1903.

Marder, Arthur J. *The Anatomy of British Sea Power.* 1940. Reprint Frank Cass, 1964.

Ponsonby, Arthur. *Henry Ponsonby: Queen Victoria's Private Secretary.* Macmillan, 1942.

Ponsonby, Rt. Hon. Sir Frederick, ed. *Letters of the Empress Frederick.* Macmillan, 1929.

— *Recollections of Three Reigns*, Eyre and Spottiswoode, 1951.

Ponsonby, Magdalen, ed. *Mary Ponsonby: a memoir, some letters and a journal.* John Murray, 1927.

Purcell, Edmund Sheridan. *Life of Cardinal Manning. Archbishop of Westminster.* Macmillan, 1896.

Rawnsley, H. D. *Harvey Goodwin, Bishop of Carlisle.* John Murray, 1896.

Thorold, Algar Labouchere. *The Life of Henry Labouchere.* New York: G. P. Putnam's Sons, 1913.

Waddington, Mary King. *Letters of a Diplomat's Wife, 1883–1900.* New York: Charles Scribner, 1904.

Ward, Thomas Humphry. *The Reign of Queen Victoria: A Survey Of Fifty Years of Progress.* Smith Elder, 1887.

Watson, Vera. *A Queen At Home.* W. H. Allen, 1952.

William II, Emperor. *My Early Life.* Methuen, 1926.

— *My Memories, 1878–1918.* Cassell, 1922.

INDEX

Abel, Sir Frederick, 144, 145
Abercorn, Duchess of, 12
Abergavenny, 1st Marquess of, *see* Neville, William
Accession Council, 248
Adams, Thomas, 170
Adelaide, Queen of England, 18
Ainger, A. C., 14
Akers-Douglas, Aretas, 1st Viscount Chilston, 50, 192
Albany, Duchess of, 7
Albany, Prince Leopold, Duke of, 7, 89
Albert Edward, Prince of Wales, *see* Wales, Prince Albert Edward, of
Albert of Saxe-Coburg and Gotha, Prince Consort, 6, 14, 19, 85, 89, 166, 178, 250; death of, 7, 24–5, 26, 68, 154, 249; equestrian statue of, 135, 136, 137, 148, 154; Great Exhibition, 124; head for management and royal ceremonial, 18, 22, 24, 151; marriage of, 17–18
Alberta (Royal Yacht), 252
Aldershot review, 201–4
Alexander II, Tsar of Russia, 61
Alexander III, Tsar of Russia, 96
Alexander of Battenberg, ('Sandro'), Prince, (later Alexander I of Bulgaria), 38, 197
Alexandra, Princess of Wales (formerly of Denmark), 23–4, 94, 155, 166, 195, 242–3
Alexandra Hotel, 97, 100, 105
Alfred, Prince, Duke of Edinburgh, 10, 57, 89
Alice, Princess, 26
All Sorts and Conditions of Men (Walter Besant), 171
Allingham, William (diarist), 3
Allsop, Sir Henry, later Baron Hindlip, 188

Ames, Captain Oswald, 243
Ancient Monuments Act, 64
Anti-Corn Law League, 160
Antiquarians, Society of, 71
Aosta, Duke of, 91, 205
Armstrong, Sir George, later Baron, 198
Arthur, Duke of Connaught, Prince, 113; breakfast party at Buckingham Palace, 2; ceremonial command of troops on Diamond Jubilee Day, 223; at Diamond Jubilee, 244; as 'favourite son' of Queen Victoria, 155; at Queen Victoria's funeral, 249; leave from India, 44–8, 55; pageantry, lack of aptitude for, 220; and subscriptions for Imperial Institute from India, 141–4
Asiatic Quarterly Review, 115
'Athalie' (Mendelssohn), 7
Athenaeum, The, 71
Athill, Charles, later Richmond Herald, 86
Atkinson, Henry J., M.P., 107
Augusta, Dowager Duchess of Cambridge, Princess, 10, 155, 166–7
Augusta, Princess, Grand Duchess of Mecklenburg-Strelitz, 92, 224
Augusta, Crown Princess of Prussia, 93

Baden-Powell, George, M.P., 177
Bagehot, Walter, 168
Balfour, Arthur J., 160, 240; as Chief Secretary of Ireland, 9, 52–3, 77, 107, 199; as Conservative Leader in House of Commons, 266; as Scottish Secretary, 79
Balmoral (Scotland), 1, 14
Banting & Son, Messrs., 4, 68–71
Barrington, Eric, 106
Battenberg, Prince Alexander of, 38, 197
Battenberg, Prince Henry of, 89, 90–1, 196

Index

Battenberg, Prince Louis of, 93, 234
Beatrice, of Battenburg, Princess Henry, 2, 7, 90, 101, 189, 196
Bedford, Duke of, 10
Benson, Edward W., Archbishop of Canterbury, 100, 108, 172; and Church House scheme, 118–24, 138–139, 140, 141; on House of Commons thanksgiving service, 56–7; and jubilee medal, 199; in procession to Westminster Abbey, 4–5; national thanksgiving service at WA, 7, 85, 162–5
Beresford, Lord Charles, 8, 204–5, 211, 213–14
Beresford-Hope, A. J. B., M.P., 118, 119, 140
Bergne, J. H., 98, 101, 109
Besant, Walter, 171
Biddulph, Sir Thomas, 28
Bigge, Sir Arthur: as Private Secretary to Queen Victoria, 216–17, 218, 219, 254; on Diamond Jubilee committee, 221, 223, 225, 226, 236, 241
Bing, Colonel, 225
Bladensburg, Ross of, 111
Blomfield, Sir Arthur, 140
Boehm, J. E., 13, 148–9, 179, 183
Bootle-Wilbraham, Lady Florence, 59
Borthwick, Sir Algernon, 11, 85, 192–3
Bounty, Queen Anne's, 119–20
Boyd Carpenter, Dr., Bishop of Ripon, 56–7
Bradford, Sir Edward, 223, 225, 250
Bradley, Rev. George Granville, 63–5
Breadalbane, 1st Marquess of, 18, 90
Brett, Hon. Reginald Baliol, 221, 223, 224–5, 250, *see also* Esher, Lord
Bridge, Dr. (Westminster Abbey organist), 6, 7
Bright, W. L., M.P., 181
British Medical Journal, 198
Broadhurst, Henry, M.P., 82, 83
Brock, Thomas, R.A., 184
Brown, John, 166
Brunner, Sir John, 227
Buckingham, 3rd Duke of, 13
Buckingham Palace, 13, 153, 173
  Golden Jubilee:
    breakfast party at, 2, 157; deputation from Women's Jubilee Offering, 10; military reviews at, 7–8, 115, 202; royal guests at, 90, 93, 98
    marriage of Queen Victoria in Chapel Royal, 18
  Diamond Jubilee:
    ceremony for M.P.s in Ball Room, 239; royal guests at, 221
  Queen Victoria's dislike of, 156
Buckingham Palace Hotel, 89, 90–3, 238
Buller, Sir Redvers, 35
Bullock, Rev. Charles, 170
Burdett, Henry, 241
Burdett-Coutts, Baroness, 5
Burke, Farnham (Somerset Herald), 250
Burleigh, Lord Balfour of, 79
Byng, Colonel, 225

Cambridge, George, 2nd Duke of, 10, 14, 26, 31, 45, 95–6, 141, 160–1
Canada, 128, 177, 201
Carnarvon, 4th Earl of, 124, 131
Carrington, Colonel, 225
Cavendish-Bentinck, William John Arthur Charles James, *see* Portland, 6th Duke of
Cecil, Lord William, 59
Chamberlain, Joseph, 34, 37, 39, 61, 159, 219–20
Chelsea Hospital, 21
Chesterfield, 7th Earl of, 25
Childers, Hugh, M.P., 47, 124, 181
Children's Jubilee Fête, 10–13
Chilston, Lord Eric, 192
China, 231, 234; Emperor of, 8, 18
Christian IX, King of Denmark, 101
Christian of Schleswig-Holstein, Princess, *see* Helena, Princess
Church House scheme, 116, 117–24, 139–40, 145, 161
Church Times, The, 12, 67–8, 121, 164–165, 180
Churchill, Lady Jane, 166
Churchill, Lady Randolph, 12
Churchill, Lord Randolph, 36–7, 38, 39, 49, 50, 158, 191
Clan-na-Gael, 72–3, 74–5
Clanricarde, 2nd Marquess of, 35
Clarendon, 5th Earl of, 249, 250
Clark, Somers, 65–6, 69
Clayton, Sir Oscar, 195
Cole, Henry, 19
Collcut, Thomas, 146
College of Arms, 152, 250, 251

Colonial & Indian Exhibition, 11, 18–19, 61, 112; 'Colinderies' (S. Ken. site), 124–7, 128, 131, 132, 145, 146; *see also* Imperial Institute

Colonial Office, 124, 125, 142, 179, 184–5

Connaught, Prince Arthur, Duke of, *see* Arthur, Duke of Connaught

Conroy, Sir John, 170

Consort, Prince, *see* Albert of Saxe-Coburg

Cooke, George, 89

Cork, Emily Charlotte, Countess of, 135, 136, 138, 148

Cork Examiner, 77

Coronation Chair (of Edward III), 6, 70–1

Corrupt Practices Act, 188

Court Journal, 128, 138, 189

Cowell, Sir John, 89, 90, 92, 95, 197, 237

Cox, Charles, 71

Cranbrook, Lord, 5

Cranworth, Lady, 24

Creighton, Mandell, Bishop of London, 223, 245

Cremer, Arthur, M.P., 54

Crewe, Baron, 5

Criminal Law Amendment Bill, 43, 45, 47, 48, 53, 58

Cross, 1st Viscount, 96–7, 114–5

Cunliffe-Lister, Samuel, later 1st Baron Masham, 192, 193

Cunliffe-Owen, Sir Philip, 95, 125–6, 144

Daily Chronicle, 85

Daily News, 5, 10, 13, 46, 51, 57, 65, 66, 71, 76, 103, 128, 131, 137, 138, 153, 154, 155, 156, 165, 171, 175, 179, 180–1, 186, 189, 198, 202, 203, 209, 213

Daily Telegraph, 6, 10, 11, 12, 51, 57, 74–5, 128, 186, 199, 211, 212, 253

Davidson, Rev. Randall, 80–1, 163, 223–4

Derby, 15th Earl of, 22, 125, 128

Devonshire, Duke of, 247, *see also* Hartington, Lord

Dilke, Sir Charles, M.P., 25, 26

Dilke, Lady Frances, 172

Dillwyn, Mr., of Swansea, 48

Disraeli, Benjamin, 17, 24, 39, 102; as a Conservative, 167, 168, 178; as Prime Minister, 38, 124, 192; and Queen Victoria, 162; *Sybil*, 86–7; *Young Duke, The*, 102

Douro, Lord, 19

Drummond, C. J., 81–3

Dufferin and Ava, 1st Marquess of, 112–3, 114, 115–6, 141, 161

Dunn, Miss Florence, 13

Eardley-Wilmot, Sir Sydney, 214

East London Observer, 172

Eaton, H.W., M.P., later Baron Cheylesmore, 193, 198

Ecclesiastical Commission, 119–20

Edinburgh, Prince Alfred, Duke of, 10, 57, 89

Edwards, Sir Fleetwood: and Westminster Abbey, 80, 104, 105; knighthood, 197; and jubilee medals, 199; on Diamond Jubilee committee, 221, 222, 227, 230, 235

Edward III, King of England, 67

Edward V, King of England, 70

Edward VII, 67, 248, 250, 251, 253, 254; *see also* Wales, Prince Albert Edward of

Effingham, Countess of, 148

Elgin, 9th Earl of, 237

Ely, Jane, Marchioness of, 166

England, Church of, 78–9, 117–24, 139–40, 164

Eric, or Little By Little (Frederick Farrar), 55

Errington, George, 107

Esher, Lord, *see* Brett, Hon. Reginald Baliol

Eton, College, 13–4

Evans, John, 184

Ewart, Sir Henry, 225, 250

Examiner, 18

Exeter, 2nd Marquess of, 20

Farquhar, Sir Horace, later Lord, 230–1

Farrar, Ven. Frederick, 55–6

Fergusson, Sir James, 79, 109

Financial News, 143–4

Fitzroy, Almeric, 247–8, 250

Flanders, Count of, 23

Forbes, William, 250

Forbes-Watson, Dr. John, 124

Fowler, Rev. Montague, 84, 131, 163

Francis, Duke of Teck, 195–6

Index

Frederick Augustus, Prince of Saxony, 232
Frederick William, Crown Prince of Germany, 7, 22, 93, 217
Fremantle, Hon. C. W., 179, 180, 182–184
Frogmore, 253, 255–6

Gascoyne-Cecil, Robert Arthur Talbot, *see* Salisbury, Marquess of
George III, King of England, 13, 60, 150, 153, 161, 211, 215
George IV, King of England, 28, 51, 167
George V, King of England, 196
George, Prince, 2nd Duke of Cambridge, *see* Cambridge, George, 2nd Duke of
Gibson, John G., 50
Gissing, George, 174
Gladstone, William Ewart, 25, 32, 36, 82, 84, 107, 109, 186, 195: and Home Rule for Ireland, 4, 35, 37, 56, 75, 90, 158, 168, 194, 228; on pageantry and monarchy, 26, 29, 30, 31, 76, 150, 151, 154, 162, 178; and Queen Victoria, 28, 34, 167–8
Gold State Coach, 153–4
Goldie, George Taubman, 185
Goldsmid, Sir Julian, 100
Goodwin, Harvey, Bishop of Carlisle, 117, 119, 122
Gordon, General Charles George, 167
Gorst, Sir John, M.P., 47
Goschen, George J., M.P.: as Chancellor of Exchequer, 9, 37, 38, 49, 50; on committee for Imperial Institute, 131; and jubilee honours, 190, 191–192; as 1st Lord of the Admiralty at Diamond Jubilee, 227, 239–40
Granville, Lord, 25
'Great Depression, The', 119
Great Eastern, The, 206–7
Greece, 233–4
Gregg, Dr. Thomas, Bishop of Verulam, 80–1
Gregory, Rev. Robert, 223
Grenfell, Sir Francis, 100
Greville, Charles (diarist), 21, 169
Grey, General Charles, 59
Griffin, Sir Lepel, 115–6

Halifax, 2nd Viscount, 152

Halsbury, Lord, 5
'Hallelujah Chorus' (Handel), 18
Hamilton, Sir Edward, 41, 162, 172, 193, 216, 218–9, 221, 230, 238, 240, 242, 243, 246
Hamilton, Lord George, 36, 57, 237
Handel, George Frederick, 6, 18
Hanotaux, M., 233
Harcourt, Sir William, M.P., 217
Hare, Augustus (diarist), 13
Harrison, Frederic, 70
Hartington, Lord, 10, 34, 193–4
Hatfield House, 37, 40, 98
Hatton, Lt.-Col. of Grenadier Guards, 2
Hawaii, 98–9, 236
Head, Barclay, 181
Healy, Timothy, M.P., 35
Heather, Mr., 95
Helena, Princess Christian, 2, 10, 90, 196, 238
Henry of Battenberg, Prince, 89, 90–1, 196
Herschell, 1st Baron, 131
Hertford, Marchioness of, 148
Hessan es Sultaneh, of Persia, 97–8, 205
Hicks Beach, Sir Michael, M.P., 217–18
Hobhouse, 1st Baron, 215, 216
Hogg, Lady Caroline Elizabeth, 134, 135, 148
Hogg, Sir James McGarel, 134, 135
Holford, G., 238
Holkar, Maharajah of Indore, 112, 113, 114, 115
Holland, Henry, 131, 177–8
Hopetoun, Earl of, 79
Hornby, Sir G. Phipps, 195
Housman, A. E., 176
Howell, George, M.P., 82, 83
Howley, Archbishop William, 17
Humphreys, Rev. A. E., 170
Huxley, Professor T. H., 133–4, 146
Hyde Park, 10–13, 201, 202, 222, 225
Hyderabad, Nizam of, 142
Hyndman, H. M., 159

Iddesleigh, 2nd Earl of, 191–2
Illustrated London News, 20, 85, 126
Imperial College of Science and Technology, 147; *see also* Imperial Institute
Imperial Indian Peerage and Almanack (Lt.-Col. A. W. Roberts), 112
Imperial Institute, 116, 123, 124–34,

135, 137, 138, 140–6, 161, 165, 174
In the Year of Jubilee (George Gissing), 174
India: imperial honours, 185; India Office, 96–7, 112, 124, 237; Indian princes at Golden and Diamond Jubilees, 3, 104, 112–6, 236–7; and Duke of Connaught as C.-in-C. of Bombay, 44–7; Queen Victoria as Empress of, 96, 105, 111–6, 142, 178–9, 237; *see also* Colonial and Indian Exhibition
Ireland: agrarian situation, 34–6; Chief Secretary for, *see* Balfour, Arthur J.; and Church of Rome, 107–8, 109–11, 110; Clan-na-Gael and terrorism, 72–3, 74, 75–6; Home Rule, 25, 34, 35, 36, 37, 48, 56, 57, 64, 75, 110, 158, 160, 168, 194; Irish Crimes Bill, 53, 55, 57, 75; Irish Nationalists, 9–10, 34, 36, 39, 46, 47, 49, 53, 54, 55, 72, 76, 77, 228; Irish representation at Westminster Abbey, 50, 77; jubilee honours, 10, 198–9; Lord Lieutenant of, 10, 199; Phoenix Park, Dublin, 10, 72; Plan of Campaign, 35, 72, 107, 111; Tenants' Relief Bill, 35; *United Ireland*, 35

Jackson, William, 64, 72
James, Sir Henry, 131
Japan, 97, 231–2
Jenkinson, E. G., 74
Jenner, Sir William, 146–7, 172, 198
Jersey, Countess of, 1
Jones, Isaac, 170
Jowitt, Benjamin, 190
Jubilee, Diamond, 215–46: colonial premiers, 219–20, 226, 230; committee for, 221; congratulatory address by Houses of Parliament, 239–40; honours, 229–31; hospital endowments, 241–3; naval review at Spithead, 214; procession to St. Paul's, 226–7, 244–5; royal guests, 231–9
Jubilee, Golden: *Intro*, 34–214; accommodation of royal guests, 4–5, 86–116; anti-activities in New York, 9–10; in Dublin, 10; in Birmingham, 158–9; budget for, 49–57, 162; celebrations in provinces, 174–6; Children's Fête, 10–13; commemorative schemes: books, 169–71; Church House, 117–24, 138, 139–40, 146; coins, 179–84; Imperial Institute, 123, 124–34, 141–2; Nursing Institute, 147–8, 242; People's Palace, 171–3; songs, 169–70; Women's Offering, 10, 134–8, 146–9; committee for, 40–3; decorations at Westminster Abbey, 68–71; fire protection at Westminster Abbey, 71–2; honours, 185–200; lack of precedent for, 60–1; in Manchester, 160; military reviews, 204–14; national thanksgiving at Westminster Abbey, 58–87, 163; presents to Queen Victoria, 8; press award, 11; procession to Westminster Abbey, 3–4, 103–4, 156–7; representation in Westminster Abbey, 77–87; state dinner at Buckingham Palace, 8; statue of Queen Victoria at Windsor, 13–14; terrorists, 72–6

Kalakauna, King of Hawaii, 98–9, 101, 104
Kapiolani, Queen of Hawaii, 7, 98–100, 104–6, 235–6
Kashmir, Maharajah of, 114
Kennedy, J. G., 109
Kent, Duchess of, 68
Kent, Duke of, 44
Khedive of Egypt, 197
Kimberley, 1st Earl of, 124
Kipling, Rudyard, 245
Knollys, Sir Francis: and Imperial Institute, 130–1; as Private Secretary to Prince of Wales, 72, 117, 124, 127, 217, 219, 221, 225, 226, 227, 236, 241; and statue of Prince Consort, 135–6
Komatsu, Prince of Japan, 97, 231
Krueger, Paul, President of the Transvaal, 217

Labouchere, Henry, M.P.: as editor of *Truth*, 11, 65, 91, 139, 156; as leader of the Radicals, 47–8, 49, 50, 52, 54–55, 56, 228
Lathom, Edward, 1st Earl of (formerly Lord Skelmersdale): on Diamond Jubilee committee, 221, 232, 235, 239, 240; and Irish Nationalists, 76–77; and jubilee honours, 185; as Lord

Index

Lathom, Edward—*cont.*
  Chamberlain, 6, 41, 42, 58–9, 62, 94, 106, 153; and representation in Abbey, 7–8, 78–87; *see also* pageantry: Lord Chamberlain's Dept.
Lawson, Edward, 10–11
Lawson, Sir Wilfred, M.P., 9
Lee, Sir Sidney, 186
Leighton, Sir Frederick, 131, 184, 189, 190
Leiningen, Prince Ernest of, 195
Leiningen, Princess of, 92
Leo IX, Pope, 107, 108, 110
Leopold, Prince, Duke of Albany, 7, 89
Lethbridge, Sir Roper, M.P., 142
Lindsay, W. A. (Windsor Herald), 250
Linton, Sir James, 189
Lipton, Thomas, 243
Lloyd, Arthur, 249
London Gazette, 14, 30, 156, 179
London Working Men's Association, 81, 206
Londesborough, Lord and Lady, 25
Londonderry, Lady, 10, 137
Lorne, Marquess of, 3, 92
Lothian, Lord, 79
Louise, Princess, Marchioness of Lorne, 3, 92
Louis, of Battenberg, Prince, 93, 234
Lowe, Robert, M.P., 27
Luard, Rev. Dr. 174
Lubbock, Sir John, M.P., 181

Macartny, Sir Halliday, 231
MacBean, Forbes, 83
McCarthy, Justin, M.P., 76
McDonnell, Schomberg, 222, 230
MacGeorge, Mr., 182–3
McGuire, James, 100, 105
Mackenzie, Dr. Morrell, 93
M'Neill, Sir John, 249
Maltby, Dr., Bishop of Durham, 17
Malvern Hills, 175
Manchester Courier, 160
Manchester Exhibition, 160
Manchester Guardian, 48, 74, 146, 209
Manchester, Louisa, Duchess of, 12
Manners, Henry John, 41, 191
Manners, Lady John, 98, 104
Manning, Henry, Cardinal, 109, 110
Mansion House, 122, 123, 128, 132, 136, 222
Marks, Harry, 227–8

Marlborough House, 89, 127, 131, 132, 135, 221
Marochetti, Baron, 135, 148
Mary, Princess, of Cambridge, Duchess of Teck, 3, 10, 105, 196, 224
Matthews, Henry, M.P., 9, 74
Maude, Colonel George Ashley, 3, 102–3, 104, 105–6, 197
Meade, Hon. Robert, 125
Meath, 12th Earl of, 215
Mecklenburg-Strelitz, Augusta, Grand Duchess of, 92, 224
Melbourne, Lord, 17
Mendelssohn, Felix, 7, 21
Menzies, W. J., 79
Merlin, 180
Methuen, Lord, 225
Metropolitan Fire Brigade, 71–2
Metropolitan Police Force, 72, 73, 74, 75, 85, 199–200, 253
Metropolitan Police Courts (Holidays) Act, 229
Millais, Sir John, 189
Mills, Sir Charles, later Baron Hillingdon, 188
Milner, Alfred, 192, 198
Milward, Victor, 175
Monkswell, Lady, 5
Monson, Sir Edmund, 232–3
Montague, Charles, 242
Montague, Andrew, 193
Monteagle, Lord and Lady, 83, 84
Mordaunt, Sir Charles, and Lady, 25
Morning Post, 11, 85, 192
Morocco, Sultan of, 232–3
Morvi, the Thakore of, 8
Mount Edgcumbe, William Henry, 4th Earl of, 40–2
Mowatt, Sir Francis, 251
Mowlem and Co., 65, 67, 71
Muller, E. B., 160
Murray, Kenric, 129, 131
Murray's Magazine, 180
Musical World, 7

Nature, 87, 189
Naval Defence Act, 214
Naval reviews at Spithead, 204–14
Nelson, Horatio, 118, 119
Neville, William, 1st Marquess of Abergavenny, 11, 192, 193
Nicholas II, Tsar of Russia, 197, 235
Nicolson, Arthur, 96, 97

Nightingale, Florence, 147
Nineteenth Century, 194
Nineteenth Century and After, The (Somers Clark), 66
Nolan, M.P., 75
Norfolk, 12th Duke of, 18, 108, 109–11, 152
Norfolk, 15th Duke of, 249, 250, 252
Norris, Archdeacon of Bristol, 120
Northcote, Sir Stafford, 1st Earl of Iddesleigh, 191

O'Connor, T. P., M.P., 54
Osborne House, 212, 248–9, 251, 252
O'Shea, Kitty, 194

pageantry: College of Arms, 250, 251; coronation of Queen Victoria, 17–18; Diamond Jubilee, 215–46; Earl Marshal, 18, 20–1, 27, 86, 152, 250, 251, 252, 254; Foreign Office, 9, 38, 88, 89, 96, 97, 98, 101, 106, 108, 205, 223, 231–2, 234–5; funeral of Queen Victoria, 248–56; funeral of Duke of Wellington, 19–24, 51; Garter King of Arms, 27–8; Gold State Coach, 153–4; Golden Jubilee, *Intro*, 34–214; heralds, 21, 22, 250, 251; Lord Chamberlain, role of, 6, 18, 20–1, 29–30, 49, 52, 58, 70, 85; Lord Chamberlain's Dept., 8, 21, 27, 59, 63, 69, 71, 73, 78, 79, 80, 81, 85, 95, 98, 101, 103, 112, 113, 151–2, 157, 226, 239, 240; Lord Steward, role of, 6, 18, 40, 42; Master of the Horse, role of, 102, 116, 248; Master of the Household, role of, 116, 221, 238; national press, influence of, 24, 30–1, 67, 85, 128, 154–5, 165, 180–1; Office of Works, 4, 5, 49, 62, 63, 65, 67, 71, 73–4, 83, 151, 202, 221, 224–225; and Prince Consort, 22; semi-state, 27–33, 151–76, and full state, 152–76; wedding of Prince of Wales, 22–4, 51, 114, and thanksgiving service, 26–33, 150
Pall Mall Gazette, 11, 12, 65, 120, 126, 128, 134, 138, 141, 144–5, 155
Palmerston, Lord, 59, 68
Parker, Eric, 14
Parnell, Charles Stewart, 9, 34, 35, 55, 72, 76, 194, 228; *see also* Ireland

Peacock, Edward, 85
Pease, Sir Joseph, M.P., 53
Peel, Sir Robert, 185, 229
Pelham-Clinton, Lord Edward, 221, 237–9
Pembroke, 14th Earl of, 221
Penrose, F. C., 29
People's Palace, 171–3
Perry & Co., 65
Persia, 96–8, 205, 236
Persico, Monsignor, 111
Philipps, Sir James, 118
Phoenix Park (Dublin), 10, 72
Piggott, Charles, 72
Pistrucci, 180, 184
Plan of Campaign, 35, 72, 107, 111
Playfair, Sir Lyon, 131, 215
Plunket, David, M.P., 51–2, 70–1
Ponsonby, Captain Frederick, 249, 251–6
Ponsonby, Sir Henry Frederick: career of, 59–62; over Church House scheme, 124, 126–9; and other jubilee commemorations, 117, 135, 136, 137, 138, 147, including Imperial Institute, 127, 129, 130, 132, 140–1; and Duke of Connaught's leave, 46; and foreign missions to Golden Jubilee, 101–6, 116; and jubilee honours, 190, 195, 197; over Prince William of Prussia, 93–4; as Private Secretary to Queen Victoria, 50, 80, 120, 148, 150, 152, 156, 159, 166, 200
Ponsonby, Lady Mary, 168
Ponsonby Fane, Sir Spencer: and accommodation for royal guests, 89, 90, 92, 95, 238; career of, 59; as Comptroller of Lord Chamberlain's Dept., 2, 28, 64, 68, 101, 155, 199, 233, 235, 240; at funeral of Queen Victoria, 250, 254; on jubilee committees, 41, 221; and Westminster Abbey, 6, 29, 60–5, 70, 79–84, 173–4
Portland, 6th Duke of, 10, 102, 221, 226, 227, 250
Potter, George, 81–3, 206
Powell, David, 184
Poynter, Edward, 184
Primrose, H. W., 63, 67, 73
Protection of Ancient Buildings, Society of, 64, 70
Punch, 93, 125, 145, 189

Purcell, Edmund, 110

Queen's Resolve, The (Charles Bullock), 170
Queen Victoria's Jubilee Institute for Nurses, 147, 242

Rainy, Rev. Robert, 79, 80
'Recessional' (Rudyard Kipling), 245
Record of an Adventurous Life (H. M. Hyndman), 159
Redmond, William, M.P., 54
Reed, Sir Edward, M.P., 209
Reform Act, 188
Reformed Church Record, 80–1
Regent's Park, 12
Reynolds's, 100, 161–2
Ridley, Sir Matthew, M.P., 216, 227
Roberts, Lord, 251, 252, 256
Roberts, Lt.-Col. A. W., 112
Rose, Sir John, 186
Rosebery, Lord, 10, 100, 152, 248
Rothschild, Leo, 135
Roustan, Captain, 213
Royal Niger Co., 185
Royal Titles Bill, 178
Roxburgh, Dowager Duchess of, 148
Rudolph, Crown Prince of Austria, 196–7
Russia, 38, 92, 197

St. James's Palace, 8, 10, 59, 82, 89, 92, 199, 248
St. James's Park, 12
St. Paul (Mendelssohn), 21
St. Paul's Cathedral, 65, 150, 151, 154, 253; Diamond Jubilee thanksgiving service, 222–5, 244; Duke of Wellington's funeral at, 21–2, 68; Somers Clark, architect for, 66, *see also* Clark, Somers; thanksgiving service for Prince of Wales, 28, 29, 32, 162
Salisbury, Lady, 5
Salisbury, 3rd Marquess of, 64, 147; at accession of Edward VII, 248; as Foreign Secretary, 38, 96–9, 104, 106–11, 157, 205, 218–9, 220, 233, 234, 235; lack of interest in ceremonial, 39–40, 150–1, 165, 231; and jubilee arrangements, 40–57, 162, 165, 228–229, including honours, 185, 187–200, and the Fleet, 213–14; and Lord Chamberlain's Dept., 58–9, 62, 98; as Prime Minister and leader of 'Unionist' party, 34–5, 158, 179; and Queen Victoria, 156, 157–9, 172–3
Sanderson, Thomas, 231, 234
Sandringham House, 25–6
Sanger, 'Lord' George, 153
Satow, Sir Ernest, 231–2
Schleswig-Holstein affair, 23
Scilla, Monsignor Ruffo, 107–10
Scotland, Church of, 78–80, 164
Scotland, Episcopal Church of, 78
Scotland, Free Church of, 79
Scotland Yard, 21, 86
Scottish Widows' Fund, 69, 80
Selbourne, Earl of, 251
Serge, Grand Duchess of Russia, 7
Serge, Grand Duke of Russia, 92, 197
Shaw, Captain Eyre Massey, 71–2
Shepheard, Alfred, 78, 79
Sheppard, Rev. Edgar, 210
Shropshire Lad, The (A. E. Housman), 126
Sing, Hee, 19
Singh, Maharajah Duleep, 23, 113–14
Singh, Maharani Duleep, 113, 114
Sing, Sir Pertab, Maharaj, 113
Skelmersdale, Lord; *see* Lathom, Earl of
Smith, Lt.-Col. Henry, 225
Smith, W. H., M.P., 36, 37–8, 46, 50, 52–3, 64, 67, 198
Somerset, Lady Geraldine, 155
South Africa (Boer War), 247
'South Kensington Gang', 125, 126, 128, 132, 134, 142, 143, 144
Spencer, 5th Earl of, 90
Spencer, Herbert, 133
Stack, M.P., 75
Standard, 12, 54–5, 57, 103, 115, 121, 123, 126, 128, 131, 132, 139, 145, 146, 151, 154, 155, 182, 187, 188, 203, 204, 208–9
Stanhope, Edward, M.P., 191, 202
Stanley, Rev. Arthur, 63
Statute Law Revision Committee, 107
Stockmar, Baron, 22
Story, Herbert, 80
Strafford, Alice, Countess of, 135, 137–138
Sun Fire Office, 71
Swaine, Colonel L. V., 93–4
Swinburne, Sir John, 48, 57

Index

Sydney, 3rd Viscount, 27, 28, 29, 30, 41, 78, 81, 249-50
Synge, R. F., 100, 101

Tanner, Dr., 54
Taylor, John, 49, 65
Teck, Francis, Duke of, 195-6
Teck, Princess Mary of Cambridge, Duchess of, 3, 10, 105, 155, 196, 224
Temple, Frederick, Bishop of London, 122-3, 139, 215-6, 223, 244, 245
Tennyson, Lord, 167, 189
Thesiger, Hon. Edward, 84
Thorne Brothers, Messrs. (royal coach-builders), 103, 153
Thorneycroft, Hamo, 184
Thunderer, The, 228
Thynne, Lord John, 17
Times, The, 4, 13, 14, 19, 20, 26, 29, 30, 31, 32, 33, 43, 47, 63, 72, 73, 87, 100, 112, 117, 119, 120, 123, 128, 129, 131, 132, 133, 134, 136, 145, 176, 177, 182, 194, 206, 209-10, 213, 215, 216, 228, 237, 240, 241, 242-3, 245
Times of India, The, 113, 115, 142-3
Trade Depression, Royal Commission on, 81
Trades Union Congress, 81
Trendell, Arthur, 85
Tritton, J. H., 131
Trollope, Anthony, 144
Truth, 11, 91, 120, 128, 139, 156, 198, 207-8
Tully, Major, 138, 147, 149
Tupper, Sir Charles, 128
Turkey, 233-5
Turner, Thackeray, 65

'Unionist' party, 11, 34, 35, 36, 37, 39, 46, 52, 75, 111, 158, 160, 194, 228, 230
United Ireland, 35
United States, 9-10, 99, 104

Vanity Fair, 58, 59
Vatican, 107-11, 235
Vavasour, Sir Henry, Bt., 86-7
Victoria, Queen of England: Birmingham, visit to, 158-9; and Boer War, 247; John Brown, 166; at Buckingham Palace, 7-10; character of, 1, 44, 62, 65, 100, 161, 165, 167-74, 199, 200, 215, 247; at Children's Jubilee Fête, 10-13; and the Church, 162-5; the colonies, 177-84; coronation, 17, 51; death, 247-56; Diamond Jubilee, 215-46; Duke of Connaught's promotion, 44-6; Duke of Wellington's funeral, 20; as Empress of India, 96, 105, 111-16, 142, 178-9, 237; and Gladstone, 28, 34, 167-8; Golden Jubilee, *Intro,* 34-214; Great Exhibition, opens, 18-19; and Imperial Institute, 130, 132, 141, 145, 146; jubilee coinage, 179-84; jubilee guests, 88-116, 232, 236; jubilee honours, 185-200; Jubilee Institute for Nurses, 147; letter in *London Gazette,* 14; Manchester, visit to, 160; marriage of, 17-18; opens People's Palace, 171-3; and Prince Consort, 6, 22, 24-5, and equestrian statue of, 135-8, 146-9; and Prince of Wales, 25-33, 140-1; Privy Purse, 27, 28, 49, 51, 88, 160-2, 218; procession to St. Paul's, 244-5; procession to Westminster Abbey, 3-4; semi-state, preference for, 27-33, 62, 134, 151-76, and dislike of pageantry, 1, 14-15, 27-8, 149, 151, 152-8, 161, 172-3, 174, 216-7, 222, 250; Spithead, visit to, 207-12; and Westminster Abbey, 6-7, 150-1; and William, Crown Prince of Prussia, 94-5; Women's Jubilee Offering, 134-8, 146-9; as staunch Unionist, 34, 44
Victoria, Princess Royal, 22
Victoria and Albert (Royal Yacht), 205, 208, 211
Villiers, F. H., 233, 235
Vincent, Colonel Howard, M.P., 12, 177
Vine, Sir John Somers, 126, 134, 143, 144
Volunteer Record, 202, 203
Volunteer Service Gazette, 201

Wade, Richard, 184
Waddington, Madame, 62, 114
Wales, Prince Albert Edward of, 10: at Diamond Jubilee, head of committee, 217, 219-21, 224-5, 227, 231, 232; and Imperial Institute, 61, 123, 124;

Wales, Prince A. E., of—*cont.*
146, 174; and Indian princes, 115–6, 236–7; and Golden Jubilee honours, 186, 195; Manchester Exhibition, opens, 160; and metropolitan hospital plan, 241–2; and Mordaunt divorce case, 25; pageantry, delight in, 2, 101, 165; typhoid illness, 25–6, and national thanksgiving for, 26–33, 150; wedding of, 22–3, 51, 114; *see also* Edward VII

Wales, Princess Alexandra of, 23–4, 94, 155, 166, 195, 242–3

Warren, Sir Charles, 9, 73–4, 85, 199

Watkin, Sir Edward, 143

Watts, George, 230

Way We Live Now, The (A. Trollope), 144

Webb, Sydney and Beatrice, 81

Weldon, W. H., 251, 255

Wellington, Duke of, 12, 19–22, 29, 51, 68, 250

Wellington, 2nd Duke of, Lord Lt. of Middlesex, 31

Westminster Abbey, 13: boycotting of, 10, 54, 75, 76, 77, 110; coronation of Queen Victoria at, 17; decorations and restorations at, 4–5, 164–71; fire protection, 71–2; Golden Jubilee service at, 6–7, 49–50, 58–87, 150–1, 162–5; prevention of terrorism at, 72–6

Westminster, Duchess of, 12

Westminster, Duke of, 10, 242

Wilder, Mr. (Vice-Provost of Eton), 13

Willes, Sir George, 204–5, 208, 210, 211

William I, German Emperor, 93, 94

William IV, King of England, 45, 155, 167

William, German Crown Prince (subsequently Emperor William II), 23, 93–5, 217

Windsor, 1, 39, 165, 190, 230: Diamond Jubilee garden party at, 240; equestrian statue of Prince Consort at, 149; Golden Jubilee celebrations at, 13–14, 113; Prince of Wales's wedding at, 23–4; Queen Victoria's funeral at, 251–4

Wolseley, Lord, 1st Viscount, 201, 227, 244

Women's Jubilee Offering, 10, 116, 134–8, 146

Wood, Henry J., 226

Woods, Sir Albert, 22, 28

York, Duke and Duchess of, 146, 224

Young Duke, The (Disraeli), 102